I0626792

SACRAMENTS IN SCRIPTURE

Sacraments in Scripture

A Symposium

T. Worden   L. Johnston   D. M. Stanley s.j.

Edward J. Kilmartin s.j.   Kevin Condon c.m.

J. Van der Ploeg o.p.   C. Spicq o.p.

Jean-Paul Audet o.p.   H. J. Richards

Edited by T. Worden

TEMPLEGATE, SPRINGFIELD, ILLINOIS

First published 1966

© 1966, Catholic Biblical Association

Nihil obstat: R. D. Desmundus Leahy, D.D., Ph.D., L.S.S., Censor Deputatus
Imprimatur: H. Gibney, Vicarius Generalis
Datum Southwarci die 21a Septembris 1965

Made and printed in Great Britain

Contents

	Preface	*T. Worden*	7
I	Old Testament Signs	*J. Van der Ploeg O.P.*	15
II	The Spirit of God	*L. Johnston*	31
III	Baptism in the New Testament	*D. M. Stanley S.J.*	45
IV	The Formation of the Bread of Life Discourse (John 6)	*Edward J. Kilmartin S.J.*	63
V	The Holy Eucharist in St John	*T. Worden*	69
VI	The Date of the Last Supper	*L. Johnston*	94
VII	The Meaning of 'Sin'	*T. Worden*	105
VIII	Sin and Repentance	*L. Johnston*	119
IX	The Remission of Sins	*T. Worden*	135
X	The Sacrament of Healing (Jas. 5 : 14–15)	*Kevin Condon C.M.*	172
XI	Priestly Virtues in the New Testament	*C. Spicq O.P.*	187
XII	Love and Marriage in the Old Testament	*Jean-Paul Audet O.P.*	210
XIII	The Mystery of Marriage	*L. Johnston*	239
XIV	Christ on Divorce	*H. J. Richards*	247
	General Index		265
	Index of Scripture References		275

ABBREVIATIONS

BDB   Brown, F., Driver, S. R., and Briggs, C. A., *A Hebrew and English Lexicon of the Old Testament*, Oxford 1952

BZAW   *Beiträge zur Wissenschaft vom Alten Testament*

DB   Denzinger-Bannwart, *Enchiridion Symbolorum*

GCS   *Die griechischen christlichen Schriftsteller der ersten drei Jahrhunderte*, Leipzig 1897–1941, Berlin and Leipzig 1953, Berlin 1954 ff.

TWNT   *Theologisches Wörterbuch zum Neuen Testament*, ed. G. Kittel and G. Friedrich, Stuttgart 1932 ff.

Preface

Since the sacraments are the seven effective symbols and visible signs of Christ's gift of life within the church, it is imperative that they should constantly be reconsidered and reappreciated. It is not that we doubt their power to give us a share in Christ's life, by effecting that birth from above whereby we become the begotten of God, and by sustaining and renewing this divine life within us. We believe that they possess within themselves an efficacy which is that of Christ himself, appointed and sent by the Father to be the saviour of the world; an efficacy which is that of God's saving will itself. God has revealed to us that these seven signs are of his own certain choosing, and in that divine choice lies the certainty of their power, a certainty which cannot be called in question by man's doubts, and a power which is not contingent on man's response. And yet we must co-operate with the saving will of God, and accept the life-giving union with Christ, knowingly and deliberately welcoming these signs of the divine determination to give us life. Throughout the Bible it is clear that the divine initiative has so often failed, not because of the impotence of God, or the fickleness of his purpose, but because men have it within their power to reject his approaches. The sacraments which are the manifest approaches of Christ to man in every age can remain without effect, not because of their own impotence but because they are not sought, or they are received without that sympathetic understanding of genuine faith which establishes the necessary conditions for a vital union with Christ. It is because this genuine faith is constantly in danger from the deadening effects of ignorance, misunderstanding and distractions, and from the stifling consequences of routine and careless repetition, that it is imperative constantly to reconsider the sacraments.

Faith is not an unchanging possession, any more than is life itself. Just as there is a true sense in which we may speak of being more alive at one time than another, so also those who possess the divine gift of faith do so to a constantly varying degree. Not all who confess the same faith, and indeed use identical formularies to make that confession, possess the faith to the same degree. We may all subscribe to the Church's teaching on the sacraments, and all carefully recite the formularies in which that teaching is presented. But our faith concerning these sacraments varies in intensity, with a variety which cannot be measured by formularies, but which shows itself in the closeness of our union with Christ. Further reflection, therefore, upon the meaning of the sacraments is no mere academic exercise; nor is it for the sake of challenging accepted formulations or calling in question popular notions. Its purpose is the revival and the strengthening of that living response in faith which will provide the necessary conditions for a closer and more stable union with Christ through the sacraments.

The reflection upon the truths of faith which holds the surest promise of a renewed vitality and a deepening of our sympathetic understanding is that which is centred on the sacred scriptures, where these truths were first recorded and offered to the reflection of God's people. It is this reflection upon the word of God which has always been the primary source of the Church's vitality and has always led to the expressing of that vitality in her liturgical action. It is true, and indeed important to bear in mind, that her prayer and her practices have also been influenced by the varying historical and social conditions of her children, and these have in turn determined the particular lines along which her reflection on the scriptures has developed. There is always a mutual influence at work, since the Church's reflection upon the scriptures is not that of the uncommitted scholar examining an ancient literature, but rather that of the beloved re-reading the letters of the lover, who has already so shaped her life that she is sensitive to the overtones and the implications which a stranger can hardly be expected to find there.

The convictions of the Church, living by the strength she draws from the word of God, have been crystallised at various times in credal formulas and doctrinal statements which have sought to make articulate her complex experience of meditating the scriptures and living by them. Because the Church is a human reality, existing within the limitations of this historical world, both her experience of living by the word of God and her capacity to formulate that experience must wax or wane according as those human circumstances from which she can never be free make her more or less attentive to the Spirit who will teach her all truth. But because the Spirit of God is the life-giving strength which preserves her she can never be overcome by such circumstances. Her experience of living according to the word of God can never be so changed that she becomes wholly alienated from her past and unfaithful to her origins. Because she lives by the Spirit there will be constant growth, implying of its very nature a constant change; but it is a homogeneous change which is simply the further development and the greater realisation of those potentialities which have been hers from the beginning.

The relationship between the scriptures and that living experience within the Church which we know as the tradition is perhaps nowhere so clearly brought out as in the doctrine concerning the sacraments. It is in this area that Catholic theology has often been condemned as unscriptural. Whilst the Church teaches that there are seven sacraments, there are many non-Catholic theologians who maintain that the sacraments are only two in number. They insist that there is clear

warrant in the scriptures for Baptism and the Holy Eucharist as
the two signs determined and made efficacious by Christ himself.
They would doubtless agree that the history of doctrine and
practice within the Church endows certain other liturgical rites
with a specially sacred character, and makes them pre-eminently
apt means for invoking God's blessing at moments of particular
need. But they might hesitate to apply the term sacrament to
these rites, because in so doing it would seem that they are being
given a status which is equal to that of Baptism and the Eucharist,
and being turned into sacramental realities which are wholly
independent of the two great sacraments. The numerical distinction in the alternative statements that there are seven sacraments,
and that there are two, may easily lead to such an inference.
When this inference is taken for granted it is not without
reason that the scriptural foundation for the doctrine of seven
sacraments is called in question. Moreover, it must be admitted
that theological teaching on the seven sacraments since the
Reformation has lent some support to the conclusion that
Catholic doctrine is unscriptural. Faced with a new scriptural
interpretation which in the name of science was deliberately
isolated from the Church's living experience of the scriptures,
and yet put forward as the complete and solely legitimate
doctrine, Catholic theologians have tended to solve the resulting
problem in either of two ways. Accepting, at least tacitly, that
the scriptures are the essential and primary source of revelation,
they have attempted to show, by a similar scientific interpretation, that in fact all seven sacraments are to be found equally
explicitly in the New Testament. But the unhappy result of the
misguided effort to do this has had no little influence at times,
and has led them to try another way, by persuading them that
the tradition is an independent source of divine revelation.
Catholic theology in the post-Tridentine period has often shown
this uneasiness. Controversy concerning the apostolic origin
of certain sacramental rites tended to become controversy

concerning the apostolic origin of certain sacraments. Since rites are clearly distinct from one another, it was natural that in an atmosphere of controversy the realities they signified and realised should be thought to be equally distinct. Since the searching of the scriptures for seven clearly distinct rites was doomed to failure, it seemed all the more imperative to search them for seven clearly distinct realities which the Church had been able as it were to clothe in their appropriately distinctive rites.

All this theological effort stemmed from the unshakable conviction that the Church's teaching, proclaimed by her practice as much as by her formal pronouncements, was the authentic proclamation of the gospel. The Church, guided by the Holy Spirit, offered to her children seven distinct signs of efficacious union with Christ, and therefore Christ himself had willed these signs. The apostles were the authentic witnesses of Christ's will, and therefore they too bore witness to these signs. Since the New Testament was the record of the apostolic teaching, then it would seem to follow that this should provide the evidence. But whilst this last conclusion was a deep conviction, it was not itself unshakable. Theologians began to wonder whether the New Testament was the only record of the apostolic teaching. Could it not well be, and the more they thought of it the more reasonable it became, that there existed another and distinct record in the unwritten tradition of the Church? The affirmative answer to this question became stronger the more difficult it was to find in the New Testament what they were looking for. It seemed that the fathers of the Church had found there what the theologians could no longer find. Must they continue to look in the same place, or could they not confine their search to the unwritten tradition? The cynical comment that one can find in the Bible anything one wants to find has never really been true.

But it is certainly true that there are different ways of reading

the Bible, and therefore many different aspects of the truth to
be found there. We now interpret the scriptures by way of
investigating with all the new wealth of historical knowledge
available to us the meaning which the human authors intended
to convey to their readers. The implications of such a method
are only slowly being realised, and the consequences have often
enough proved unwelcome when they have first been made
known. Not unnaturally this has often led to a questioning of
the historico-critical methods of interpretation. But it is by now
far more clearly understood that this method is the only sound
and satisfying way of reading the scriptures for our own age:
an age whose mentality has been determined by that very same
method in all the other aspects of its search for truth. The great
encyclical letter of Pius XII, *Divino afflante Spiritu*, gave the
needed assurance and encouragement which has helped Catholic
exegetes to revitalise the Church's meditation of her sacred
scriptures and thus, among many other things, to throw new
light on the significance of the sacraments for her daily life.

The articles which comprise this book, therefore, are the
result of historico-critical investigation of the scriptural foundations for the Church's belief in the sacraments. Since the writers
have concentrated upon the scriptures, they only touch indirectly
upon other aspects of the Church's teaching which are the fruit
of her meditation and practice over the centuries. The purpose
of this collection is not to provide a complete treatise on the
sacraments, but rather to offer new insights which may perhaps
throw light on doctrines already well known and cherished, but
which have possibly become banal and ineffective. The study
of the development of doctrine shows that this takes place
through a series of efforts starting from the scriptures, rather
than by a continuous and logical process of deduction from what
has immediately preceded. The Church's teaching resembles a
never-ending series of concentric circles round the Bible, rather
than a chain the links of which depend only on what immediately

precedes. The circle of doctrine which is being boldly described within the Church today is at the same time part of a more complex pattern which has been growing since the beginning. It depends upon its centre, the scriptures, for its true shape, and it depends upon those earlier circles of doctrine concentric with it for its ability to give a complete and an inspiring picture of the unchanging faith entrusted to the Church. It is in this way that the Church fulfils her responsibility as both the custodian and the interpreter of God's word. Thus for example the renewed study of the scriptures brings out more clearly the interrelation between the seven sacraments and the body of Christ, the great sacrament of God's saving power in our midst. We realise more clearly the intimate connection that the five other sacraments have with Baptism and the Holy Eucharist. We are enabled to see the whole sacramental system as our initiation into that life of union with Christ, as our strengthening of that union or our re-establishing of it when it has been broken by sin. We do not lose sight of the fact that the Church has clarified and made easier the understanding of the sacraments by developing her rites and her explanations. But this clarification and this practical development can result in a shallow understanding and too mechanical a reception of the sacraments. Men are historical beings and the way in which they attempt to grasp truth varies from epoch to epoch The Church, however, bears responsibility towards the men of every age, who have always continued to beseech Jesus 'that they might touch even the fringe of his garment' (Mk. 6 : 56). It is the Church's task to put the fringe of his garment within our reach so that touching it we may be made well.

Perhaps this book may play some part in making the sacraments more deeply appreciated and more eagerly sought after. It is in no way a complete treatment of the scriptural sources of sacramental doctrine. Moreover the articles were written in some cases as much as ten years ago, and it has been possible to

make only minor changes. But it has seemed worth while
nevertheless to make them more readily available, especially since
we celebrateed in 1965 the silver jubilee of the Catholic Biblical
Association, in whose quarterly *Scripture* they were originally
published.

T. WORDEN

I

Old Testament Signs[1]

J. van der Ploeg O.P.

THE use of signs or tokens pervades the whole of human life in our day as in the past, though the identity or nature of these signs may differ according to the time or the place. Broadly speaking, a sign is an action or a thing which has a meaning for us differing from the action or the thing taken by itself. The Middle Ages used to express this clearly when its philosophers said that a sign is a thing by which we may know something else. Taken like this, signs may be natural or conventional: natural when they have a natural connection with that of which they are a sign; thus smoke is a sign of fire, and footsteps in the snow signs that someone has passed that way; conventional, when there is no such relation and the sign has been chosen at random to mean something else. For the most part signs are not chosen completely at random, because the human mind wishes to see some similarity between the sign and its meaning. But this similarity is not necessary, and is often completely lacking when a sign has been used over a long period. Nevertheless we may say that the distinction between conventional and natural signs is rather a distinction between different types; transitional forms are possible and a sign may be partly natural, partly conventional.

The most common signs among men are the words they speak. Most words have now become purely conventional signs, but originally many were more than this. Words have always been the sign *par excellence* for making known one's ideas to

[1] First published in *Scripture*, 1956, pp. 33–44.

other people. Among the ancient Hebrews the word or name of
a thing was thought to be something more than a purely conventional sign; the name was closely connected with the thing
and almost a part of it, often expressing one of its characteristic
qualities. Thus we read in the story of Paradise that the first
man gave names to all the animals and that God stood by to see
what he would call them. This was no idle or arbitrary game,
for it thereby became clear that no animal could be the help
God desired to give to Adam. The highest of all names was that
of God: Yahweh, that mighty, awe-inspiring name which in
later times the Jews feared even to pronounce.

Words spoken in solemn circumstances, such as words of
blessing or cursing, and especially the word of God, were
thought to be instinct with power. This primitive idea has not
yet completely disappeared. A Dutch proverb says that he who
speaks of the devil steps on his tail, which means that if you
pronounce a person's name he may suddenly appear. There are
many who still fear to pronounce the names of certain diseases,
lest they be struck down by them. It is difficult to say by what
mental or psychological mechanism words are thought to be so
closely connected with things or events that they are credited
with power over them, or with a share of the power of those
who pronounce them; but it is certain that the connection was
felt by the ancient Israelites as a very strong one.[1] When Isaac
had blessed his son Jacob in error for his elder son Esau the effect
of the blessing could not be taken away (Gen. 28 : 33).[2] In
Is. 55 : 10–11 we read that as rain and snow do not return to

[1] The reason might be that the word is closely connected with the image
of the thing, and in primitive thought the image is partly or wholly
identical with the thing itself. Cf. J. Maritain, 'Signe et symbole chez les
primitifs', *Revue Thomiste*, 1938, pp. 299–330.

[2] If we interpret this story as a part of the whole book of Genesis it seems
clear enough that the author sees divine providence at work, choosing
Jacob, i.e. the people of Israel, in spite of the sins and shortcomings of
Jacob and his mother. It is nevertheless clear that in the old folk-tale the
power of the blessing played its part.

heaven but drench and fertilise the earth, so the word which proceeds from the mouth of God shall not return idle to its lord, having achieved nothing; but it shall fulfil and execute the will of God. A late text illustrates this as follows: 'Whilst a deep silence surrounded everything, and the night rapidly reached the midst of its course, thy almighty word came forth from heaven, from the royal throne, as a grim warrior in the midst of the land doomed to destruction; as a sharp dagger it carried thy irrevocable command; whilst it stood it filled every thing with death; it touched heaven, walking on the earth' (Wis. 10 : 14–16). Thus a word, though essentially a sign, could be more; it could be instinct with power, and bring to pass what it symbolised.

There were many signs and symbols beside those belonging to language, though language very often accompanied them as their complement. There was, for instance, the covenant. When a covenant was made, a sign was chosen to be its token. This sign was like a silent witness, continually recalling the covenant. In Babylonia no contract was valid unless it had been written on a tablet and duly sealed. People like Laban and Jacob acted in a more primitive way: having concluded a treaty they heaped up stones and called the crude monument 'the heap of witness' (Gen. 31 : 47). This heap of stones was to remind later generations of what had taken place. When God made a covenant with men, signs of that covenant were determined.

But before speaking of these signs we must speak of what 'covenant' meant for the ancient Israelites.[1] It must be explained in

[1] Modern theologians often explain the word in accordance not with Israelite ideas, but with their own, and sometimes go so far as to clothe it with completely modern thought. For modern man it is strange that God should conclude a covenant or treaty with men, since to our mind this can only be concluded on a basis of a certain equality. There is no equality between God and man, and when God manifested his will, as he did when offering a covenant to the Patriarchs or to Israel, they were physically free to refuse, but morally bound to accept.

relation to the social customs of the world in which the patriarchs
and the people of Israel lived. Amongst the nomad tribes of the
Arabian Desert there was, and perhaps there still is, a state of
latent war, or more exactly of absence of peace. Within the
family, clan or tribe (and clan and tribe were thought of as big
families) ruled the ties of kinship. Here there was a solidarity
which obliged everyone to help his 'brother', and it was considered normal that the individual should share the fate of the
community. Within the totality of the family there was peace.
But there was no such peace in their relations with others unless
a covenant had been made with them. The stranger was always
the enemy, real or potential, and in many languages the word for
stranger or foreigner is the same as that for enemy.[1] It is abundantly clear that in the world in which ancient Israel lived, or
had lived in still earlier times, and which was afterwards considered as an ideal one (just as the civilised modern Arab idealises
the life of the Bedouin in the desert), the absence of peace
between tribes and peoples was considered normal. Only a
pact or covenant could change this; it established a solidarity
and a common interest between those who had previously
nothing in common, not even the same human rights. There
was, moreover, the possibility of a man having to flee from his
own family or clan or tribe; if he lived in the desert alone he
would be like Cain after he had killed his brother; as a stranger
to everybody, his life and his possessions would be at anybody's
mercy. In order to avoid this miserable state so like to death, he
would seek the protection of a powerful man. He would take
refuge in his tent and protection would normally be granted to
him. Then a covenant could be made by which the refugee
became, quite artificially, a member of the family of the protector. He would be obliged for his part to accept the rules and

[1] In Hebrew *nokrî* means stranger, but the related *nakru* in Accadian
means enemy; the Latin word *hostis* originally meant stranger, but more
commonly signifies enemy.

customs of the community of which he had become a member. This explains the type of relationship which God established with men when he made a covenant with them. Israel did not flee to God, but God came to their rescue. He offered his covenant and the people freely accepted it.

The first covenant mentioned in the Bible is that which God made with creation after the great flood. God had destroyed humanity because men had separated themselves from God and thus the state of peace which had existed in Paradise had come to an end. After the flood he is represented as resolving to do this no more; to assure humanity of this he made a covenant, by which an end was put to the enmity between God and men which had caused the flood: 'I establish my covenant with you; neither shall all flesh be cut off any more by the water of the flood, neither shall there any more be a flood to destroy the earth' (Gen. 9 : 9–11). The covenant had also a sign, the rainbow, which links heaven and earth, the abode of God and that of men, and which appears in the clouds after the storm. From now on the rainbow had the character of a sign; it was a reminder of this covenant. This is probably a theological reflection of a later time, expressing in the form of a covenant the theological truth concerning what had happened, with the rainbow as a very apt sign of it.

The second covenant mentioned in the book of Genesis is that of God with Abraham, the first and ideal ancestor of the Israelites. This covenant, first mentioned in Gen. 15 : 18 (J) and then in 17 : 2 (P), is presented as a unilateral promise made by God and accepted by Abraham who believed in God.

The covenant contained, moreover, a commandment, which was also its sign. Abraham must be circumcised with all his descendants, and even the male slaves belonging to them. Circumcision was to be a fundamental law in the society of which God was the father and protector. The Israelites knew that it was practised by other peoples such as the Egyptians. But among the people of God it acquired a new meaning, that of a divine command expressly given to Abraham and through him to the whole of Israel. Of its nature it was also an apt token of the indestructibility of the bond between those who were his by covenant and promise. Much has been written about the original meaning of circumcision. It seems probable that among many peoples or tribes it is an initiation ceremony by which a boy attains the status of manhood; this may have been its original signification among the early Semites. But in Israel it was performed when the child was only eight days old, and this was perhaps peculiar to the Israelites.[1] Its special practice in Israel on the eighth day was at the same time a token of the covenant. Was it also the token of a special relationship set up between God and the individual? This question seems out of place in the Old Testament, for the covenant with Abraham and his offspring who formed the people of Israel was not with the individual as such. Though each individual had to observe the commandment of circumcision (cf. Gen. 17 : 10), the people formed a unity, or corporate personality as it has been called, and it was with the people as a unity that the covenant was made. If any individual refused to observe the commandment, and if he were not, for this refusal, cut off (killed or eliminated) from the community, then the whole community was responsible for breaking the covenant. So the covenant was made with the individual in and through the group, not with the individual directly. Thus it is quite superfluous to ask why girls were not circumcised, as they are in certain savage tribes. Only the males represented the people in the covenant with God, and circumcision as a sign of the covenant of the whole people with God was not necessarily imposed on every single individual. In the dispensation of the New Testament circumcision no longer exists, because it was

[1] The Israelites greatly scorned the Philistines because they were not circumcised, with the suggestion that uncircumcised meant impure. This is an additional explanation of why circumcision was so important.

the sign *par excellence* of the old Law and, we may say, a positive commandment of it.

In the book of Exodus we read of another covenant concluded between God and his people at the foot of Mount Sinai. Moses built an altar and erected twelve stones beside or round about it, in accordance with the number of the tribes of Israel (Ex. 24 : 4). That such an altar could have served as a token is well proved by the story related in Jos. 22 : 10 ff. and that the stones could have had that meaning is clear from their very number. Their primary purpose was for worship, but they were also to be perpetual witnesses of what had happened once in the past. A second sign to confirm the covenant is the singular rite with the blood of animals, mentioned only in Ex. 24 : 5 ff. Half of the blood was for Yahweh and was sprinkled on the altar, half of it on the people, and *between* those two acts (if we may interpret the text strictly in this way) the book of the Law was read. Thus the sprinkling of the blood and the reading of the Law were closely united and formed one sacred ceremony. It has been said that the sprinkling of the blood on the altar and on the people was done after the pattern of a blood-ceremony, which established kinship between two persons, clans or tribes,[1] and there may be some truth in this statement. Of course, real kinship between Yahweh and his people was impossible, but strong ties were to keep both together, or rather to keep the people united with their God, and this unity was symbolised by the ceremony. It established a real bond between God and his people, and though the bond was before everything a moral one, which could be both broken and repaired, the ceremony of the double sprinkling of blood was a sacred act which was not without effect of itself. By it Israel was in a certain sense consecrated to God and acquired a special holiness.

[1] Cf. W. Robertson Smith, *Kinship and Marriage in Early Arabia*, new edn, London 1903, pp. 59 ff.

Other important signs are the many sacrifices of the old Law. According to the Old Testament, sacrifices were offered from the beginning and they are thought by many scholars to have been a feature of every religion.[1] Certainly their origins are deeply rooted in human nature. But it is not sure that all the ceremonies which are classified as sacrifices are expressions of one and the same fundamental idea. However, we need not examine this here. We wish to confine ourselves to the idea of sacrifice as it is found in Lev. 1–7, chapters whose ultimate formulation is to be regarded as the result of a long development, certainly as far as details are concerned, and perhaps also in some important ideas. Except for the oblation of incense (and the *ḥerem*) that which is offered is always food, either animal or vegetable. This, however, does not necessarily imply that it is always offered precisely as food, or that the final author of Leviticus regarded it as such. It is with his intention, rather than with the primitive meaning of such sacrifices, that we are concerned here. Clearly it cannot be doubted that the author of this book shared the belief expressed in Ps. 50 : 13, where God asks: 'Shall I eat the flesh of bulls or drink the blood of goats?'[2]

The priestly author first distinguishes three kinds of sacrifice: the holocaust, the meal offering, and the sacrifice of communion; then two other kinds are added: the sin offering and the guilt offering. Of the holocaust, the sin offering and the guilt offering, it is explicitly stated that they are offered to obtain expiation. The smoke of the sacrifice, even of the meal offering and the sacrifice

---

[1] This is however denied by so eminent an author as W. Schmidt s.v.d., *Ethnologische Bemerkungen zu theologischen Opfertheorien*, Wien 1922, pp. 21 ff.

[2] In Lev. 1 : 9 ff. the sacrificial substance is called *'iššeh*, which is generally translated as 'offering made by fire'; but some link it with the root *'nš* to be friendly. Recently it has been translated by H. Cazelles as *mets consumé* (*Le Lévitique: Bible de Jérusalem*, Paris 1951, p. 13 etc.), though he concedes that the Israelites actually linked the word with *'eš*, fire.

of communion, is called the soothing or tranquillising perfume.[1]
The old versions, Latin, Greek, Syriac and Aramaic, ignore the
sense of 'soothing' and translate the expression by sweet odour
or, according to Onqelos, 'that which is favourably received'.
But the Hebrew word means probably 'causing to rest' and
therefore 'appeasing'. Possibly this meaning had been lost by
the time the Greek version was made, or it may have been considered too anthropomorphical. Anything may be soothing or
placating for two reasons: it averts the anger of God which
has been roused, or it prevents it from being roused. In one of
these two senses all the sacrifices mentioned in Lev. 1–7 are
thought by its final author or redactor to be soothing. But if we
try to penetrate more deeply into the exact meaning of the
different sacrifices we find it difficult to give adequate explanations. The meaning of a sign may vary according to the time
when it is used. We have to keep in mind that such very old
signs and symbols as sacrifices may have had an original meaning
which was replaced by another later on. Many religious ceremonies, as we know from our own practices, are performed
simply because they are traditional and have been handed down
from generations long past. Those who perform them do what
they have seen done by others as acts of religion, to honour God,
to fulfil his will and to implore his favour. For the Israelite, the
Law was above all the expression of the will of God; if the later
Jew offered sacrifices it was first of all because God had ordered
him to do so; if he did it of his own initiative he still had to do it
according to the precise rules which had been laid down for him
in the Law. But this does not mean that sacrifices had no further
meaning.

The particular significance of the sin offering and the guilt
offering is clearly indicated by their very names, though it

[10] rê^aḥ nîḥô^aḥ: 'soothing, tranquillising odour' (BDB), *parfum d'apaise-
ment* (Cazelles); Zorell hesitates, translating the second of the two words by
placans, pacans, Deo placens.

surprises us to find that the 'sins' for which such sacrifices must
be offered were sometimes unconscious infringements of the Law
(cf. Lev. 5 : 17). This must not, however, lead to the conclusion
that the legislator had no strictly moral concept of sin, a conclusion clearly at variance with many other places in the Old
Testament. The idea in Lev. 1–7 is rather that the holiness of
God is so great that every offence, even an inadvertent one,
committed against such holiness ought to be repaired. Violations
of the Law which were not considered as violations of the
covenant[1] could be repaired by sacrifices, which took away
the consequences of cer monial uncleanness. Thus they were a
means of preserving the co rect procedure to be observed in the
worship of God, and served 'o emphasise the strict rights which
God enjoyed by reason of his sanctity.

The sacrifice of the holocau t is probably much older than
the two mentioned above, and consequently its meaning is less
clear in the Law. According to Lev. 1 it seems to have been
offered to expiate for sins and to obtain the general favour of
God. The sins are not limited to any specific examples, and the
holocaust was probably considered the highest ritual act of
religion. By it the complete dependence of man on God was
recognised. Hence it belongs to the daily service. It was offered
to God by Noah after the flood, by kings before a battle, and so
on. It is nowhere stated that by virtue of this sacrifice sins disappeared, and the prophets protested against the idea that man could
win the favour of God merely by external acts such as sacrifices.
So it is not clear precisely what efficacy was attached to the

[1] When an individual had transgressed the covenant he had to be
eliminated, usually by death. The Law possessed no system of greater or
lesser penalties, such as we find for instance in the *Manual of Discipline* of
the Covenanters of Qumran, or in a modern penal code. Death was practically the only true penalty, and it is not considered as a punishment in the
modern sense of the word. This penalty could not be commuted by
the imposition of sacrifices in its place. Cf. J. Van der Ploeg, 'Studies in
Hebrew Law', *Catholic Biblical Quarterly*, 1951, pp. 166–9.

sign. They were external acts by which man could show his submission to God, and they emphasised the need of winning God's favour. The Israelite believed that by offering sacrifice with a pure intention he had at least improved his relations with God. What was the exact role played by the sacrifice? It seems to have been considered as more than a mere sign, but how much more? The prophets were strongly opposed to the more or less magical conception many Israelites had of the efficacy of sacrifice. But the author of Lev. 1–7 was much more interested in the exact ritual of sacrifices than in the idea which lay behind them; and because the whole Law stressed so much the fulfilment of the will of God, which was also stressed by the Prophets, we have no reason to suppose that the idea of the lawgiver was fundamentally different from that of the Prophets, as regards the efficacy of sacrifice.

In the case of the meal offering, the prevalent idea was that of offering a gift to God in his sanctuary. Nobody would dare to appear before a great personage to ask his favour or simply to speak with him, without offering a present. It is understandable, therefore, that gifts were presented to God in the same circumstances. The giving of the first fruits to God is a custom found even among such primitive peoples as the Pygmies, and the purpose is to recognise his dominion. The Israelite peasant, who had to give a good part of his harvest to the landlord, was not surprised that he had to give the first fruits to God; they belonged to God, and it was by his permission that man could make use of them. The sacrifice of communion was followed by a sacred meal in which man ate, as it were, with his God. To eat and drink together is a sign of peace. If anyone enters the tent of a Bedouin and eats the slightest morsel of food with him, or drinks only a cup of coffee, he knows that he will suffer no harm, and the lord of the tent is bound to protect his guest against every enemy. Hence the sin mentioned in Ps. 41 : 10, and later committed by Judas, could hardly be more heinous.

The sacrifice of communion then, combined with the sacred meal in the house of God, was a token of intimate friendship. It presumed that the participants were fulfilling the will of God, and behaving in their daily lives as his friends. It was because the contrary was all too frequent in practice that the prophets hated such sacrificial ceremonies, for when sinners participated in them they were lying mockeries. The sacrifice of communion was moreover offered privately in fulfilment of a vow (cf. Ps. 22 : 23–7). When God had granted what had been asked, and thus shown himself the good friend of the one who had taken the vow, it was natural that the latter should eat and drink with God.

It is therefore clear that some kinds of sacrifices had a special significance because of their resemblance to the customs of everyday life. But regarding the holocaust and sin offerings it is difficult to say much more than that the later Israelites and the Jews knew them to be in accordance with the will of God.[1] Animals for sacrifices, except those for the sacrifices of the poor, were costly, and this also made clear that the favour of an offended God was not easily regained; to sin against God was indeed a serious crime. It is not easy to say how far the sacrificial animal was thought to be offered in place of the person who presented it. That the idea of vicarious suffering was not unknown is clear from Is. 53, but we have already seen that, generally speaking, true violations of the covenant could not be repaired by sacrifices.

Finally something must be said about two other very important rites—purification with water and anointing with oil. The symbolic meaning of the first seems clear; as water washes away the impurities of the body, so it may also take away ritual uncleanness. But what is such uncleanness? From

[1] Cf. O. Schmitz, *Die Opferanschauungen des späteren Judentums*, Tübingen 1910, p. 119.

later rabbinical discussions we may conclude that it was something quasi-material which could be contracted by the slightest contact with impure things. Its opposite was holiness, and of this also, other things being equal, the same may be said. Thus clothes which were worn by the priests in the sanctuary were holy, because they had been in contact with the holy objects of the holy place. Though it was dangerous to come into close contact with holy things, it was not dangerous to become unclean. The idea of uncleanness was originally a merely ritual one and had in itself nothing to do with morality, though it could be a consequence of immoral deeds. In later times ritual and moral uncleanness were confused and even identified, as is not surprising, since most people find it easier to identify things which are similar rather than to distinguish between them. Various things, considered disgusting to God, were unclean. But within this category were included also the exercise of very vital functions, such as of sex and childbirth. It cannot be doubted that very primitive ideas and taboos are at the root of all this, but it is very hard to say how far these actually influenced the idea of uncleanness in later times.

Uncleanness made a person ritually unfit to take part in the cult. Only holy persons, in the widest sense of the word, could approach God, because he himself is holy. Uncleanness could be removed from a person or thing in various ways, and most commonly by a complete or partial bath. As in the case of sacrifices, we do not know precisely how the water removed the uncleanness. In later times the legislation on ritual purity and the means whereby uncleanness was to be removed were considered simply as the expression of the will of God. As God created all things, he had also instituted the means of purification. The Law taught the Israelites that God is so great that even certain material conditions are required in order to approach him in worship. Moral cleanness was, of course, required first. But in dealing with the great ones of the earth, the observance of certain external ceremonies is necessary. To teach the Israelites that God is greater than the most exalted on earth the Law required them to be clean, even in the ritual sense of the word. If rightly understood this requirement also taught them purity of heart. A particular ceremony of purification was that which was done with a kind of holy water (Num. 19), made for special purposes and in a special way. Because of the way in which it was prepared it was certainly thought to be more powerful than ordinary or even 'living' water, though nothing of this is stated in the Law. The command to use it was again an expression of the will of God. The origin of the custom is probably quite primitive.

A custom of which the primitive origin has not yet been explained is that of anointing with oil.[1] Oil was poured out on holy stones or even rubbed into them. Kings, prophets and priests were anointed with it, and also holy objects (Ex. 30 : 26 ff.). It may be that in early times oil was used for reasons not altogether unlike those for which blood was used in different circumstances. The blood was thought to be the seat of life, or even life itself (Deut. 12 : 23), in the vague way the ancient Israelites used to speak. Similarly the fat of an animal seems to have been considered as a vital part of it, and the seat of life. The oil of the olive may have been considered, in a similar way, as the spirit of life, and therefore the unction may have been regarded as a means of giving life or more life to the person anointed. Later on this idea was lost; the holy oil of Ex. 30 : 22–5 was prepared in a special way, and it was forbidden for lay-people to use the holy recipe on no less a penalty than death, since it was sacrilege (Ex. 30 : 23).

Anointing with sacred oil conferred holiness, in the sense defined above. It brought the person into closer contact with

[1] See E. Kutsch, 'Salbung als Rechtsakt im Alten Testament', *BZAW* 87, 1963.

the divine, because in Israel Yahweh alone was the Holy One
and the source of all holiness. Several times prophets who had
the spirit of God anointed a man as king. Samuel took oil and
poured it over David, and from that day 'the spirit of Yahweh
rested on David' (1 Sam. 16 : 13). From this it might be inferred
that the pouring of oil on the head of the elect was a sign of the
giving of the spirit and produced this effect in some mysterious
way. But in the history of Saul we read that he was first anointed,
and only afterwards, though probably the same day, did the
spirit of Yahweh come over him (1 Sam. 10 : 6). The anointing
of Saul by Samuel had been accompanied by powerful prophetic
words which were to produce what they expressed. The unction
of Jehu was also accomplished by a prophet, and accompanied
by a word of Yahweh: 'Thus says Yahweh: I have anointed thee
king over Israel' (2 Kgs. 9 : 3). In Is. 61 : 1 a prophet says: 'The
spirit of the Lord Yahweh is upon me, because Yahweh has
anointed me'; this recalls 1 Kgs. 19 : 16 where we read that Elias
received the command to anoint Eliseus. Thus we see that a
primitive custom, the first scope of which may have been to
strengthen and confer a new vitality, is later used as a symbol
which indicated the transfer of the mysterious quality of ritual
holiness, or even of the spirit. In Israel the spirit of God was not
transferred by oil and unction, though a certain connection
remains; it is God who gives the spirit or the spirit itself which
comes upon a person. Solemn and powerful words had to
accompany the anointing.

These examples taken from the daily life of the Israelites
show abundantly the paramount significance of signs and
symbols in their religious practice. It is also clear that in the
true religion of Yahweh those signs and symbols lost more and
more of their original, primitive and quasi-magical significance,
to a point where they became simply expressions of the will of
God. But even as such they were thought to have, by the will

B

of God, some mysterious power, the character of which cannot be determined. Being signs and symbols of the old dispensation, they were also shades of things to come. The new dispensation which has come through our Lord Jesus Christ is considered by the Christian as a continuation, an amplification and a fulfilment of the old one. In this supernatural order of things it is only to be expected that various signs which guided the faithful in the time of the old covenant should have been taken over with a more perfect meaning in the new. But these new meanings are not wholly new; they are the 'fulfilment' of the old and in harmony with them. The people of God has become the Church, gathered from all nations; and its holy signs are the sacraments.

II

The Spirit of God[1]

L. Johnston

IF THE essence of religion can be summed up in one phrase it is this: the union of God with man. This was God's plan for mankind from the beginning, when he walked in the garden with our first parents, until they hid themselves from him by sin. The rest of the history of the world as the Bible gives it, the history of the Redemption, is the process of restoration of this state of harmony, until it was achieved in an even more perfect form than at first, in the Redemption by our Lord. It is this which God signified to his people by the concept of 'covenant': the act of union, the act of alliance. And inside the covenant relationship God's presence among his people was realised in various ways. It was realised by the Law—this is an aspect of this institution which is often overlooked, that 'There is no other nation which has its God so close to it as our God is to us; for what other nation has statutes and precepts like all this law which I, Moses, put before you now' (Deut. 4 : 7). It was realised in Temple and Tabernacle ('Tent of Meeting'), where God personally came down and dwelt in their midst. And it was realised still more perfectly in the gift of God's 'spirit'.

In order to appreciate all that 'the spirit of God' means in the Old Testament, it will be necessary to begin further back than our English word; in fact it will be as well to forget for the moment the connotations of the English term—soul, ghost, disembodied spirit, and so on. The Hebrew word *rûah* means first of all 'wind'. It is the word used in Genesis when God

[1] First published in *Scripture*, 1956, pp. 65–74.

walked with Adam and Eve in the cool breeze of evening. It is
the word for the wind which dries up the flood. It is the word
for the mighty gale which smashes up great ships (Ps. 48 : 8).
It can mean breath: the psalmist (135 : 17) scoffs at idols which
can neither see nor hear nor breathe—they have not 'spirit' in
their nostrils.[1] Both meanings can be seen in Ps. 104: verse 4
speaks of God making the winds ('spirits') his messengers; and
verse 29, he takes away the breath ('spirit') of his creatures and
they cease to exist. And in both of these verses we see the danger
of reading the text with preconceived, non-biblical, ideas:
reading the Latin version, or the Latin commentators, in verse 4,
for example, we would be led to think that it meant that God
used 'spiritual beings' as messengers, or angels; and in verse 29
we would be inclined to take it simply in our sense of
'soul'.

It is true, however, that from this last sense of 'breath' it is
an easy step to the meaning 'breath of life'—breath being that
which is most obviously characteristic of a living being. Qoheleth,
lamenting the inevitability of death, says: 'man cannot retain
his spirit, he has no power over the day of his death'. God sends
the flood 'to destroy all that possessed the breath of life'—that
is, every living thing. In passages like these it is tempting to
translate the word simply as 'soul'. But Hebrew uses another
word for 'soul', which it uses to denote the thing which is living;
when it uses this word 'spirit', *rûaḥ*, it has in mind rather the
'livingness' of a thing: not, however, conceived in an abstract
way, but on the contrary thought of in a very physical,

---

[1] It is doubtful which of these senses comes first: is the breath thought
of as a little wind whistling through man's nostrils? Or is the wind thought
of as a breath of God? The latter is suggested by several texts (for example,
Ps. 18 : 16: 'The foundations of the world are laid bare by the blast of the
breath of God's nostrils.') But the evolution of sense suggested above—
from wind, a movement of air, to breath—seems probable; and in any case
it does not affect the next and more important step in the argument—from
breath to breath of life.

concrete way—the breath which shows that a thing is living.

Man is living because he draws breath, because he has 'spirit' in him. And God also is living, because of *his* spirit. His spirit, like the spirit of man, is his 'livingness'. God is thought of—or rather spoken of—as if he drew breath like a man; and as in man, this breath, this spirit, is the sign of his life. Now when God creates he communicates his own infinite power of life; and the Bible portrays this for us in an extremely graphic manner as God 'breathing into the nostrils of man' so that man becomes a living being. God 'sends' forth his spirit and all things are created (Ps. 104 : 30). That which is, breathes: and its breath is a breath of God. Man depends on God's breath for existence; if it is withdrawn he dies. Job, for instance, protests his life-long innocence 'as long as there is breath in me, as long as God's spirit is in my nostrils'. So truly is it breath of God's breath that Qoheleth says that at death 'the dust shall return to the earth as it was, and the spirit to God who gave it'.

Our idea of spirituality or immateriality is not the main impression we are to take from the 'spirit of God'. It is true that there are texts where this might seem to be the sense. Isaiah for instance warns Israel against trusting Egypt, for 'Egypt is a man and not God; their horses are flesh, not spirit'. The contrast, however, is not between the corporeal and the spiritual, but between the weak and the powerful; 'all flesh is grass, and the glory thereof is like the glory of grass' which fades with the first heat of summer; 'flesh' is man in so far as he is weak and transitory and corruptible. What Isaiah is saying, then, is that man and all his strength are weak and incapable of resistance against the strength and vitality, the 'spirit' of God. The 'spirit of God' therefore means, not the spiritual, immaterial nature of God, but his strength, his vitality. It means 'God the living'; it means 'Yahweh'—he who is. And the sacred writers are not concerned with insubstantial metaphysical definitions. Life for them is a dynamic quality. It implies vital and vigorous action.

If Yahweh is he who is, he is also he who acts: he is the Lord of life, creator, omnipotent.

We have seen that it is by God's spirit breathed into man that man lives. Now the same spirit can give him a share of the divine activity also. It descends on Othoniel and Jephte, it clothes Gedeon, it rushes upon Samuel and Saul, to urge them on to the work which they had to do. It may manifest itself in quite prosaic ways, as when the craftsmen in charge of the building of the tabernacle are given God's spirit. It may be given even to pagans, like the prophet Balaam, or foreign kings invading Israel as the agents of God's vengeance (2 Kgs. 19 : 7). But in every case we notice that it is directed to the furtherance of the covenant, the union of God and man. It descends on Moses, that he may found God's nation; it descends on the Judges that they may fight God's battles and deliver his people; on the Kings, that they may rule God's people in God's name; on the Prophets, that they may direct his people by God's own word. This is the people among whom he has desired to dwell, through whom he will be present on earth; and he forms and moulds them to that privilege with preparatory and partial manifestations of it—as we light a fire with fire.

It is sometimes said that the 'spirit of God' is no more than a figurative way of expressing God's action, like the 'arm of the Lord', or the 'hand of God'. There is certainly some truth in this; but the very comparison with such phrases brings out the difference: 'spirit' indicates something much more internal and vital than 'hand' or 'arm'; it suggests God himself acting in a person, not merely moving him by external assistance or compulsion.

The internal and even moral efficacy of God's spirit becomes more and more evident as the history of Israel progresses.[1] It

[1] This is not to be taken as implying that there is any attempt to establish the chronological succession of the texts which follow; it is meant only in

is the spirit which guides our steps (Ps. 143 : 10), thus perform-
ing the work of the Law. In the book of Wisdom, it is the spirit
of wisdom, identified with the gift of wisdom, infused into us
to show us God's will and to help us to perform it: 'For who
can know thy counsel unless thou givest wisdom, and sendest
thy holy spirit from above . . . that it may work with me, and
lead my actions wisely' (Wis. 9 : 17, 10, 11). In Ps. 51 it is even
the principle of moral life: just as God created man by breathing
his spirit into him, so it is by his spirit that the sinner recovers
from his sins and lives anew: 'Create a clean heart in me, O my
God, put a new and upright spirit within me; take not away thy
holy spirit from me.'

The description of the spirit in this last text as God's *holy*
spirit is significant. A covenant with a holy God demands
holiness in the people: 'Be ye holy, as I the Lord your God am
holy.' But the people have sinned, they have broken the covenant,
rendered it null and void. So God prepares a new and more
perfect covenant: 'Behold the day is coming, says the Lord,
when I shall make a new covenant with the house of Israel and
the house of Juda: not like the covenant which I made with
their fathers, the covenant which they have made void; but I
shall write the law in their hearts, and they shall be my people
and I shall be their God.' And just as it was by his spirit that
God formed and moulded the people for the first covenant, so
his spirit will work the reformation necessary for the new
covenant—his spirit, and in particular, the spirit of his holiness.
God's holiness is often represented under the figure of fire,
burning away all that is opposed to it: 'The light of Israel shall
be the fire, the Holy One of Israel shall be the flame which shall
burn down the lofty trees of the forest of Assyria' (Is. 10 : 16 f.).

the most general sense—that in an earlier stage of the biblical literature the
spirit seems to be looked on particularly as the source of 'superhuman' acts,
while in a later stage the stress is on the moral activity of the spirit.

And so also God's holy spirit, like a burning wind, shall sweep away the impurity of the people to prepare them for the new covenant. 'On that day all those who are left in Sion shall be called holy: for the Lord will wipe away the filth of the people by the spirit of judgment, a burning spirit' (Is. 4 : 2–4).

And just as we have seen that Moses, judges, Prophets and Kings were invested with the spirit of God for the perfection of the first covenant, so he who is to usher in the new covenant is to be filled most perfectly with this spirit. 'Behold my servant, he whom I have chosen to be the covenant of the people—to him I have given my spirit' (Is. 42 : 1, 6). On him the manifold gift of the spirit comes to rest—it does not merely rouse him like a sudden gust of wind; it imbues him, it becomes his permanent possession (Is. 11 : 2). But although the Messiah has the fulness of the spirit, it is not an exclusive possession; from him it flows over the whole land and transforms it: 'The spirit is poured out on us, and the desert becomes a garden and the garden an orchard; and justice will dwell in that desert, and righteousness in that garden; and justice will bring peace' (Is. 32 : 15–18). This transformation is in fact a new creation; that is the point of Ezechiel's vision of the valley filled with bones. At God's command, bone is joined to bone, becomes clothed in sinews and flesh and then, with the sound of a mighty wind, the spirit of God enters into them and those utterly dead things stand up as living men. So in the new age God will give new life to men. But it will be a spiritual recreation: 'A new heart I will give you and a new spirit I will put in you. I will take away your heart of stone and give you my spirit, and you shall walk according to my law' (Ezech. 36 : 23–8). In fact, Jeremiah has told us, this Law will be written in their hearts. When the first covenant was given, Israel humbly expressed their gratitude that God should be so close to them, guiding them by his Law (Deut. 4 : 7–8); now, how much closer is he when his own spirit is in them to guide them. Before, they had prophets to teach them God's will

and exhort them to do it. Now each of them is to possess that
spirit of prophecy himself: 'I will pour out my spirit on all flesh,
and your sons and daughters will prophesy: young and old,
maid and servant, shall receive my spirit' (Joel 2 : 28 f.).

The new age dawned. 'There came a sound like a rushing of
a mighty wind, filling the whole house where the apostles were.
And parted tongues like flames settled on each of them; and they
were filled with the Holy Ghost, and they began to speak with
the utterance that the Holy Ghost gave them' (Acts 2 : 2–4).
God has kept his promise; St Peter proclaims that this is the fulfilment of the prophecy of Joel. The Spirit is poured forth in
wind and flame, the breath of God's life and the fire of his
holiness.

The terminology, the symbols and the actions they signify
are the same as in the Old Testament. But between the end of
the Old Testament and the writing of the New, a most important
step in revelation has been made. It has been revealed that God's
life is so great that it needs three Persons to contain it; and that
the 'spirit' which they had looked on as being an aspect of the
divine activity is in fact a Person. Not that this revelation
abolished all previous ways of thought and expression. In the
synoptic gospels particularly it is often difficult to decide
whether 'spirit' refers to the Third Person of the Blessed Trinity,
or whether the author is using it in its Old Testatment sense, of
God's energising action. When Simeon is directed to the
Temple 'by the spirit', or when our Lord is led out into the
desert 'by the spirit', there is no very obvious difference from
the spirit which took Ezechiel to Chaldea (Ezech. 11 : 24). In
fact, when Matthew says that our Lord cast out devils by the
'spirit of God', Luke in the parallel passage says that it was due
to the 'finger of God', that is to say, simply by God's power.
But the fact remains that the revelation has been made (for
instance, it is in the name of the Spirit, as well as in the name of

the Father and Son, that the apostles are to baptise). Therefore, even when the word spirit is used in a sense not very different from that of the Old Testament, it seems safe to say that the New Testament revelation would not be far from their minds. They realise that the 'Spirit of God' is not merely a synonym for God, even a particularly expressive one; it does not merely indicate a modality of the divine action: it is in fact the divine nature itself expressed in one of a Trinity of Persons.

All that has been said of the spirit of God in the Old Testament, then, is now transferred to this Person. God breathed his spirit into man so that he became a living being, created 'in the image and likeness of God'. Now the Holy Spirit comes down on a Virgin and the result is not a man in the likeness of God, but God himself incarnate. In the Old Testament, we have seen, the infusion of the spirit of God was a partial manifestation of that union between God and man which God desires. Here that union is perfected—God becomes man.

But our Lord is not alone: he is the 'only-begotten of the Father', but he is also 'first-born among many brethren'. To all who believed in him he gave power to be like himself, sons of God. And how does he do this? By giving them a share in this same Spirit. Isaiah had said that God would 'pour out the spirit on parched ground, his spirit upon all flesh.' And our Lord cries out: 'If any man thirsts, let him come to me. If anyone believes in me, living waters shall flow in him'—the living water, St John explains, of the Holy Spirit. But this Spirit was not to be given till he himself had gone. Just before his death, our Lord consoles his disciples by telling them that it was better that he should go, for if he went then he would send the Holy Ghost to them. During his life, he would only be with the men of his time as a friend is with a friend; but when he has died he will make possible a much closer union—they will be joined to him, and his Spirit will be their Spirit. And that is what does happen;

we are baptised into Christ Jesus, and 'the Spirit of Life in
Christ Jesus' becomes our Spirit also. That perfect union
between God and man which was achieved in our Lord's
Incarnation is realised also in all those who are one with Christ.
Just as God signified his presence among Israel by descending
into the Temple, so now the Christian himself is the temple of
God and the Holy Ghost dwells in him (cf. 1 Cor. 3 : 16; 6 : 19).
'We know that we are in him and he in us, because he has given
us his Spirit' (1 Jn. 4 : 13). The Holy Ghost is in fact God giving
himself—he *is* the gift, the *donum*. St Peter exhorts his first
converts to be baptised, 'and you will receive the gift of the Holy
Ghost': not merely a gift from the Holy Ghost, but the Holy
Ghost himself, who can be defined as the 'gift', the self-giving
of God. Similarly, Simon Magus is rebuked because he wanted
to buy the power to give the Holy Ghost: 'He thought the gift
of God could be bought with money.'

The New Testament revelation allows us to go even a step
further in this mystery of God's own giving of himself. The
Old Testament knew God as creator, almighty, source of all
life; they even knew that he was loving. But it is the final step
of the New Testament revelation concerning the nature of God
to tell us that he is not only loving, but that he *is* love. 'God is
love.' When God gives us himself, therefore, he does so not
merely by breathing into us the Spirit of life—it is also the
Spirit of love. 'The Love of God is diffused in our hearts
through the Holy Spirit who is given to us.' God gives us
himself—his own love for himself, and his own love also for
men: 'Brethren, if God has so loved us, we ought to love each
other. And if we love each other, God dwells in us—dwells in
us, because he has given us his Spirit' (1 Jn. 4 : 11–14). The
Holy Ghost, then, is not only the principle of union between God
and man, but also between man and man. The same life flows
in all those who are one body with Christ, and this life is the
life of love. So St Paul ends his second epistle to the Corinthians

with the blessing that 'the grace of our Lord Jesus Christ, and the love of God, and the communion of the Holy Ghost be with you all'. He begs the help of their prayers 'through the charity of the Holy Ghost' (Rom. 15 : 30). He urges them to charity for each other 'through the communion of the Spirit'. They should be anxious 'to preserve the unity of the Spirit in the bond of peace—one body and one Spirit' (Eph. 4 : 3).

They are one body animated by one Spirit. They are sons of God, as our Lord is Son of God, because they are directed by the Spirit (cf. Rom. 8 : 14). The Spirit descended on individuals in the Old Testament to direct them to activity in God's cause; and so it does in the New Testament. It is by the Holy Spirit that the first deacons are selected; it is by the Holy Spirit that Philip is directed to his contact with the Ethiopian. Saul and Barnabas are picked out for the work God has for them by the Spirit; and the same Spirit also directs Paul continually in his work, leading him across Asia to Greece, and finally back to Jerusalem for the last trial. The Spirit in the Old Testament filled the rulers of God's people, and fills the rulers of God's people in the New Testament. 'The Holy Spirit has appointed you overseers to rule the church of God,' Paul tells the elders of Ephesus. And just as the heroes of old were given strength by the Spirit of God to do wonderful deeds, so 'the gospel message has been confirmed by the signs and wonders and manifold deeds of power and gifts of the Holy Ghost' (Heb. 2 : 4). The various extraordinary charisms which graced the church at Corinth are the overflow of the life of the Spirit in the community, giving to each according to his will.

The New Testament has its judges, heroes, kings: it also has its prophets. There were prophets of the same kind as those of old—like Agabus, who foretold by the Spirit that there was to be a famine (Acts 11 : 28); and who told Paul, with a symbolic gesture which recalls those of Ezechiel, that the Holy Ghost wished him to know that prison was waiting him in Jerusalem.

But the New Testament gift of prophecy is much more far-reaching than this. The Old Testament prophets spoke in virtue of the knowledge which the Spirit infused into them for that purpose. But now that Holy Spirit is the permanent posession of the Christian; it is God in us knowing himself. 'I will ask the Father and he will send you another Paraclete who will remain with you for ever, the Spirit of Truth . . . you know him, because he is staying with you, he will be in you' (Jn. 14 : 16 f.). All that Christ has been to his own during the years of his earthly career the Holy Ghost will be to the Church for ever. Our Lord revealed God to the world: the Holy Ghost takes this revelation and deepens it, allows them to see all that it contains and involves: 'I have spoken thus while I have been among you; but the Paraclete, the Holy Spirit, will teach you everything, and bring back to your minds all that I have said.' He is to be 'another Paraclete'. Our Lord is the first paraclete or advocate: 'We have as advocate with the Father, Jesus Christ, the Just' (1 Jn. 2 : 1). He stands by us, fights our cause, pleads our case. What more effective advocacy could we have than God himself praying for us: 'We know not what to ask for nor how to ask it; but the Spirit himself prays for us with wordless petition. And God who searches hearts knows what the Spirit desires' (Rom. 8 : 27). But the Holy Ghost is not only in us pleading our cause with the Father—he is in us pleading Christ's cause to the world: 'I will send you the Paraclete, and he will convict the world of sin and justice and judgment.' He will show them that sin consists essentially in the failure to accept Christ. He will show that Christ's death, which was not an ignominious defeat but a victorious union with the Father, has established him as the Just One; and that moreover he has thus established a new principle of justice—not one depending on the fulfilment of the Law, but one which attains union with God through union with Christ. He will show them that the judgment they passed on Christ, condemning him to die, was actually judgment on themselves and on the devil who prompted their actions: 'Now is the hour for the Son of Man to die, now is the Prince of this world cast out.' Christ's work, his role as revealer of the Father and guide of mankind, 'the way, the truth and the life', is not ended with his death but is continued by his Spirit. And so it is that the Church gives fearless testimony to the truth, through the Spirit. Peter is filled with the Holy Spirit to address the crowds after the curing of the lame man; the deacons are 'full of the Holy Ghost and of wisdom'. St Stephen spoke with wisdom and the Spirit so that he could not be resisted. They are giving testimony to Christ; they have no need to be timid or afraid, for 'it is not they who speak, but the Holy Spirit which is in them'.

Spirit of action, Spirit of prophecy; and we saw that in the Old Testament the Spirit was also the source of a new spiritual life. And so it is in the New Testament. The adjective 'Holy', with which the Spirit was qualified in the Old Testament occasionally (not more than half a dozen times in all), is now the regular attribute of the Spirit of God. For this Spirit really unites them to God, gives them a real participation in the divine life, and therefore gives them a share in the holiness of God. They are the temples of the Holy Ghost—a sanctified, consecrated dwelling for God. We possess this principle, this seed of holiness; and the rest of our lives should be the development of this seed. St Paul begs his converts not to grieve the Spirit by any imperfection in their lives. Our vocation gives us holiness and lays the obligation of holiness on us: 'If you despise this, you are not despising man but God who put his own Holy Spirit in you' (1 Thess. 4 : 8).

So finally we come to that which is the most characteristic effect of the Holy Ghost's dwelling within us: joy and peace. These words abound in the Acts of the Apostles, the 'gospel of the Holy Ghost'. The disciples of St Paul and Barnabas are

filled with joy and the Holy Ghost (Acts 13 : 52). The Christian
has a source of rejoicing, not in drunkenness but in the new wine
of the Holy Ghost (Eph. 5 : 18). The Thessalonians receive the
word of God 'with the joy of the Holy Ghost' (1 Thess. 1 : 6).
Even in persecution we should see not a cause for sorrow but
for further rejoicing, because the Holy Ghost is with us
(1 Pet. 4 : 14).

This last note brings us back to Christ and to the key to the
whole doctrine. Our Lord told his own apostles that suffering
and persecution were to be the mark and characteristic of their
apostolate; and that when they met opposition they were to
rejoice, because it was the guarantee of their apostolate: 'The
servant is not greater than his master. If they have persecuted
me, they will persecute you. And rejoice and count yourselves
blessed when men persecute you, for so they persecuted the
prophets' and so must suffer all those who bear witness to the
truth. The union between God and man reached its climax and
fulfilment in our Lord. He is the true temple of God, he is the
Holy One of God. In his every action and every word he
revealed and showed God to men. In so doing, he met with
opposition and hatred, which led finally to his death; but by
that very death, he achieved the work he had come to do. Now,
the role of the Holy Ghost is to make the Church the continuation of Christ. They, like him, live with the life of God. They
are the temple of God. The Church is holy, the spotless bride
of Christ. And like Christ it reveals God to men; in fact, it *is*
the continuation of Christ's witness. 'The Paraclete will bear
witness to me and you will bear witness.' Christ reveals God
to the world, and the Church with the Holy Spirit displays
Christ to the world. In so doing, the Church will meet opposition; but the Spirit is in the Church reassuring them, infusing
them with the peace which Christ left them, giving them joy
in the following of Christ.

'Rejoice, because your reward is great in heaven.' The

Christian rejoices to follow the road of Christ, knowing that this road does not end with the cross but continues to resurrection and new life with the Father. The Spirit is the pledge of this new life—not merely promise, but initial possession. 'You are signed with the Holy Spirit of promise, the pledge of our inheritance' (Eph. 1 : 13). 'We wait with confidence for the resurrection of our bodies, knowing that God will do this who has given us the pledge of the Spirit' (2 Cor. 5 : 5). 'We who have the first-fruits of the Spirit long for the completion of our adoption, the resurrection of our bodies' (Rom. 8 : 23).

We end as we began, with the spirit of God being breathed into the face of man; we end with a new breath of life from the Holy Spirit of God giving us a life which is supernatural and eternal. St John also ends by taking us back to Genesis and putting the life-giving action of the Spirit in a new perspective. The whole of St John's gospel is a new interpretation of the meaning of creation. He begins with the opening words of all revelation: 'In the beginning . . .'; and at the end we have the echo of those other words of Genesis, when our Lord breathes on his apostles and says: 'Receive ye the Holy Spirit . . .' To them henceforward is entrusted not merely the life of the Spirit but the perpetual power of conveying that Spirit to others.

III

Baptism in the New Testament[1]

D. M. Stanley S.J.

THE history of Christian Baptism takes its origins from the mission of John the Baptist. In our day, when that saint has long ceased to hold the prominent place in Christian popular devotion which he occupied until the close of the Middle Ages, we are perhaps in danger of underestimating his significance in the story of Christianit   specifically the part he played in pointing out the meaning of the future sacrament of Baptism. It is sad to recall that the age-old, universal Christian cultus enjoyed by John appears to have terminated at the time of the Reformation, in what might be called an act of misguided veneration. Zwingli, Calvin and eventually Luther declared that Johannine Baptism had the same efficacy as the Christian sacrament, an erroneous view which the Council of Trent defined as heretical.

Yet in any discussion concerning Baptism in the New Testament it is necessary to remind ourselves of the place of special honour which each of the canonical gospels reserves for the Baptist. St Mark considers John's work as 'the beginning of the good news of Jesus Christ the Son of God' (Mk. 1 : 1). In order to grasp the meaning of John's role in the Christian revelation, it is helpful to keep in mind the various characterisations of him suggested by the evangelists. Broadly speaking, we may say that there are two distinct presentations of him in the New Testament. In the synoptic gospels he appears as *Elias redivivus*, as a prophet who announces the imminent coming of the Christ.

[1] First published in *Scripture*, 1956, pp. 44–57.

An integral part of this conception, as we shall see, is the representation of John as the prophet of Christian Baptism. In the Fourth Gospel, on the other hand, it is as a witness, testifying to the identity of the Christ, that John plays his part in the drama of salvation (cf. Jn. 1 : 6–8, 15). A brief study of each of these characterisations of John the Baptist will reveal important aspects of Christian Baptism.

John makes his appearance in the first three gospels as a prophet. Matthew, Mark and Luke each depict John's principal function as the preaching or 'heralding' of the Kingdom. John's is the 'voice crying in the desert' (Is. 40 : 3) proclaiming 'the word of God' which 'came to him', as it had come to the Old Testament prophets (Lk. 3 : 2). John appears in the garb which had characterised Elias the prophet (2 Kgs. 1 : 8; Mt. 3 : 4). Indeed Gabriel had announced to Zachary before John's conception that the child would be 'endowed with the spirit and power of Elias' (Lk. 1 : 17). Christ himself declared to his disciples after John's death that in his person Elias had returned and had 'restored all things' (Mt. 17 : 11). This 'restoration', the work of the returning Elias, which is a recurrent theme in later Old Testament tradition (Mal. 3: 1–5, 22–3; Sir. 48 : 1–11), was to become an article of faith in post-biblical Judaism.

John effected this 'restoration of all things' by his invitation to *metanoia*, a change of heart or repentance on Israel's part which, by re-establishing good relations with Yahweh, was the necessary preparation for the coming of his Christ. The symbol of this restoration was Johannine baptism, a lustration performed in the River Jordan. John himself called it a baptism 'with water, aimed at a change of heart' (Mt. 3 : 11). The second evangelist describes it as 'a baptism in token of a change of heart, which looked to the forgiveness of sins' (Mk. 1 : 4). Long after John's death, Paul was to explain to a little group of the Baptist's disciples whom he had discovered at Ephesus how 'John practised a baptism of repentance, telling the people they should make an act of faith in him who was to come after him . . .' (Acts 19 : 4). The evangelists also tell us that the reception of Johannine baptism was accompanied by a confession of sins (Mt. 3 : 6; Mk. 1 : 5). Thus the New Testament reveals John's baptism as a sign of a fundamental change of heart, involving sincere repentance of sin and renewed faith in the proximate advent of the Christ. Moreover, it was by means of this baptism that John effected the 'restoration of all things', and was accordingly revealed as a prophet, the second Elias.

John is, in addition, presented by the synoptics as the prophet of Christian Baptism. 'I am baptising you with water in token of repentance', John tells the crowds who gathered to hear him. 'He who is coming after me is mightier than I. I am indeed unworthy to carry his sandals. He will baptise you with a Holy Spirit and fire' (Mt. 3 : 11). The value of this text lies in its description of the Baptism Christ was to institute as essentially eschatological—that is, as pertaining to the 'last times', the Messianic age. The Old Testament prophets had characterised the era ushered in by the Christ as an age when Yahweh would pour out his Spirit in abundance upon mankind (Joel 3 : 5 ff.). They also designated it as the terrible 'Day of Yahweh' when he should pass judgment upon all humanity—a judgment whose searching, relentless character they symbolised by fire (Am. 7 : 4; Is. 30 : 27–30; Mal. 3 : 2). Faithful to this prophetical tradition, John associated these world-shaking events with the coming of the Christ. His originality consists however in connecting them with what was later to be known as Christian Baptism. Subsequent history was to teach the disciples of Christ to distinguish different moments in this Messianic period which John, like his predecessors, had depicted with prophetic fore-shortening as contemporaneous. During the period subsequent to Christ's resurrection, the apostles learned that there was to be a second coming of Jesus Christ, while the interval between, inaugurated by the Pentecostal descent of the Holy Ghost, was designated as the period during which the Church should practise this Baptism 'with a Holy Spirit and fire'.

Yet the eschatological note picked out by the Baptist's prophecy of Christian Baptism remains important for the New Testament conception of this sacrament. It deserves to be recalled here, particularly as the modern Christian, unlike his brethren of the apostolic age, has a tendency to overlook the relation which the sacramental system bears to Christ's *parousia* or second coming. Paul, writing to the Corinthian church, describes the eucharistic sacrifice in terms of the second coming. 'As often as you eat this bread and drink the chalice, you proclaim the death of the Lord until he comes' (1 Cor. 11 : 26). In Paul's view, the eucharistic coming of the risen Christ is a reminder of, and a preparation for, his coming at the end of time. At Pentecost Peter had made it clear to his audience that the 'baptism with the Spirit' received by the apostolic assembly and accompanied by the charismatic gifts of ecstatic prayer and prophecy, had inaugurated 'the Day of Yahweh' and was, in consequence, a sign of the imminence of the eschatological judgment (Acts 2 : 16–17; Joel 3 : 1 ff.). The apostolic experience during the first years of the Church's growth will, as we shall see, clarify this eschatological character of Baptism. For the moment, it is sufficient to realise that in the New Testament the Christian sacraments appear as signs of 'the end'.

In addition to this prophetic description of Christian Baptism, another prophetic function of the Baptist's was pointed out in the apostolic preaching: the Messianic anointing of Jesus by his baptism in the Jordan (Acts 4 : 27; 10 : 38; cf. Lk. 4 : 18; Heb. 1 : 9). This event occupies a place of first-rate importance in the synoptic tradition. As described in the first three gospels, the scene culminates in a theophany (sensible manifestation of the divine presence), in which 'the Holy Ghost descended in bodily form like a dove' (Lk. 3 : 22a, a text which contains the most explicit reference to the Third Person of the Trinity), while Christ heard the voice of his Father declaring the Messianic royalty of his Son (Mt. 3 : 17; Mk. 1 : 11; Lk. 3 : 22b). In this inaugural vision of Jesus' public life, as the fathers of the Church perceived, all the elements which are to constitute the future sacrament of Baptism stand revealed: the washing with water, the Spirit, the reference to the Triune Godhead. In order to obtain, however, a deeper insight into the meaning of the Messianic anointing of Jesus and of John's part in it, we must turn to the fourth gospel.

The fourth evangelist assigns the Baptist's message to the category of *testimony*. 'I have come baptising with water in order that he might be made known in Israel' (Jn. 1 : 31). This manifestation of the Christ by John is represented as the result of the theophany which occurred at Jesus' baptism. 'He who sent me to baptise with water had said to me, "He upon whom you see the Spirit descend and rest, is he who baptises with a Holy Spirit". And I have seen, and I have continued to testify that he is the Son of God' (Jn. 1 : 33–4). As these words indicate, John's testimony was primarily concerned with the person of Jesus Christ, and only secondarily with the Baptism which he would institute. The fact that they contain only an implicit reference to Jesus' baptism by John, an incident which is central in the synoptic tradition, indicates the view which the fourth gospel takes of John's function. Earlier in this same chapter the Baptist is represented as contrasting his baptism, not as in the synoptics with that of Christ, but with the presence of Christ himself (Jn. 1 : 26–27).

By focusing attention upon Christ rather than upon Christian Baptism in these opening scenes of his gospel, St John the evangelist presents a facet of that sacrament which did not appear in the synoptic accounts: the relation of Baptism to Christ's

death. 'Behold the Lamb of God! He who is taking away the
world's sin' (Jn. 1 : 29). John attests that Jesus is at once the
new Paschal Lamb, anti-type of that lamb which was the
perennial symbol of Israel's redemption out of Egypt, as well
as the Suffering Servant of Yahweh, compared with a lamb in
undergoing that redemptive death in which 'he bore the sins
of many' (Is. 53 : 12). By thus adding a new dimension to the
Baptist's message, the last of the gospels provides a deeper
insight into the 'Baptism with the Spirit' which Christ is come
to impart. Its efficacy depends upon the fact that it is he who, by
his redemptive death, will liberate the world from sin.

In the synoptic narrative of Jesus' public life there is little,
at first sight, that seems to throw any light upon the sacrament
of Baptism. Twice, it is true, Christ refers to his coming death
as a 'baptism'. When the sons of Zebedee demand the places
of honour in his 'glory', Jesus asks: 'Can you drink the cup I
shall drink, or be baptised with the baptism with which I am
to be baptised?' (Mk. 10 : 38). In the context (cf. Mk. 10 : 45)
it is clear that he means his death. In Lk. 12 : 50 there is a similar
reference. 'I have a baptism with which I am to be baptised.
What anguish do I experience until it be consummated!' This
'baptism' is a prelude to the accomplishment of his mission,
'to cast fire upon the earth' (Lk. 10 : 49). That 'fire' is the
judgment, as the verses following indicate (Lk. 10 : 51–3). Luke
is moreover probably thinking of the pentecostal fire, to which
he will refer in his second volume (Acts 1 : 5). These sayings of
Jesus both insist upon an essential feature of Christian Baptism,
its orientation to Jesus' redemptive death, as well as to the
judgment already mentioned by John the Baptist.

While the synoptic tradition has retained little in its record
of Christ's teaching during the public ministry which may be
considered as bearing directly upon the later apostolic baptismal
theology, it has preserved a conception of the miracles performed during Jesus' mortal life which the fourth gospel will

develop into a most remarkable sacramental theology. On the synoptic view Jesus' miracles of healing are, not less than the exorcisms he performed, an initial assault upon Satan's dominion over men. As a prologue to his narrative of the Galilean ministry, Luke has prefixed the *récit* of Jesus' visit to Nazareth, in which we find recorded the words he read on that occasion from the scroll of Isaiah, and which he declared fulfilled in himself. His mission is 'to announce release to the captives, recovery of sight to the blind, to set the oppressed at liberty' (Is. 61 : 1–2; Lk. 4 : 16 ff.). Matthew's introduction to the public life, which contains a citation of Is. 9 : 1–2, suggests the same campaign against evil in terms of light and darkness (Mt. 4 : 14 ff.). His account of the exorcism of the Gadarene demoniacs presents that miracle as an anticipation of the definitive blow which, by his death, Christ will strike at Satan's kingdom. 'Are you come here to torture us before the time appointed by God?' (Mt. 8 : 29). The Greek word, here translated as 'the time appointed by God', is in the New Testament a quasi-technical term for Jesus' passion and death. Perhaps the clearest statement of this miracle-theology by Matthew is found in his description of Christ's mission of the twelve. 'And calling his twelve disciples, he gave them power over unclean spirits, so as to cast them out and heal all manner of disease and sickness' (Mt. 10 : 1). In Luke's account of the triumphant return of the seventy-two to announce to Jesus the miracles they had performed, even over the demons, Jesus remarks: 'I was watching Satan falling from heaven like flashes of lightning' (Lk. 10 : 18). The miracles performed by Christ as well as those performed in his name are, then, a pledge of his ultimate victory over Satan. In other words, the miracles of the public life are an initial step in the founding of the Kingdom upon earth.

In the fourth gospel we see this view of Jesus' miracles developed into a theology of the Christian sacraments, especially the Eucharist and Baptism. Just as the Old Testament prophets

applied the great events of Israel's past (the exodus out of Egypt,
the creation of the world) to contemporary or future happenings
in order to explain their religious signification, so too John
employs Jesus' miracles to propound the doctrine of the sacramental system. Just as these miracles inaugurated the Kingdom
in this world and, as such, look forward to Jesus' salvific death
and resurrection (the definitive coming of the Kingdom), so
the sacramental practice of the apostolic Church, the chief
means for the spread of that Kingdom, looks backwards to the
central act of man's redemption. Space permits the mention here
of only one example of John's baptismal theology, the cure of
the blind man at the pool of Siloe (Jn. 9 : 1 ff.).[1] John relates
how Jesus 'anoints' the blind eyes with mud as he pronounces
the words, 'I am the the light of world' (Jn. 9 : 5), and then
sends the blind man to wash in the pool of Siloe. This place-
name, which actually means 'conduit', is interpreted by the
evangelist as 'the One sent', that is, the Christ (Jn. 9 : 7). By
such a symbolic interpretation John informs his readers that he
has perceived, in this command to wash in a pool which bears
Christ's name, an action which prophetically signifies Baptism.
The miracle points to those waters which bear Christ's name
because in them Christ's sacramental action of regeneration is
operative. In such a context Jesus' reference to himself as 'the
light of the world' becomes clear, Baptism being regarded by
the apostolic Church as an illumination (Eph. 5 : 14; Heb. 6 : 4;
10 : 32). Christ's concluding remarks in this episode again
draw attention to its baptismal signification. 'I am come into
this world [to effect] a discrimination: that the sightless may
obtain the gift of sight and that those who see may become

[1] The interpretation followed here is that of Père M.–J. Lagrange O.P.,
in his commentary on St John's gospel. More recently, Oscar Cullman has
developed this sacramental theme of the fourth gospel in a fascinating
monograph, *Les sacrements dans l'évangile johannique*, Paris 1951. The
English translation of this forms the major part of *Early Christian Worship*,
S.C.M. Press, London 1953.

blind' (Jn. 9 : 39). The Church has always taught that faith is required in him who would receive baptismal illumination.

The fourth gospel also records two discourses of Jesus which contain his baptismal teaching. In the first of these, the conversation with Nicodemus, Baptism is described by a characteristically Johannine *double entendre* as a birth 'anew' or 'from above'. The rest of the dialogue makes it very clear that what is meant is a new, supernatural birth. It is the work of 'the Spirit' (Jn. 3 : 8); its author is 'the Son of man who descended from heaven' (Jn. 3 : 13); it effects 'eternal life', to be conferred by Christ once he is 'exalted' upon the cross and, ultimately, at the right hand of the Father. This last point is illustrated by the brazen serpent which Moses 'exalted' in the desert (Jn. 8 : 14) and which, in late Old Testament theological thought, had been regarded as a 'symbol of salvation' (Wis. 16 : 6). The most important item in this instruction of Christ's is however the description of the new birth as effected 'by water and the Spirit' (Jn. 3 : 5). This is the clearest statement in the New Testament of the role played by these two essential elements in Christian Baptism. Another conversation, that between Jesus and the Samaritan woman near the well, contains important Baptismal doctrine. The distinction Jesus makes on this occasion between well-water and 'living water' (water flowing in a brook or from a spring) would appear to be the source of the Church's insistence from earliest times upon the use of flowing water in the administration of Baptism (cf. *Didache* VII,I). In John's narrative, 'living water' is a symbol for a mysterious, supernatural reality. 'Any man who drinks this water' (that drawn from Jacob's well) 'will be thirsty again. Whoever drinks the water I shall give him, will never again experience thirst. For the water I shall give him will become in him a fountain of water that leaps up unto eternal life' (Jn. 4 : 13–14). Among the fathers of the Church, Justin and Irenaeus understand these words of Baptism. Moreover, the evangelist himself explains this 'fountain' or 'rivulets' of 'living water' as 'the Spirit whom those who came to believe in him were destined to receive' (Jn. 7 : 38–9). This 'living water' which symbolises the Spirit is the sacrament of Baptism. Christ's promise that this divinely given 'drink' will slake thirst for ever is a reference to a quality of Baptism which distinguishes it from the Eucharist: the impossibility of its being repeated.

The scene which closes Jesus' mortal life in the fourth gospel, the piercing of his sacred side, is of the greatest significance for John, as his insistence of his own veracity as an eye-witness shows (Jn. 19 : 35). Moreover, John makes use of this same episode in his description of 'Jesus Christ the Son of God' in his first epistle (1 Jn. 5 : 6–8). 'He who is come by water and by blood, Jesus Christ; not with water only but with water and with blood. And it is the Spirit who testifies, because the Spirit is the truth. There are accordingly three who bear witness, the Spirit, the water, the blood; and these three are in agreement.' John clearly regards the water and the blood which issued from Christ's side as miraculous, and therefore as most meaningful, like the other 'signs' recounted in his gospel. John Chrysostom and Cyril of Alexandria, with other fathers of the Church, regard the water as a symbol of Baptism, while the blood signifies the Eucharist. St Augustine asserts that the birth of the Church, the new Eve, occurred on the cross because of this emission of blood and water 'in which we perceive the sacraments by which the Church is built up'.

St Matthew's gospel reaches its conclusion and its climax in the mandate of the risen Christ to his apostles. 'Universal power in heaven and upon earth has been granted to me. Therefore, go and make disciples of all peoples, baptising them in the name of the Father and of the Son and of the Holy Spirit . . .' (Mt. 28 : 18–19). In virtue of his investiture with supreme and universal domination, conferred by God the Father in conse-

quence of his death and resurrection, Christ now declares himself
author of the Church and of the sacrament of Baptism. The
precision and the liturgical character of the formula, 'in the
name . . .', have led modern Catholic scholars to perceive in these
words a reflection of the liturgical practice already in general
use throughout the apostolic Church by the time our canonical
Greek version of this gospel came to be written. Whether or
not this formulation of Trinitarian faith had supplanted an
earlier custom of baptising 'in the name of Jesus' is a question
we shall discuss later.

It is remarkable that nowhere in the New Testament are the
apostles said to have received Christian Baptism, according to
the rite which, from the day of Pentecost itself, they administered
to the first converts to Christianity. The silence of the sacred
text upon this point would not, of course, constitute an argument by itself, were it not for other evidence provided by Acts.
St Luke makes it clear that the apostolic group in the upper
room were baptised with the Holy Ghost in the fires of Pentecost.
He first carefully records Christ's promise of this 'baptism'.
'Whereas John baptised with water, you will be baptised with a
Holy Spirit not many days hence' (Acts 1 : 5; cf. also Lk. 24 : 49).
Then in his description of Pentecost itself he shows how this
prediction was fulfilled by the appearance of 'tongues like fire,
which, being divided, rested upon each of them. And they were
all filled with a Holy Spirit' (Acts 2 : 3–4). What is of greatest
significance, however, in Luke's account, is the presentation of
the unique character of this 'baptism'. By it the 'new Israel' was
created out of the little band of disciples in the upper room.
That the apostolic group at once perceived the significance of
what had happened to them is evident from Peter's Pentecostal
discourse in which he cites a passage from Joel describing the
wonders of 'the last days' where mention is made of the surviving
remnant of Israel (Joel 3 : 5). This was that holy nucleus which
Isaiah had foretold would, in the Messianic age, include 'everyone

enrolled amongst those destined for life in Jerusalem' (Is. 4 : 2–3; cf. Acts 2 : 47).

This consciousness of the singular nature of their Pentecostal experience led the newly created community to practise a completely new rite in admitting to their ranks those who wished to join them: Baptism with water, and the imposition of hands by which the Holy Spirit was visibly imparted. The 'Baptism with the Spirit' which they themselves had received in fulfilment of Christ's promise and which had constituted them the Messianic community was, of its very nature, impossible of repetition. Yet they were aware, as Acts shows, that by Christian Baptism they could bring new members into the Church and so impart to them a share in that same Spirit who had descended upon themselves in a special manner. Perhaps the episode of Cornelius's conversion is the one which best illustrates the apostolic awareness of the distinction which obtained between their Pentecostal 'baptism' and sacramental Baptism. Before this pagan and his household were baptised they received the Holy Ghost (Acts 10 : 44–6). Peter's description of the extraordinary event, in his speech to the Jerusalem congregation, is to be noted. 'The Holy Spirit fell upon them exactly as upon us in the beginning' (Acts 11 : 15). Yet Peter's subsequent decision, caused by this very manifestation of the Spirit, puts a somewhat different construction upon his statement. 'He ordered them to be baptised in the name of Jesus Christ' (Acts 10 : 48). Despite his insistence upon the similarity of Cornelius's experience to that of the community at Pentecost, Peter recognised an essential difference. He knew that the first descent of the Spirit had been a Baptism which transformed the disciples into the 'new Israel'. In the case of Cornelius and his household, Peter saw that the coming of the Holy Ghost was proof of God's will that they should be aggregated to the apostolic community by Christian Baptism.

.   .   .   .   .

One further point concerning the primitive community's conception of Christian Baptism deserves to be mentioned here. It would appear, on the evidence of the very ancient sources which Luke employed in writing the first part of the Acts, that in the first years the gift of the Holy Spirit was looked upon as an effect of the imposition of hands, the rite which normally accompanied Baptism, rather than as the direct result of Baptism itself. The well-known story of Philip's evangelisation of Samaria seems to exemplify such a viewpoint (Acts 8 : 5–17). Thus it would appear that while admission into the Messianic community was regarded as the primary effect of Baptism, the explicit reference to the Spirit was reserved for the imposition of hands. At the same time, it must be remembered that 'remission of sins' was also regarded as an effect of Baptism (Acts 2 : 38), and it is quite clear that from the beginning the Church distinguished this sacrament from the purely symbolical nature of Johannine baptism. Further reflection upon Christian Baptism moved the Church to make explicit what perhaps had only been implied in her earlier view, viz. that by Baptism the Holy Spirit was communicated to the Christian. It may well be that such a theological development was largely due to the reflection of St John the evangelist, who recognised in the waters of Baptism a symbol of the presence of the Spirit. At any rate, by the time the Fourth Gospel was written, apostolic Christianity had consciously adverted to the operation of the Holy Ghost in Baptism itself and had formulated a definition of the sacrament as a rebirth of 'water and the Spirit' (Jn. 3 : 5).

We may now ask a question which we mentioned earlier and which has long been a subject of discussion amongst students of the New Testament: what is meant by 'Baptism in the name of Jesus'? At Pentecost Peter remarks to those who found faith in his preaching: 'Repent, and let each of you have himself baptised in the name of Jesus Christ for the remission of his sins, and you will receive the gift of the Holy Spirit' (Acts 2 : 37–8). The Samaritans converted by Philip were 'baptised in the name of the Lord Jesus' (Acts 8 : 10), as were also the Ephesian followers of John the Baptist whom Paul converted to Christianity (Acts 19 : 4–6). It is perhaps Paul's account of his own Baptism by Ananias in Damascus which gives the best insight into the meaning of this expression (Acts 22 : 16). Ananias is represented as saying to the blinded Saul: 'Arise, be baptised, and be washed from your sins by invoking his name.' From this it is evident that the invocation of 'his name' is made, not by the minister of the sacrament, but by the candidate for Baptism himself. The supreme importance which the apostolic Church attached to this baptismal profession of faith resulted in the designation of Baptism as 'Baptism in the name of Jesus'. Paul has preserved one version of this *credo* for us in his letter to the Romans: 'If you confess with your mouth 'Jesus is Lord' and you believe in your heart that God has raised him from the dead, you will be saved' (Rom. 10 : 9). A few verses further on, the apostle provides what appears to have been the scriptural basis for this element in the baptismal liturgy (Rom. 10 : 13). It is the same text of Joel mentioned in Peter's Pentecostal sermon: 'Whoever invokes the name of the Lord will be saved' (Joel 3 : 5).

What is the meaning of such a formula, 'Jesus is Lord'? The answer to this question is provided by Philipp. 2 : 9, where Jesus' exaltation is described as the conferring upon him by God the Father, of the divine name 'Lord'. This characteristically Semitic way of stating that Jesus' divinity was revealed to the first disciples by his resurrection and elevation to the right hand of God indicates that the baptismal invocation of 'Jesus' name' (i.e. 'Lord') was a profession of faith in the fact that he is divine. It is to be observed that such a credal formula implied, moreover, the Trinitarian faith of the primitive Church. For it was to the revelation of Jesus' glorification that the apostolic community owed its belief in the Trinity. Through her contemplation of the risen Lord, the Church was led to acknowledge the Father as source of Jesus' glory and to confess the Holy Spirit, principle of all holiness, as the gift of her ascended Master. Thus the invocation of 'the name of the Lord Jesus' was a memorial of the newly found Christian faith in the Triune Godhead.

It was this baptismal confession which gave meaning to the reception of Baptism as the means of entering into union with the risen Christ, and consequently (although this implication seems to have dawned only gradually upon the early community) with the Spirit and with the Father. We catch glimpses of this comprehension of the nature of Baptism in the Pauline epistles. To the Corinthian Church whose unity was being compromised by the appearance of a partisan spirit ('I am Paul's. I am Apollo's. I am Cephas's', 1 Cor. 1 : 12), St Paul remarks: 'Surely Paul was not crucified for you? Surely you were not baptised in the name of Paul? I am grateful that I have baptised none of you except Crispus and Gaius, lest any man say you have been baptised in my name' (1 Cor. 1 : 13–15). In Paul's view, the unity of the Church derives from the personal union with Christ entered into by each Christian at his Baptism. In urging the Ephesians to preserve the 'unity of the Spirit', Paul explicitly refers this union to each of the Persons of the Trinity. [There is but] 'one Body and one Spirit, just as you have been called by one hope in your vocation. [There is but] one Lord, one faith, one Baptism, one God and Father of all . . .' (Eph. 5 : 3–5). Baptism, then, makes the Christian one with the glorified Lord, Jesus Christ, since he is united to him by the operation of the Holy Ghost, and through this union with Son and Spirit, one with the Father. This doctrine implies a deep theological development which the baptismal teaching of the Jerusalem Church underwent at the hands of St Paul, a development we shall presently investigate.

A word must be said concerning the eschatological aspect of
the apostolic community's understanding of Baptism: that
character of the sacrament to which the Baptist had referred in
prophetical terminology by calling it a 'Baptism with the Spirit
and fire'. According to the Old Testament scheme, history was
to find its consummation both theologically and historically in
the coming of the Messiah. He would usher in the final judgment
of God upon humanity, since in his person the good must win
a definitive triumph over evil. The New Testament revelation
which crowned the Messianic expectations of Judaism modified
this theology of history profoundly. Jesus' ascension into
Heaven after his death and resurrection taught the apostles
that there was to be a second coming, in glory, of the risen
Lord. As to the period intermediary between Jesus Christ's
first and second coming, it was the descent of the Holy Spirit
that revealed its significance. This intercalary era was indeed
part of the 'Messianic times'. It was, however, specifically a
time of preparation for the final *parousia*. The preparation con-
sisted chiefly in the building up of God's Kingdom upon earth,
the Church, by means of the Christian sacraments. Baptism
had its place in such a scheme of things as a rite of initiation into
the Kingdom which washed away men's sins and imparted the
divine gift promised during the 'last times', the Holy Spirit.
As John the Baptist had predicted, it was a 'Baptism with the
Spirit'. It was also a 'Baptism with fire', symbol of Yahweh's
final judgment at the end of time, because by destroying sin it
anticipated that judgment and assured men of salvation. This
effect is described by Acts with the remark, 'the Lord added
to the community those who were numbered amongst the
saved' (Acts 2 : 47).

We have already seen that the orientation of Baptism to
Christ's redemptive death is traceable to the public teaching of
Jesus himself. The reference of Baptism to his resurrection, as

we also saw, was recognised by the apostolic Church who called it 'Baptism in the name of the Lord Jesus' and who cherished the tradition of her risen Master's mandate to 'make disciples of all nations by baptising them'. It was left to St Paul, however, as one of Christianity's first and greatest theologians, to work out the doctrinal implications contained in the deposit of the Church's faith and to create what we may call the first baptismal theology. Two passages in his epistles epitomise his view of Baptism. 'All you who have been baptised into Christ have put on Christ' (Gal. 3 : 27). In the primitive preaching, Baptism was indicated as the ritual initiation into the 'new Israel', the community of the risen Christ. In writing to the Galatians, Paul expresses his profound intuition of this sacrament as a being baptised *into* Christ'. In his eyes it is an act of incorporation into the Body of the risen Lord, by which the Christian becomes identified with him as one of his members. Or, as he states to the Corinthians, the baptised becomes 'one Spirit' with the risen Lord (1 Cor. 6 : 17). 'For indeed by one Spirit we have—all of us—been baptised into one Body' (1 Cor. 12 : 13). Such is the dynamic realism of the Pauline conception of 'the Body of Christ', Paul's theological transposition of the notion of 'the Kingdom of God' in its terrestrial phase. Accordingly, in the text we have cited from Galatians, the phrase 'to put on Christ' signifies to become a member of the Body of Christ, to become one with Christ. And this identification, as Paul states, is accomplished by Baptism.

Just how this union of the Christian with the glorified Lord is effected through Baptism, is explained by the second text we wish to recall, the only other place in the Pauline letters containing the expression 'to be baptised into Christ'. 'You are surely aware that we, who were baptised into Christ Jesus, were baptised into his death. We were then buried together with him by this Baptism into his death, in order that just as Christ was raised from the dead by the glory of the Father, so also we may

c

live by a new kind of life. For if we have grown together with
[him] into the likeness of his death, so also shall we grow with
[him] into the likeness of his resurrection' (Rom. 6 : 3–5).
Baptism unites the Christian with Christ by uniting him with
the two acts through which Christ accomplished our redemption, his death and resurrection. In writing to the Corinthians
Paul had sketched this same baptismal theology in terms of
Israel's redemption from Egypt. Because they shared the
experiences which, under the leadership of Moses, had liberated
them from Egyptian bondage (the guidance and protection of
the cloud, the crossing of the Red Sea), God's people had been
in effect 'baptised into Moses' (1 Cor. 10 : 1–2). Similarly in the
text we are considering, Paul teaches that the double act of the
Father's by which Christ 'was handed over for our sins and
raised for our justification' (Rom. 4 : 25) reaches out, in
Baptism, to include the neophyte, and thus through this baptismal experience of the act of man's redemption the catechumen
is 'baptised into Christ', united with his glorified saviour.

With this magnificent conception we reach the climax of New
Testament baptismal theology. The eschatological note first
sounded by the message of the Baptist in an endeavour to foretell
the nature of Christian Baptism, was developed by the apostolic
teaching, which regarded it as the act of initiation into the
Messianic community of the elect. Finally, it appears fully
orchestrated by St Paul's genius as an integral part of his theme
of 'the Body of Christ'. The other New Testament writings
concerning Baptism merely provide variations on this Pauline
theme, describing it as a 'rebirth', an 'illumination', a 'sealing'
with the Spirit, a 'washing white in the Blood of the Lamb'.

IV

The Formation of the Bread of
Life Discourse (John 6)[1]

Edward J. Kilmartin S.J.

IN New Testament times it is clear that manna was considered a type of the Eucharist.[2] That this should be so is readily explained by the stress upon the relationship: manna—Messiah, in contemporary Judaism.[3] This relationship of course finds its best scriptural expression in Jn : 6, where the manna of the desert plays an important role in the course of the development of what appears to be a eucharistic catechesis.[4] Thus the all-important function of Christ on the day of the miracle of the loaves is to give bread: he takes the initiative (v. 5); he gives the bread himself (v. 11). Furthermore Christ is pictured as giving this miraculous bread at the time of the Passover (v. 4) when according to Jewish speculation the Messiah would come and deliver the heavenly manna.[5] The messianic enthusiasm of the crowd seems to have been aroused precisely because they saw in Jesus' miracle the long-awaited return of the manna.[6] The murmuring crowd which appeared the next day to demand a

[1] First published in *Scripture*, 1960, pp. 75–8.

[2] 1 Cor. 10 : 3 ff.

[3] J. Jeremias, *The Eucharistic Words of Jesus*, Oxford 1955, pp. 152–9; C. H. Dodd, *The Interpretation of the Fourth Gospel*, Cambridge 1953, p. 335; B. Gärtner, *John 6 and the Jewish Passover*, Coniectanea Neotestamentica XVII, Lund 1959, pp. 18–25.

[4] Cf. E. J. Kilmartin, *The Eucharist in the Primitive Church*, Englewood Cliffs, N. J. 1965, pp. 93–140.

[5] B. Gärtner, op. cit., p. 19.

[6] Ibid., p. 21.

sign calls to mind Israel wandering in the desert and thus completes the exodus motif of the chapter.

But if Jesus is pictured as the Messiah who gives bread in a miraculous way, nevertheless it is unmistakably pointed out that this bread is a type of the future gift which Jesus *will give* (vv. 27, 51c). As a type it is gathered up lest it be lost (v. 12) and remains incorrupt though it nourished the whole crowd (v. 13).[1] A further hint that this bread miracle is only a type may be derived from the consecration phrase of vv. 11 and 23, which looks forward to the action of Christ at the Last Supper. Thus John describes the multiplication of the loaves in terms of a eucharistic banquet organised and directed by Jesus and served by him.

Other evidence that the author of the fourth gospel was already in the spirit of the Last Supper when he wrote this pericope may be drawn from v. 51: 'And the bread I will give is my flesh for the life of the world,' which recalls the words attributed to Christ at the time of the institution of the Eucharist.[2] Again, the dissociation of the two phrases: 'to eat my flesh'/ 'to drink my blood', is a clear reference to the double consecration of the Last Supper (vv. 53–8). Even the mention of the fact that the discourse on the bread of life took place in a synagogue at Capernaum has eucharistic overtones (v. 59). We are justified in supposing that the author of the fourth gospel dates this discourse on Friday evening or Saturday morning. In which case the multiplication of the loaves must be placed on Thursday, the day which, according to johannine chronology, Christ celebrated the Passover meal.

With the importance of the relationship between manna and Eucharist established, it would not be surprising if the bread-of-life discourse was a midrash, an exegesis of the text of scripture

[1] D. Daube, *The New Testament and Rabbinic Judaism*, London 1956, p. 43.
[2] 1 Cor. 11 : 24; Lk. 22 : 19.

which is put in the mouths of the Jews and which refers to well-attested Jewish speculation about messianic manna (v. 32). Yet this point has not been emphasised in the past.[1] Recently, however, P. Borgen has called attention to it.[2]

According to Borgen the discourse of Jesus following Jn. 6 : 31, i.e. vv. 32–58, is a midrash of the reference to the manna miracle with the quotation from scripture: 'Our fathers ate manna in the wilderness; as it is written, "He gave them bread from heaven to eat".' R. Bultmann claims that vv. 51b–58b are an interpolation made in the interest of eucharistic doctrine. A close study, however, of vv. 32–52 reveals that the words 'bread', 'from heaven' and 'He gave' are quite sufficiently developed. But the word 'to eat' occurs only from v. 49 onward. Now if we suppose that vv. 53–8 are an interpolation, then the word 'to eat' had not received a development comparable to the rest of the words of Ps. 78 : 24. The conclusion, therefore, is drawn that vv. 52–8 are not an interpolation but that vv. 26–58 form a unified whole, for only in vv. 53–8 does the word 'to eat' receive adequate treatment.

In the light of this observation it seems best to say that the plan of the discourse is ruled by the words of Ps. 78 : 24. The development of the exegesis follows the general form: revelation —objection—further revelation, as X.-L. Dufour has pointed out.[3] In this form the objection yields up in abbreviated fashion the theme of the revelation surrounding it and points to a further revelation (vv. 28, 30–1, 42, 52). This method is also employed

---

[1] The detailed investigation of H. Schürmann, for example, did not hit upon this point as a proof of the unity of the discourse. Cf. 'Jn. 6 : 51c—ein Schüssel zur johanneischen Brotrede', *Biblische Zeitschrift* II (1958), pp. 244–62; 'Die Eucharistie als Repräsentation und Applikation des Heilsgeschehens nach Jn. 6 : 53–8', *Trierer Theologische Zeitschrift* LXVIII (1959), pp. 30–45, 108–18.

[2] P. Borgen, 'The Unity of the Discourse in Jn. 6', *Zeitschrift für die Neutestamentliche Wissenschaft* L (1959), pp. 277–8.

[3] X.-L. Dufour, 'Le mystère du Pain de Vie', *Recherches de Science Religieuse* XLVI (1958), pp. 496–500.

in Jn. 3 and 4, and points out the incapacity of human reason before the revelation of the Word.[1] Reason rejects revelation which it cannot explain or justify.

Regarding however the questions asked in vv. 28, 30–1, 42, 52, it should be noted that although a question method is used which finds its parallel elsewhere in the fourth gospel, still it remains possible that the question arrangement *in this passage*, if not the method itself, was inspired by the four questions which the four sons asked in the Jewish Passover Haggadah.[2]

First of all there are four distinct inquiries, each of which is placed between revelations made by Christ. Secondly, each inquiry has a special character.

The question of v. 28 seems to be a simple *halakhic* question concerning a point of law. It parallels the question of the wise son in the Jewish Passover Haggadah and stands apart from the questions of vv. 30–1 which suppose the revelation of v. 28.

The questions of vv. 30–1 ask for a sign like that which proved Moses' power of mediation, namely the manna. The reference to Ps. 78 : 24 indicates that the Jews interpret this verse as referring to the sign which the Messiah will give to prove his authenticity. These questions, then, are of the *haggadah* type, involving precisely the interpretation of Ps. 78 : 24, and thus parallel the question presumed to be asked by the child who is too young to be able to ask a question in the Jewish Passover Haggadah.

Having stated that he is the bread of life and that faith, a gift of the Father, is required to understand this, Jesus finds himself confronted with a question aimed more at ridicule than anything else (v. 42). This is a *boruth* question which finds its counterpart in the question which the wicked child asks in the Jewish Passover Haggadah. It makes light of the interpretation which Jesus gives to the words 'bread from heaven'.

[1] Ibid., pp. 498, 500–1, 504.
[2] B. Gärtner, op. cit., pp. 26–8.

In vv. 43–51 Jesus reiterates the necessity of faith to compre-
hend his interpretation and introduces the notion of *eating* which
is found in the verse of Ps. 78 under consideration.

The question of v. 52 again hinges on the understanding of
the exegesis of Ps. 78 : 24 with the emphasis on the word 'eat'.
The notion of eating, introduced by Christ into the discourse,
makes concrete the idea of participation and leads to the practical
question of how this may be applied to daily life. This question
of the Jews is a *derekh 'ereṣ* question which finds its counterpart
in the interrogation of the sincere child asked in the Passover
Haggadah. The fact that the Jews 'disputed among themselves'
concerning the revelation which Jesus had made in the previous
verse seems to indicate that the question is to be understood as a
sincere one.

So from the nature of the questions asked, it remains possible
that the author of the fourth gospel is following the Passover
Haggadah arrangement.[1] This probability is strengthened by
the fact that there exists synoptic material which seems to have
been directly influenced by the Passover Haggadah question
scheme.[2] Mk. 12 : 13–37 (Mt. 22 : 15–46) contains a series of
questions identical in character with the questions asked by the
four sons at the Passover, and the order of inquiry is the same.
The identity is so close that Jesus himself asks the last question
of those who dared not asked (Mk. 12 : 34), thus paralleling the
question presumed to be asked by the infant son 'who does not
know how to ask'. From this analysis D. Daube concludes
that the passage of Mk. 12 : 13–37 shows a direct influence of
the Passover-eve ritual and 'very likely came into existence, or
at any rate was published, on the occasion of a Jewish-Christian

[1] Other possible points of contact between the Jewish Passover
Haggadah and Jn. 6 : 26–58 are the use of the liturgical formula EGO
EIMI and the parallel between Jn. 6 : 35 and the words of the father when
he raises the Seder dish at the beginning of the Passover meal. Cf. B.
Gärtner, op. cit., p. 28.

[2] Cf. Daube, op. cit., pp. 158–69.

Seder'.[1] This possibility is further enhanced by the fact that vv. 31–58, which begin with the *haggadah* question concerning the interpretation of scripture, seems to be formally a midrash of Ps. 78 : 24: a text concerning a Passover theme important for a Jewish Christian Passover ritual modelled on the Jewish Passover Haggadah.[2]

---

[1] Ibid., p. 168.

[2] Concerning the probability of the existence of such a Christian Passover ritual and the further probability of a connection between Jn. 6 and such a ritual, see B. Gärtner, op. cit., pp. 14–38. Lately, moreover, G. Ziener has argued convincingly that a Christian Passover Haggadah probably served as a basis of John's gospel, cf. 'Johannesevangelium und urchristliche Passafeier', in *Biblische Zeitschrift* II (1958), pp. 263–74. For a summary of the evidence for (1) the existence of a primitive Christian Passover Haggadah modelled on the Jewish counterpart, (2) the correspondence between Jn. 6 and the Jewish Passover Haggadah, (3) the dependence of Jn. 6 on a Christian Passover Haggadah, see E. J. Kilmartin, 'Liturgical Influence on John 6', *Catholic Biblical Quarterly* XXII (1960), pp. 183–91.

V

The Holy Eucharist in St John[1]

T. Worden

In 1 Cor. the Holy Eucharist is presented as the liturgical action of the believing community: the repetition of the action performed by Jesus at the Last Supper. It is the liturgical action which is done as the memorial of Jesus' sacrificial death, in obedience to Jesus' command 'Do this in remembrance of me' (1 Cor. 11 : 24). St Paul tells the Corinthians: 'As often as you eat this bread and drink the cup, you proclaim the Lord's death until he comes' (11 : 26). The Holy Eucharist therefore is essentially an *action* performed by the community, an action having the power to re-present or renew the saving event of Christ's death, in the same way that the Jewish Pasch had always been the action whereby the saving event of the deliverance from Egypt had been renewed for each generation of God's chosen people. The action in each case involved eating and drinking, and what was eaten and drunk had in each case its symbolical reference. But that which essentially constitutes the Holy Eucharist according to St Paul is the action performed, not the things eaten and drunk.

This liturgical and effective remembrance of Jesus was without doubt the most prominent feature of the Christian community's life from the beginning. It was the essential community act, reiterating that this group of people was the people of God, for whom the blood of Christ had been shed: the people of the new covenant in Christ's blood. It was the act which united

[1] First published in *Scripture*, 1963, pp. 97–103, and 1964, pp. 5–16.

them into one whole: 'Because there is one loaf, we who are
many are one body, for we all partake of the same loaf' (1 Cor.
10 : 17). But because it was a community action, the individual
Christian tended to lose sight of his personal responsibility
towards it. It may come as something of a shock to find that
within a very short time the personal interests and animosities
of the Corinthian Christians were intruding themselves into the
celebration of the Eucharist to such an extent that Paul had to
rebuke them strongly: 'When you come together, it is not for
the better but for the worse. . . . There are divisions among
you. . . . Each one goes ahead with his own meal, and one is
hungry and another is drunk' (1 Cor. 11 : 17, 18, 21). Personal
interests, personal ambitions and the desire for personal benefits
were intruding themselves into this community act. We may
imagine an unspoken question in the minds of the Corinthians:
what benefits do I personally obtain from the gathering of the
Church to celebrate the Eucharist? Some hoped that their
influence and prestige would be enhanced. Others looked simply
for a good meal. It is clear enough from the whole of Paul's
letter to the Corinthians that the latter found the greatest
difficulty in subordinating personal interests to the good of the
community: they had been quarrelling among themselves
(cf. 1 : 11); the more educated and powerful resented the
presence of so many of the lower class (cf. 1 : 26-8), and tended
to despise Paul himself (4 : 8 ff.); personal interests of one sort
or another had influenced their indulgent attitude towards the
man living with his father's wife (5 : 1 ff.), and had led them to
prosecute their brethren 'before the unrighteous' (6 : 1): 'To
have lawsuits at all with one another is defeat for you. Why not
rather suffer wrong? Why not rather be defrauded? But you
yourselves wrong and defraud, and that, even your own
brethren' (1 Cor. 6 : 7-8). That personal interests, militating
against the unity of the 'one body' were not slow to make their
appearance ought to be no cause for surprise. We all know from

sad experience how difficult it is to control our own individual interests and ambitions.

But the emergence of such personal interests, in so far as they were a threat to the unity of the Christian community in general, and to the worthy celebration of the Eucharist in particular, are the occasion for a further consideration of the significance of the Holy Eucharist, precisely in terms of each individual member of the community celebrating it. The Eucharist as a liturgical action is the action of the community, attributable to no individual in particular. But in that community action there is a point at which each individual takes for himself a morsel of the bread and a share of the wine; each individual eats and drinks. Those actions are not community actions but personal ones, and the *personal* benefit depends upon the answer to the question: *What* have I eaten, *what* have I drunk? Already St Paul, realising that personal interests were profaning the celebration of the Holy Eucharist, had warned the Corinthians that personal responsibilities were involved in this community action, because of *what* each individual eats and drinks, namely the body and blood of the Lord: 'Whoever, therefore, eats the bread or drinks the cup of the Lord in an unworthy manner will be guilty of profaning the body and blood of the Lord. Let a man examine himself, and so eat of the bread and drink of the cup. For any one who eats and drinks without discerning the body, eats and drinks judgment upon himself' (I Cor. 11 : 27–9). The community in celebrating the Eucharist performs an action which proclaims the Lord's death until he comes; each man in the community, after examining himself, eats and drinks of the body and blood of the Lord.

It is with this second aspect of the Eucharist that St John is concerned. Paul had only touched on it from a negative point of view, as a warning of the dire consequences of eating and drinking in an unworthy manner. St John gives a positive

answer to the Christian's question: What do I eat and drink at
the celebration of the Eucharist, and what benefit accrues to
me? With the question, What are we doing when we celebrate
the Eucharist? he is not concerned. He writes his gospel within
the Christian community, where the celebration of the Eucharist
is the centre of its life, accepted unquestioningly as the bond
of unity and the pledge of redemption. But he writes his gospel
within a community the personal interests of whose members
are surely no less assertive than those of the Corinthians;
within a community moreover which has waited for its communal
redemption far longer than had the Corinthians at the time
when Paul had written to them. Even in the early fifties the fact
that many of the Corinthians were weak and ill, and some had
died, had called for an explanation (1 Cor. 11 : 30). The delay
in the *parousia* must raise questions with regard to the Eucharist,
with its implied expectation of the Lord's coming. Many
individuals who had formed the community celebrating the
liturgical action were no longer sitting round the table of the
Lord. The liturgical action continues unquestioned; but its
significance for each individual becomes more important as
the community outlives its members. John chooses to consider
the latter, while leaving aside the former. Of the liturgical action
which is the renewal of the banquet celebrated by Jesus on the
night before he died he says nothing. Instead, he tells us *what*
the bread and wine are which each eats and drinks, and what
benefits accrue to each individual recipient.

This is consistent with John's main preoccupation throughout
his gospel, namely to expound the significance of Jesus Christ
for the contemporary believer: not so much the significance of
what Jesus said and did during his earthly life, as the significance
of what Jesus *is*, here and now, for each one of us. The events of
Jesus' life and his teaching are the source and foundation, but to
show their relevance to the individual Christian of succeeding
generations demands that those events and that teaching be

applied and developed. Thus, for instance, John chooses to relate only a limited number of events; and he does so precisely in so far as they are 'signs', or significant actions, namely, actions that actually take place but carry 'a meaning deeper than the actual happening',[1] not, in John's mind, to be grasped by the eye-witnesses of the actions, but by John's contemporaries, to whom the Spirit of truth has been given. Moreover, they reveal what Christ is, here and now and eternally, rather than what Christ did on this or that particular occasion. They are manifestations of his glory (cf. 2 : 11), not in the superficial sense of showing him to be a wonder-worker, but of showing forth to those who see his signs with faith the glory which makes him to be what he is: the only Son from the Father (1 : 14). As C. K. Barrett says: 'It would not be impossible for the casual reader of the synoptic gospels to pick out from them miracle narratives which he could regard simply as the work of a strolling magician. It would be much more difficult to do this in the fourth gospel. With the miracles, as with other elements of the tradition, John has seized the christological interpretation which is implicit in the synoptics, clarified it, and stamped it upon the material in such a way that the reader is not allowed to escape it. The miracles of this gospel are a function of its christology. Rightly to understand them is to apprehend Christ by faith (10 : 38; 14 : 11). The miracles once grasped in their true meaning lead at once to the christology since they are a manifestation of the glory of Christ' (2 : 11).[2]

The feeding of the 5,000 is one of the few incidents John chooses to narrate, because it is a sign of what Christ is for all believers, namely the bread of life, the bread of God 'which comes down from heaven and gives life to the world' (6 : 34). That Jesus is the source of life, or the true and eternal life, is the

[1] C. H. Dodd, *The Interpretation of the Fourth Gospel*, Cambridge 1953, p. 300.
[2] C. K. Barrett, *The Gospel according to St John*, London 1955, pp. 62–3.

dominant theme of the gospel. 'I came that they may have life and have it abundantly' (10 : 10). It is this theme which is presented through a series of variations, in the doctrinal discourses which form the core of the gospel (ch. 3–12). We have first of all the idea of rebirth of water and the Spirit; then there is the water 'that I will give him, [which] will become in him a spring of water welling up to eternal life' (4 : 14). After the cure of the sick man at Bethzatha we have the claim: 'For as the Father raises the dead and gives them life, so also the Son gives life to whom he will. . . . Truly, truly I say to you, he who hears my word and believes him who sent me, has eternal life' (5 : 20, 24). After the bread of life we have the proclamation: 'If anyone thirst let him come to me and drink. He who believes in me, as the scripture has said, Out of his heart shall flow rivers of living water' (7 : 38). Then we have the variation of the theme in terms of 'I am the light of the world: he who follows me will not walk in darkness, but will have the light of life' (8 : 12). There follows the promise: 'Truly, truly I say to you, if anyone keeps my word, he will never see death' (8 : 51). Jesus the shepherd has come 'that they may have life, and have it abundantly' (10 : 10). 'My sheep hear my voice, and I know them, and they follow me, and I give them eternal life, and they shall never perish, and no-one shall snatch them out of my hand' (10 : 27–8). Finally we have the solemn declaration: 'I am the resurrection and the life; he who believes in me, though he die, yet shall he live, and whoever lives and believes in me, shall never die' (11 : 25–6).

In the sixth chapter we have that particular presentation of this theme which is announced by the narrative of the feeding of the 5,000: Jesus is the source of life in so far as he is the bread of life, the food which endures to eternal life. He is the supernatural, the heavenly food, of which even the bread from heaven, the manna, was only the faint and imperfect type. More significant still, the loaves which he had multiplied to feed the 5,000 had been simply an invitation to believe that Jesus could and would give them another bread which if any man eat of it, he would live for ever (cf. 6 : 51).

It is the supernatural character of this bread that must be emphasised, for it is all too easy to take the Eucharist for granted, to eat of it as of ordinary bread and expect it to work its life-giving effect in the same, natural and inevitable way as earthly food. It must be realised that this bread is the bread of life only for those who come to Jesus with faith: 'This is the will of the Father that every one who sees the Son and believes in him should have eternal life' (6 : 40). The fundamental source of eternal life is Jesus Christ; the fundamental and essential link between Christ and men is faith; fundamentally, therefore, he who has faith has eternal life; 'Truly, truly I say to you, he who believes has eternal life' (6 : 47), because belief in Christ means union with Christ the source of life. Here, as throughout John's gospel, we have that emphasis on faith which is reinforced by the insistence that faith itself is impossible to man unless it be given him by God: 'No one can come to me unless the Father who sent me draws him' (6 : 44). John's insistence on the need for faith which is the gift of God, and his parallel insistence on the need for knowledge of God are surely the corrective for the irresponsibility of the individual within the community, and for too crude a reliance upon the sacramental efficacy of the community's status as God's redeemed people.

To strike a correct balance between the notions of salvation through knowledge and salvation through sacramental union was a problem from the beginning, and one with which John was particularly preoccupied. When therefore he speaks of the Holy Eucharist, he is concerned first to insist that here too, and perhaps here especially, we must never lose sight of the truth that salvation is through knowledge, namely that experiential knowledge which John prefers to call faith, an act demanding the conscious submission of the individual to the divine attraction.

Jesus is the bread of life; but it is only he *who comes to* Jesus who shall not hunger, and he *who believes in* him who shall never thirst.

However, that salvation is not through knowledge alone is a truth evident to John's contemporaries from their experience within the Church. Regularly they celebrate the Holy Eucharist as the reaffirmation of their salvation through Christ, and the pledge of his coming to perfect it. Yet this action of the community is at the same time the means whereby each individual completes and perfects his own union of faith with Christ, by the sacramental act of eating the flesh of the Son of Man and drinking his blood. Jesus is the bread of life, not only because in seeing him and believing, their minds are fed with the life-giving wisdom from heaven, but also because in eating of the bread which they break together they eat of his flesh. Mind and body are united in the one complex and human act. When they come to Jesus with faith, drawn by the Father, and partake of the Eucharist, they are eating of the bread of life not only with their minds but also with their mouths, for the bread is the flesh of Christ and the wine his blood. In this way the Eucharist gives eternal life, here and now, to each individual recipient. The eschatological hope which the community expresses in its liturgical action of celebrating the Eucharist is not superseded, but the Eucharist is the food which here and now gives eternal life to everyone who eats and drinks: 'He who eats my flesh and drinks my blood *has* eternal life, and I will raise him up at the last day' (6 : 54).

John's doctrine concerning the Holy Eucharist stresses therefore the significance for each member of the community, of his eating the bread and drinking the wine. It is for each, here and now, eternal life, because he eats the flesh and drinks the blood of the Son of Man who is the source of life. Let it not be said that such a thing is monstrous and impossible, for the Son of Man is a heavenly as well as an earthly being (cf. 3 : 13): the partaking of the Eucharist is truly the eating of the bread of life for it is the eating of the flesh of Christ: but only he can eat of this heavenly food to whom faith is granted by the Father. Whereas the synoptic gospels and St Paul had concentrated on the significance of the liturgical action of the Church in celebrating the Eucharist, St John's doctrine provides us with the answer to the question, What does each one of us eat and drink when we share in the community's celebration of the Eucharist, and what does it give to each one of us?

This has been an attempt to give a brief summary of the doctrine of St John concerning the Holy Eucharist, in a positive and coherent way. But it will be quite clear to anyone aware of the formidable difficulties facing the interpreter of John 6 that the summary rests upon a number of previous conclusions. Naturally, then, this understanding of John 6 stands or falls by the validity of the positions previously adopted. It is true, moreover, that completely apodictic arguments are not forthcoming to establish the validity of these positions. In such a situation it might well be thought desirable to deal with the problems first. But all too frequently the contribution of the biblical theologian seems negative. We ought, I think, always to try as best we can to expound in a positive way the doctrinal content of the scriptures which alone matters in the end, even though we cannot always do this with certainty.

On the other hand, the difficulties and uncertainties must not be glossed over, at the risk of facile, subjective and unsound doctrinal syntheses. It will therefore be necessary to indicate the underlying conclusions and the reasons why they were adopted.

Briefly they may be reduced to two: first that the whole of the discourse which follows the narration of the feeding and the

walking on the sea is a discourse on the Eucharist; and second,
that this discourse is written for the instruction of the Christians
who frequently celebrate the Eucharist at the time the fourth
gospel was finally completed. It was on account of these conclusions that the Johannine doctrine of the Eucharist was stated
to be concerned with the benefit accruing to the individual
Christian when he partakes of the Eucharist, and with the need
for belief, precisely in regard to this sacrament.

But many would not agree with this doctrinal synthesis,
precisely because they would reject the foregoing conclusions.
Perhaps there are some who would wish to accept the doctrinal
synthesis whilst still repudiating the conclusions reached by the
preceding exegetical and literary study of the text. This latter
course seems impossible; but the attitude of the former has
much to commend it, for in point of fact there have always
been those who have denied any reference whatsoever to the
Eucharist in Jn. 6. This may be surprising, since the weight of
ecclesiastical tradition has always considered Chapter 6 to be
concerned with the Eucharist, and has usually referred to it
more precisely as the promise of the Eucharist. And yet, a more
careful and more thoughtful reading of the text could easily
make us much less certain of this. Among the fathers, Clement
of Alexandria, Origen and Eusebius of Caesarea saw no reference
to the Eucharist in Jn. 6; Augustine, to say the least, was somewhat uncertain. In the sixteenth century Cajetan, Luther and
Calvin adopted the same view.[1] At the present time it is a
common position, held by many outstanding scholars, to consider that only vv. 51c–8 refer to the Eucharist. Moreover, a
few would consider that these verses are a later addition made
after the gospel was written, in order to include a eucharistic
reference in a discourse from which it had been wholly absent.
For my part, not only have I rejected, along with most commen-

[1] Cf. A. Wikenhauser, *Das Evangelium nach Johannes*, Regensburger
N. T., 1957, p. 134.

tators, this last opinion, but I have maintained that the whole of the discourse, and not simply vv. 51c–8, is eucharistic in its reference.

Without any doubt the reasons for the contrary opinion are strong. Thus, there is first of all no explicit mention of the Eucharist, namely the celebration of the Lord's Supper, nor of the breaking of bread; nor is there any explicit reference to the Last Supper itself. Why then should vv. 26–51, first of all, be considered eucharistic? The statement 'I am the bread of life' has no necessary reference to the Eucharist, simply because 'bread' is mentioned. The statement immediately calls to mind other descriptions in this gospel, of what Jesus is when it is a question of the salvation of men: 'I am the light of the world' (8 : 12); 'I am the door of the sheepfold' (10 : 7); 'I am the good shepherd' (10 : 11); 'I am the resurrection and the life' (11 : 25); 'I am the way, the truth and the life' (14 : 6); 'I am the genuine vine' (15 : 1). These are so many metaphorical expressions and symbolical descriptions of what Jesus is for us. Similarly then, 'I am the bread of life' would be a metaphorical description, without any reference to real bread, but descriptive of Jesus as our spiritual food, attained by our believing in him, and thereby giving us eternal life. This understanding of the phrase seems to be borne out by the text: 'I am the bread of life; he who comes to me shall not hunger, and he who believes in me shall never thirst' (6 : 35). And it is supported by the fact that already in the sapiential books the image of eating bread had been used as a description of receiving heavenly wisdom, of which, according to John, Christ is the very incarnation (cf. 1 : 14). Wisdom says, for instance: 'Those who eat me will hunger for more, and those who drink me will thirst for more' (Sir. 24 : 21). Or again: 'Come, eat of my bread and drink of the wine I have mixed' (Prov. 9 : 5). The first part of John's discourse at least (viz. vv. 26–51b), would therefore be concerned simply with presenting Jesus to us as the object of our faith, and through faith, as the source of life: to believe in Jesus is to eat of the true, heavenly bread of life. It is the common opinion that only after this does John refer to the Eucharist, in vv. 51c–8, for now he speaks, not of Jesus the bread of life, but of the bread which Jesus will give which is his flesh. The mention of bread, given for the life of the world, and of flesh and blood, are said to be obvious references to the Eucharist, the sacrament of Christ's sacrificial death.

But we ought not to lose sight of the fact that this last remark is true only when we recall the words of institution: 'This is my body given for you' (Lk. 22 : 19 longer text), and 'This is my blood of the covenant poured out for many' (Mk. 14 : 24). If we were to read Jn. 6 : 51c–8 without reference to the words of institution, and let us bear in mind that John has no account of the institution, then vv. 51c–8 have no more explicit reference to the Eucharist than have the preceding verses. If Jesus is the bread of life in the metaphorical sense explained above, then to eat the bread of life is metaphorically to eat Jesus, namely, if we carry the metaphor to the extreme limit, to eat his flesh and drink his blood. Bernard, for instance, whilst admitting that the *language* is sacramental, could write: 'This does not mean that a non-sacramental explanation might not be placed by a Christian reader upon the mystical phraseology of the passage. No-one would deny that there may be ways of "eating the flesh and drinking the blood" of Christ in a spiritual manner which do not involve sacramental feeding.'[1] The point I am trying to make is this: vv. 51c–8 are eucharistic, precisely because they echo the words of institution, given to us by the other three gospels, and we suppose that John intends them to do so. This is a correct supposition; but if, wrongly, we refused to allow it, John's words would not then become meaningless: they are susceptible of a metaphorical interpretation. Now I consider it to be altogether more consistent to make the supposition that

[1] J. H. Bernard, *The Gospel according to St John*, I.C.C. 1928, p. clxix.

John had the same intention whilst composing the whole of this discourse, and therefore that he had in mind the eucharistic banquet from the very beginning, namely from the very moment he narrated the feeding of the 5,000. Therefore the whole of the discourse and not just its closing verses are eucharistic in reference. It is wrong to divide vv. 51c–8 from what goes before, and speak of them as introducing a fresh thought. To argue to this, from the contrast between 'My Father gives you the true bread from heaven' (6 : 32) and 'The bread which I shall give' (6 : 51), as though there were two breads: Jesus the object of faith, and the eucharistic bread: the former sent by God, and the latter given by Jesus, seems to be over-literal. The eucharistic bread might well be considered as given in two stages, if we wish, as John does, to compare it, first with the manna: it is given by the Father and from heaven, in so far as he has sent his son to earth: without the incarnation there is no Eucharist; but at a later stage it is given by Jesus, in that he gives himself, saying, 'This is my body; this is my blood.' It is not to be ignored that the discourse concludes in the same terms with which it began. 'This is the bread which came down from heaven, not such as the fathers ate and died; he who eats this bread will live for ever' (6 : 58).

The discourse as we now find it in the gospel is one whole, and the whole of it is eucharistic, not because of the words in themselves (even those of vv. 51c–8), but because John is writing fully conscious that the only bread of which the Church thinks, as soon as bread is mentioned in connection with Jesus, is that bread which Jesus took, and pronouncing the blessing broke. The living water offered to the Samaritan woman, the door of the sheepfold, the light of the world and so on, have no sacramental significance, because in fact there were no such sacraments within the life of the community. On the other hand, the water of which a man must be born again certainly has (Jn. 3 : 5). But why? Not because of any supposedly sacramental language, but because we rightly accept that John and those for whom he writes are conscious of the sacrament of Baptism, whereby they are reborn to life in the kingdom. What John insists upon is that Baptism is a birth of the Spirit, made possible only by the descent from heaven of the Son of Man, and demanding faith in him. So, too, in Chapter 6 the feeding of the 5,000 is narrated because it is the accepted 'sign' of the Holy Eucharist, the living bread sent from heaven by God in the person of his son, but only accessible through faith. John is not speaking of two things: first that act of believing in Jesus which might metaphorically be called eating the bread of life; and second, that eating of the flesh and drinking of the blood of Christ which is called the Eucharist. He is speaking of the eating of the bread of life which is Jesus, flesh and blood, an eating which must be an act of faith, if he who eats this bread will live for ever.

The second conclusion on which the synthesis of John's eucharistic doctrine is based has already begun to appear. The discourse as we find it in Chapter 6 was composed from the standpoint of the post-resurrection community, with its frequent celebration of the Eucharist. That obviously implies that this discourse as it now stands, and according to the intention of the author who has given it to us, has been put into a literary setting which is unhistorical, for it is said to be addressed to the people who had followed Jesus from the other side of the lake (6 : 24–5); the Jews interrupt the discourse at various points, and at the end of it we read: 'This he said in the synagogue, as he taught at Capernaum' (6 : 59). Clearly this conclusion is of considerable importance, and doubtless it is one that may easily be misunderstood. But it is also clear that it makes all the difference to our understanding of the discourse, for the interpretation of the text would of necessity have been very different if, instead of supposing that the discourse has in mind the Christian contemporaries of John toward the end of the first century, it had been taken for granted that it was addressed to the Jews of Capernaum about the year A.D. 30.

But perhaps the importance of this may be overshadowed by the fear that this foregoing conclusion impugns the historical reliability of the whole of St John's gospel. To give a full answer to this second and more general problem is obviously beyond the scope of this article, for the question concerns the relation of the whole of John's gospel to the history of Jesus. It is, however, significant to see how much more cautious commentators are becoming in this respect. Until recently many interpreters of John dismissed his historical reliability very quickly, and considered his gospel to be the free speculation of a theologian who felt little responsibility towards the historical teaching of Jesus. This attitude has changed, because it is becoming increasingly apparent that below the superficial dissimilarity between John and the synoptics, there is considerable identity of material; it has also changed because the synoptics can no longer be regarded as the yardstick with which to measure the historical reliability of John. Let us therefore remember that the historical reliability of John's material is not to be called in question too easily. But it still remains true that John adapts and rearranges and develops that material with the greatest freedom.

C. K. Barrett puts it well: 'John probes into the meaning of the synoptic narratives, and expresses it in other terms. It follows on the one hand that the differences between John and the synoptic gospels must not be exaggerated. John does not so much import foreign matter into the gospel, as bring out what was already inadequately expressed in the earlier tradition. On the other hand, the consequences of this process for the question of the historicity of the fourth gospel must be understood and faced. It is of supreme importance to John that there was a Jesus of Nazareth who lived and died in Palestine; but to give an accurate outline of the outstanding events of the career of this person was no part of his purpose. The critical and scientific writing of history was no common art in the ancient world, and it was certainly not a primary interest with John. He sought to draw out, using in part the form and style of narrative, the true meaning of the life and death of one whom he believed to be the Son of God. It is for this interpretation, not for accurate historical data, that we must look in the fourth gospel.' And further: 'He (John) did not hesitate to repress, revise, rewrite or rearrange. On the other hand there is no sufficient evidence for the view that John freely created narrative material for allegorical purposes. His narratives are for the most part simple, and the details generally remain unallegorised. This means that the chronicler can sometimes (though less frequently than is often thought) pick out from John simple and sound historical material; yet it may be doubted whether John would approve of the proceeding, for he wrote his gospel as a whole, combining discourse material with narrative, in order to bring out with the utmost clarity a single presentation, an interpreted history, of Jesus. Neither of these factors, history and interpretation, should be overlooked; nor, for a full understanding of what John intended, should they be separated.'[1]

The clear inference is that there must be sound reasons for questioning the historicity of even the lesser details. What grounds are there then for the conclusion at which we arrived concerning Chapter 6? The answer in brief is that a study of the discourse reveals that it has a looser connection with the preceding historical narrative than appears at first sight; and that the discourse itself is composite, and therefore has a history of its own. In other words we do not find in Chapter 6 a stenographic-like record of Jesus' instruction in the synagogue at

[1] C. K. Barrett, *The Gospel according to St John*, 1960, pp. 44; 117. Cf. J. A. T. Robinson, 'The Relation of the Prologue to the Gospel of St John', *New Testament Studies* (1963), pp. 128–9.

Capernaum, but a highly theological presentation of the doctrine of the Eucharist.

First of all the discourse, and we must continually make clear that we are at present speaking of the discourse as it now exists in Chapter 6, does not have close historical connections with the situation described in the opening narrative. The immediate link between the two, in vv. 22–4, is confused and gives the impression of a hurried attempt to provide some sort of connection. But more important, the discourse begins: 'You seek me, not because you saw signs, but because you ate of the loaves and were filled' (6 : 26). But we have just read at the end of the feeding narrative: 'The men therefore, having seen what sign he had done, were saying that this was truly the prophet coming into the world' (6 : 14). And they were for making him king. Why are they now credited with no higher ambition than to fill their bellies? Is not the reason simply that John intends the feeding to be a sign to his readers, not that Jesus is the prophet coming into the world, nor that he is the king, but that he is the bread of life? Moreover, is not the expression 'Labour not for the food that perishes' a rather strange way of referring to their search for Jesus? It reminds us rather of the synoptic saying: 'Do not seek what you are to eat and what you are to drink, nor be of anxious mind. For all the nations of the world seek these things; and your Father knows that you need them. Instead, seek his kingdom, and these things shall be yours as well' (Lk. 12 : 29–31).

Perhaps a more obvious connection between narrative and discourse would seem to be 'Our fathers ate the manna in the wilderness' (6 : 31). The last words perhaps remind us of the feeding which had taken place in a deserted place. But this information is in fact absent from John. It is supplied by the synoptics. No connection therefore with the Johannine narrative is to be found through the words 'in the wilderness'. But it could be insisted that there is a clear similarity between the manna in the wilderness and the feeding of the 5,000. Certainly there is a logical or, may we say, a homiletical connection; but surely the raising of the subject of the manna does not depend very closely on the narrative of the feeding. What I mean is this: the subject could just as easily have been brought up without the foregoing narrative, as an example of a 'work', i.e. a sign, done by Moses and as a challenge to Jesus: Can he equal it? In fact, if we suppose a close connection with the feeding narrative, then it seems foolish to choose this example of the manna, since Jesus has on this hypothesis done something at least similar in feeding the 5,000. In order to make sense of this remark about the manna on the supposition that there is an immediate historical connection between narrative and discourse, we would be forced to make the contrast between manna: bread from heaven, and earthly bread though miraculously multiplied: the former a greater sign than the latter; so that although Jesus had worked a sign (6 : 14), it is not as great as the manna sign. Yet the discourse does not take up this contrast: there is no reference to the lesser sign worked the previous day. Rather, Jesus says it was not Moses who gave the bread from heaven but 'my Father, (and my Father) gives you the genuine bread from heaven. . . . I am the bread of life. . . .' This first reference to the manna therefore does not seem to have any close connection with the narrative. The second (6 : 49) and third (6 : 58) are simply linked with the first (6 : 31). Note that there is no other reference of any kind to the narrative, not even in order to strengthen the faith of the disciples.

We now turn to the most important reason for thinking that the discourse does not strictly belong to the narrow historical setting of the synagogue at Capernaum. Chapter 6 : 26–58 is a composite text, namely John in giving us this gospel in its final form has written this discourse by weaving together what Jesus said on at least two different occasions. This will seem a very strange procedure to those unfamiliar with the way in which the material now forming all four gospels was first handed down by word of mouth, and only later formed into the literary works. But even a casual reading of Chapter 6 : 26–58 cannot fail to create the impression of a certain confusion, a certain obscurity, a certain amount of strange repetition. This composite character has been noted in other parts of John's gospel,[1] so that some would speak of a first and second edition. Whether there actually existed a first edition before our present gospel is a moot point. But the composite character of the eucharistic discourse is so important that we must attempt to make it clear by suggesting a possible determination of its two component parts, which we will call A and B:

A	B
(vv. 26, 30–5, 37–9, 41–4, 48–50, 58–9)	(vv. 27–9, 36, 40, 45–7, 51–7)

A

[26]Truly, truly I say to you, you seek me not because you saw signs, but because you ate your fill of the loaves.

[30]So they said to him: Then what sign do you do, that we may see and believe you? What work do you perform?

B

[27]Do not labour for the food which perishes, but for the food which endures to eternal life, which the Son of Man will give to you; for on him has God the Father set his seal.

[28]Then they said to him: What must we do to be doing the work of God?

[29]Jesus answered them, This is the work of God, that you believe in him whom he has sent. [36]But I said to you that you have seen me and yet do not believe.

[1] M.–E. Boismard, 'L'évolution du thème eschatologique dans les traditions johanniques' *Revue biblique* (1961), pp. 507–24; 'Les traditions johanniques concernan t le Baptiste', *Revue biblique* (1963), pp. 5–42; 'Le lavement des pieds', *Revue biblique* (1964), pp. 5–24.

A   B

³¹Our fathers ate the manna in the wilderness; as it is written: he gave them bread from heaven to eat.

³²Jesus then said to them, Truly truly I say to you, It was not Moses who gave you the bread from heaven; my Father gives you the true bread from heaven.

³³For the bread of God is that which comes down from heaven, and gives life to the world. ³⁴They said to him: Lord give us this bread always.

³⁵Jesus said to them: I am the bread of life; he who comes to me shall not hunger, and he who believes in me shall never thirst.

³⁷All that the Father gives me will come to me; and him who comes to me I will not cast out. ³⁸For I have come down from heaven, not to do my own will but the will of him who sent me;

³⁹and this is the will of him who sent me, that I should lose nothing of all that he has given me, but raise it up at the last day.

⁴⁰For this is the will of my Father that everyone who sees the son and believes in him should have eternal life; and I will raise him up at the last day.

⁴⁵It is written in the prophets, And they shall all be taught of God. Everyone who has heard and learned from the Father, comes to me.

⁴⁶Not that anyone has seen the

A

B

Father, except him who is from God; he has seen the Father.

⁴⁷Truly, truly I say to you, he who believes has eternal life.

⁵¹I am the living bread which came down from heaven; if anyone eats of this bread he will live for ever. And the bread which I shall give for the life of the world, is my flesh.

⁴¹The Jews then murmured at him because he said, I am the bread which came down from heaven.

⁴²They said,

Is not this Jesus the son of Joseph, whose father and mother we know?

How does he now say,

I have come down from heaven?

⁴³Jesus answered them:

Do not murmur among yourselves. No one can come to me unless the Father who sent me draws him;

⁵²The Jews then disputed among themselves, saying,

How can this man give us his flesh to eat?

⁵³So Jesus said to them:

Truly, truly I say to you, Unless you eat the flesh of the Son of Man and drink his blood, you have no life in you;

⁵⁴he who eats my flesh and drinks my blood has eternal life;

and I will raise him up at the last day.

and I will raise him up at the last day.

⁵⁵For my flesh is food indeed, and my blood is drink indeed. ⁵⁶He who eats my flesh and drinks my blood abides in me and I in him.

A	B
	[57]As the living Father sent me, and I live because of the Father, so he who eats me will live because of me.
[48]I am the bread of life.	[58]This is the bread which came down from heaven;
[49]Your fathers ate the manna in the wilderness and they died.	not such as the fathers ate and died;
[50]This is the bread which comes down from heaven, that a man may eat of it and not die.	he who eats this bread will live for ever.

If we compare A and B we find first of all that they are closely parallel and they are both concerned with the need for believing in Christ. They both present Christ as the one who has come down from heaven, sent by the Father to save men from death. Both insist on the close union existing between the Father and Christ, and they both emphasise that no-one can come to Christ unless he is drawn or instructed by the Father. But there are also certain differences. In A, Christ is the true bread that comes from heaven, the bread of God and the bread of life. There is a greater emphasis on the need to *come* to Christ, and only at the end is there a mention of eating this bread. In B, Christ is the living bread (not the bread of life), which came down from heaven; immediately the need to eat this bread is stated, and the bread is the flesh of Christ. Although both A and B twice have the refrain 'And I will raise him up at the last day,' only B uses the expression 'eternal life'.

It is also of interest to compare the two discourses A and B with the composite discourse at the last supper (Jn. 13–17). Just as both A and B insist on the need to believe in Christ, so too at the Last Supper Christ emphasises this (cf. 14 : 1, 24 with 6 : 29, 38). But the Supper discourse is closer to B than to A.

In 14 : 8–10 we read of Philip's request: 'Lord, show us the Father.' Our Lord then complains that although he has been with them so long they still do not know him, for they do not realise that in seeing him they see the Father also: 'I am in the Father, and the Father in me.' Now in B (6 : 36, 40, 45–6) we have the same doctrine in similar terms: Christ complains that although they have seen him they yet do not believe. He asserts an intimate relationship between himself and the Father, so that everyone who has learned from the Father comes to Christ, even though they have not seen the Father. Moreover in 15 : 4–7 Christ speaks of the need to abide in him, a need which according to 6 : 56 is met by eating his flesh and drinking his blood. Lastly, in 17 : 2–3 Christ speaks of giving eternal life, and defines it as the knowledge of the Father and himself; in B, Christ promises eternal life to him who believes and eats his flesh and drinks his blood.

The one discourse therefore which we find in Chapter 6 is John's composition, but in no sense his own free, creative teaching on the Eucharist. Essentially the words are Christ's, preserved by the tradition. But John, as untrammelled by any artificial and rigorist idea of historical veracity as all his successors engaged in teaching the gospel truths, feels free to adapt these words to one particular purpose. It is difficult to discover their original historical settings. Perhaps one is the occasion of the feeding of the multitude. Mark tells us that on the occasion of the feeding of the 5,000: 'He began to teach them many things' (6 : 34). Moreover after Mark has described the feeding of the 4,000[1] he tells us that the Pharisees sought from Christ a sign from heaven (8 : 11), and that 'He left them, and getting into the boat again he departed to the other side. Now they had forgotten to bring bread; and they had only one loaf with them in the boat. And he cautioned them, saying: "Take heed, beware

---

[1] It is possible that this is a doublet, namely an alternative tradition to the feeding of the 5,000 narrative.

of the leaven of the Pharisees and the leaven of Herod." And
they discussed it with one another, saying: "We have no bread" '
(Mk. 8 : 13–16). Then Jesus complains of their lack of understanding (cf. also Mk. 6 : 52). How are we to explain this
extremely enigmatic passage? Is it not reasonable to suppose
that Jesus had been preaching just previously on the theme: I
am the true bread? That moreover he had preached on this
theme at Passover time, as a commentary on the unleavened
bread to be used at the Passover? That the only bread the
disciples had taken with them in the boat was that true bread,
that bread from heaven, Christ the unleavened bread (cf. 1 Cor.
5 : 7)? That in failing to understand Christ's teaching the
disciples were continuing to eat the leavened, the corrupted
bread of the Pharisees? Matthew explicitly interprets Jesus'
warning as concerned with the teaching of the Pharisees
(Mt. 16 : 12). Is it not reasonable, lastly, to suppose that Jesus'
proclamation of himself as the bread of life, the true wisdom,
took place at Passover time[1] in the synagogue at Capernaum
(cf. Jn. 6 : 4, 59)? These suggestions are admittedly conjectural.
But the second historical setting is much less so. It is almost
certainly the Last Supper, and perhaps we may suggest the
reason for the surprising omission by John of the institution of
the Eucharist on this occasion. John regards the celebration of
the Eucharist in his own community as the Christian celebration
of the Passover.[2] But in his view Jesus' Last Supper was not a
celebration of the Passover,[3] and therefore from the Christian,
theological point of view as distinct from the historical, the
eucharistic references in Christ's last discourse are better placed

---

[1] Bertil Gärtner, *John 6 and the Jewish Passover* (Lund 1959), propounds
the interesting thesis that Jn. 6 is modelled on the Passover instructions
given in the synagogue either for the feast itself or on the four preceding
Sabbaths. Cf. the preceding chapter.

[2] 'Investigation has shown that the primitive church celebrated the
Passover according to the Jewish liturgy.' Gärtner, op. cit., p. 30.

[3] Cf. Jn. 18 : 28.

within the discourse given at the time of Passover (cf. Jn. 6 : 4).

The determining of the original historical contexts of Jesus' teaching is bound to be conjectural, but this has not been our real task. We have undertaken to interpret the text of Jn. 6 as it now stands; to determine what its author intended to convey, and not what the words meant at the time they were first uttered. But we must emphasise strongly that this does not mean that John makes use of Christ's words to signify something different and altogether new. As we have tried to show, John has composed this discourse in this way, to teach us that Christ is the bread of life pre-eminently when, as the climax to hearing his heavenly wisdom, we believe in him and eat of the bread of the Eucharist, so that we are united with the source of life by faith and by sacrament together.

VI

The Date of the Last Supper[1]

L. Johnston

THE date of the Last Supper is one of the most notorious difficulties in the New Testament. The synoptic gospels describe it as a paschal meal, while John tells us that the Jews were to eat the Pasch the next day, the day our Lord died—they refused to enter Pilate's court lest they be defiled and so debarred from eating the Pasch. Commentators have generally been content to opt for either John's date or that of the synoptics, and then to suggest explanations of how the other dating came about. Another solution, attempting to justify both methods of dating, was to suggest that there may have been two ways of reckoning the Pasch, and that our Lord was following one, described by the synoptics, and the 'Jews' who put our Lord to death were following another, and it is to this that St John refers. This theory would certainly be very convenient, if true; but it sounds rather too convenient—as if, in fact, it were invented in order to solve the difficulty. Certainly the arguments hitherto used to support it have failed to carry conviction. Recently, however, new arguments have been brought forward which it is suggested give an objective foundation to the theory.

The arguments are based on the Dead Sea Scrolls.[2] It has long been recognised that the calendar was something about

---

[1] First published in *Scripture*, 1957, pp. 108–15.

[2] The originator of this theory is A. Jaubert; for more detailed information the reader is referred to her articles, 'La date de la dernière Cène', in *Revue de l'Histoire des Religions*, CXLVI, 1954, pp. 140–73; 'Le Calendrier

which the Qumran sect felt very strongly; this was one of the points on which they were fiercely opposed to the official Jewish priesthood, and several passages in the documents exhort their followers to preserve jealously their own calendar and their own manner of reckoning the liturgical feasts. They even refer to the book on which their calculations are to be based—it is the *Book of Jubilees*, many fragments of which were found at Qumran. Without entering too much into technicalities concerning this calendar, we can say this much: the year was a solar year of exactly 364 days, which divided up into exactly 52 weeks. Thus 1 January would always be the same day of the week; if the year began on a Monday, the next year would begin exactly 52 weeks later on a Monday again. Further, the year was neatly divided into four parts, each having two months of 30 days plus one of 31 days; again, an exact number of weeks (13 each quarter), so that each quarter would begin on the same day of the week. In other words, if we knew the day on which any feast fell in any year, we could immediately tell on what day of the week it would fall in any other year. Now, by a series of complicated calculations it has been worked out that the year, according to this calendar, began on a Wednesday, and that the Pasch also fell on a Wednesday.

What is the history of this calendar? It seems probable that it is an old priestly calendar—how old, it is as yet impossible to say. In Hasmonean times the ordinary lunar calendar of 365 days was adopted. This gradually became current, but seemed like apostasy to the more zealous among the Jews, another lapse into hellenist ways. Among such circles the older calendar would remain current and even, as we see from the Qumran

des Jubilés et de la Secre de Qumran', in *Vetus Testamentum*, III, 1953, pp. 250–64. The latter is summarised in *Theology Digest*, V, 1957, pp. 67–72. It is discussed by E. Vogt in *Biblica*, XXXVI, 1955, pp. 408–13. Mlle Jaubert published her findings in *La date de la Cene. Calendrier biblique et liturgie chretienne*, Paris 1957 (English translation: *The Date of the Last Supper*, New York 1965).

documents, be a source of violent disagreement with the official priesthood.

Now how does this affect our reading of the gospels? According to the Old Testament the paschal lamb had to be eaten on the evening of the 14th Nisan, the next day, the 15th, being the Pasch, a feast which continued for a week. On the first and seventh days no servile work was permitted. The same week was also the feast of the Azymes: on the afternoon of the 14th Nisan the house was scrupulously cleared of leavened bread and throughout the week unleavened bread only was permitted. Now all the evangelists agree that our Lord died on a Friday, the eve of the Sabbath. But for John this day was the 14th Nisan, since the Jews were to eat the paschal victim that night. For the synoptics, on the other hand, our Lord and his disciples had already celebrated the paschal meal, 'on the night on which he was betrayed' (1 Cor. 11 : 23); this day, then, was for them the 14th Nisan. The difficulty is solved if we allow that the synoptics are describing the sequence of events according to a calendar similar to that of Qumran; while St John describes events according to the official Jewish calendar, in order to bring out the symbolism of our Lord the paschal victim. Thus following the Qumran dating, our Lord and the disciples ate the paschal meal on Tuesday evening before the Pasch, the 15th Nisan, a Wednesday; for the Jews, Friday evening was the 14th Nisan, the evening on which the paschal meal was to be eaten.

This immediately offers a solution to other difficulties also. In the first place it must be recognised that the events described in the gospels are with difficulty squeezed into the course of one night and a morning: the paschal meal, the arrest at Gethsemane, the double trial before the Jews, the trial before Pilate, with a visit to Herod followed by another session before Pilate; and only finally the sentence, the journey to Calvary and death.[1]

---

[1] Mark (15 : 25) says that our Lord was crucified at 'the third hour'. This is another difficulty in the chronology of the Passion which the

It is of course not absolutely impossible to fit them into the time-scheme which has become traditional, a period of only some fifteen hours; but it is very much easier if we can allow two whole days for the events, from Tuesday evening to Friday afternoon.

Further, according to the Mishna, capital cases must be tried during the daytime and, moreover, sentence could only be passed in a separate session. Hitherto it has either been said that this rule was not in force at the time of our Lord (the Mishna is a second-century document, though it embodies earlier traditions), or that the Jews in their haste to do away with our Lord acted illegally. But if we accept the present suggestion, there is once more ample time to allow for all the formalities of the law. Finally, this theory fits perfectly with another curious discrepancy between the synoptics and John. Mark describes the anointing of our Lord at Bethany after the words, 'The Pasch was to take place after two days'; John says that this anointing took place six days before the Pasch. If we allow that this anointing took place on Saturday, then the Pasch which Mark has in mind is indeed two days later, and at the same time it is six days before the official Jewish Pasch which St John describes.

The main objection to this would seem to be the completely novel interpretation of the gospel account of our Lord's last day, or days, on earth. In spite of the disagreements mentioned— particularly the nature of the Last Supper—it has always seemed that all four evangelists agree in packing the last events into the few hours between the last meal and his death the following afternoon. And now we are suggesting that these events actually took several days. Does this fit the gospel narrative? In considering this difficulty two factors should be remembered. First,

present theory helps to dispel. But since it is not insoluble by other means —see the commentators ad loc.—it seems to be an unnecessary complication to deal with it here.

we must bear in mind that the gospels in their present form are
not free and original compositions. They are not the beginning
but the end of a fairly long process of preaching, teaching and
collecting of various traditions. The Passion history itself is
probably one of the earliest parts of the gospel to be formed,
probably to explain the scandal of the cross and to bring out the
central doctrine of the resurrection. But this narrative would
probably be quite brief and simple in its original form; and in
the course of time other elements would be added to it—added,
moreover, without much in the way of careful reshaping and
editing but rather merely by means of insertion. Take the
incident at Bethany just referred to. Mk. 14 begins with a
reference to the plotting of the Jews; the story of the anointing
follows, but there is no organic connection between this story
and the preceding two verses; in fact it interrupts the next step
in the plot, the collaboration of Judas. Luke, for example
(22 : 1–3), links the two closely together, omitting the story
of the anointing (a similar incident to that which he has already
recorded in 7 : 36–50). It seems quite likely that this story of
the anointing was inserted at a later stage of the gospel formation, after the bare outlines of the Passion history—plot,
betrayal, trial, death—were already determined. Now the same
is probably true of other incidents in the present form of the
gospel of the Passion.[1] And while this by no means discredits
the trustworthiness of these 'secondary' elements, it does mean
that we can allow ourselves more latitude in estimating their
historical connection with the main thread of the story.

In any case of course, and this is the second consideration,
the main purpose of the evangelists was not to give an historically connected account. This is a statement which must be
understood very carefully. It does not mean that the evangelists

[1] For the criticism of the anointing at Bethany, see V. Taylor, *The Gospel
According to St Mark*, London 1953, p. 529 f.; for his discussion of the whole
chronology of the Passion, see p. 524 f., and Additional Note J, pp. 653–64.

were not concerned to give a factual account of what happened. But they were not concerned to give a history, a chronicle, a diary of the events as they happened. Their main purpose was theological—what precise theological point they had in mind may be stated with slight variations by different interpreters,[1] but there is no doubt about the main fact. The evangelists are not writing history for the sake of history; they are writing history, but for the sake of the theological meaning which God has inserted into it. This means that although they neither invent facts nor falsify the facts at their disposal, they feel a certain liberty in their arrangements of the facts and in their manner of telling them, and relatively unconcerned with precise details of place and time. This happens continually throughout the gospels. Quite early in our Lord's life Matthew describes three conflicts with the Pharisees (Mt. 12 : 1–30)—when the disciples were plucking ears of corn, when he healed the man with the withered hand, and 'then' when he cast out the devil from the dumb man. Luke agrees with Matthew for the first two incidents, but gives the third very much later, during his journey to Jerusalem (Lk. 11 : 14–23). No-one would accuse either evangelist of being untrustworthy—neither of them is concerned primarily with the precise historical sequence of events, and Matthew's 'then' is not to be taken too literally; it means simply, the next incident which he chooses to narrate. And the same is true of the history of the Passion. The evangelists are intent on the history of salvation; the incidents they narrate are selected and arranged with this in mind; and considerations of chronology are of secondary and negligible importance.

The evangelists, therefore, agree on the main facts—that our Lord was betrayed, tried by the Jewish authorities, found guilty of nothing else than of being the Messiah, handed over to the

---

[1] As an example of different ways of looking at the theology of salvation in the New Testament itself, see the articles by D. M. Stanley, *Catholic Biblical Quarterly*, XVIII, 1956, pp. 231–54; pp. 345–63.

Roman governor and condemned to die. This is sufficient for their main theological purpose. They are not then very much concerned with details—when exactly the trial took place, how many trials there were, when exactly the various details took place (denial of Peter, insulting by the priests), how long the trial before Pilate took and so on. They even feel free to describe these details from different points of view—Luke's account of Peter's denial is different from that of the other gospels. They feel free to pass over one or other of them—only Luke tells us of the visit to Herod, only John tells us about the visit to Annas. We need not feel any difficulty, therefore, about accepting a theory which demands an expansion of the compressed account of the Passion given in the gospels. We should expect to find that it has been compressed; and in fact, as we have already seen, we should already have suspected that it was unduly compressed and be far from unwilling to find some means of relieving the pressure.

The chronology of the Passion, then, on the basis of the gospel account combined with the Qumran calendar, would be as follows:

Saturday night: anointing at Bethany ('two days' before Mark's Pasch; 'six days' before John's).

Sunday: solemn entry into Jerusalem: Palm Sunday; return to Bethany.

Monday: return to Jerusalem, cursing the fig tree on the way.

Tuesday: to Jerusalem again; fig tree withered; preparation of the Pasch; last supper, which was a paschal meal according to their calendar, but not for the Jewish authorities who were therefore free to arrest our Lord that night in Gethsemane and take him to the house of Annas. It is probably during this night session that Peter's denials took place, so that at the end, as he was being led off at cock-crow, the Lord turned and looked at Peter (Lk. 22 : 61).

Wednesday: at cock-crow, plenary session of the court before Pilate. Probably here, when the formalities were over, the mockery of our Lord took place.

Thursday: another session of the court early in the morning, merely to pass sentence according to the Mishna ruling; our Lord taken to Pilate, who after a preliminary enquiry sent him on to Herod.

Friday: second appearance before Pilate; this was the 14th Nisan according to the official calendar, so the Jews refused to enter Pilate's court; the whole morning given up to wrangling before Pilate, the incident of Barabbas, the scourging and condemnation; and finally, the crucifixion.

This interpretation is so novel that some people will be inclined to condemn it on that ground alone; 'untraditional', they will say and consider that this is sufficient condemnation. But is it so untraditional? The *Didascalia Apostolorum* (a work of about the third century which incorporates even earlier documents) bears traces of a similar tradition. It explains the fast days of holy week by connecting them to the various events of the Passion, which it describes in the following order: on *Tuesday* evening the Last Supper, then the arrest of our Lord; *Wednesday*, detention in the house of Caiphas and council of priests; *Thursday*, appearance before Pilate, by whom he was kept in prison that night; and *Friday*, Pilate condemns him and delivers him to be crucified. The author is obviously aware of the difficulty arising from John's statement that the Friday was the day when the Pasch was to be eaten, and offers a far-fetched explanation of how this came about; but this does not modify the importance of his *independent* witness to a four-day chronology of the Passion. His statement, moreover, is taken up by Epiphanius in the fifth century. Epiphanius clearly depends on the *Didascalia*, but it would be very surprising if he accepted this tradition on the sole ground of this one source. One might well, then, suspect that the tradition was rather more widespread than our present documentation reveals. This idea receives confirmation from the fact that Victorinus of Pettau, who died in 304, accepts the same tradition in his *De Fabrica Mundi*, and clearly without dependence on the *Didascalia*. Not very much evidence, one might say. But the important thing to notice is that it is completely independent of the gospels; this tradition could not have arisen from a reading of the gospel texts—and it must have an origin somewhere. Whereas the whole body of contrary tradition, holding the normal chronology of a last supper and arrest on the Thursday night followed by trial and death on the Friday, is entirely based on the gospel text. Now we have already seen that the gospel text does not necessarily demand this interpretation and is not irreconcilable with a longer chronology; therefore the tradition which depends on the gospel text is likewise not necessarily binding. A tradition which depends on the gospel text cannot be used to support that text itself. Moreover, since the shorter chronology is the natural and simple way of regarding the gospel account, if there were no other evidence to the contrary, it can quite easily be understood that a tradition which at first sight appeared to conflict with the gospel account should fairly soon have disappeared. We hear no more of it, explicitly, after Epiphanius in the fifth century.

It will be agreed that this theory offers a better solution to the difficulties of the gospel text than any other so far suggested. It does not depend on any arbitrary alteration of the date of the Pasch by either our Lord or the Jewish authorities, but rests on the evidence of a calendar we know did exist. But it cannot yet be said to have been proved conclusively. In the first place, the calendar on which it rests was that of the community of Qumran; but we do not know that our Lord and his disciples followed it. Against this it should be admitted that there is a steadily growing body of evidence which points to fairly close contact between the Qumran sect and early Christianity. We need not say that this contact was direct and immediate; nor do we need to say the same concerning the calendar. It would be sufficient to say that the Qumran documents show us that there were ideals and ideas current in Israel in the first century which are not reflected in the documents of official Judaism; and that it is quite possible that Christianity drew its first followers from circles which had at least as much in common with these 'marginal' elements as with official Judaism. In other words, we do not need to say that our Lord followed the calendar of Qumran; all we need to say is that we now know there was such a calendar, that it may well have been current in other places besides the Qumran community, and that our Lord may have followed this body of opinion which preferred the ancient priestly calendar to the later official civil calendar. It must be admitted, however, that the words 'may be' occur rather too often in such an explanation for us to be quite certain about it.

A second point on which we would like further explanation is the question of intercalated days. Even in our year of 365 days we have to insert an extra day every few years in order to make up for the fact that the year is actually slightly longer than 365 days. In a year of 364 days the difference between the days and seasons of the year would become more noticeable even more quickly than in our year. This would be of particular importance in a calendar which was meant to preserve the regularity of the liturgical feasts, when those feasts were so closely connected with the seasons. If the year were computed inflexibly according to 364 days, there would come a time when they were celebrating the offering of first fruits before the seed was even sown. Moreover, if they were to preserve the regularity of the recurring days (New Year's day always falling on the same day of the week), it could not be a question of inserting merely one day, as we do in our calendar. At least a complete week, if not a complete month, would have to be inserted. Now we have as yet no information how or when this was done. Therefore, in spite of the apparent mathematical certainty of the computation of the Qumran calendar, we cannot be absolutely sure of the occurrence of any given feast in any given year. We know that the Pasch, the 15th Nisan, would certainly be a Wednesday; but we do not know if it would necessarily be in the same week as the official Jewish 15th Nisan.

For the moment, then, this theory must remain no more than a very attractive possibility.

VII

The Meaning of 'Sin'[1]

T. Worden

No one would deny that the word 'sin' is used in the Bible to cover many different aspects of the idea of wickedness or opposition to the will of God. This is obvious to anyone who examines the different Hebrew words, all translated in the Septuagint by the same word *hamartia*, and in the English versions by the one word 'sin'. It is true that we also find such variants as injustice, lawlessness, evil, guilt, but there is no consistency in the way such words are used.[2] There is a place within the concept of sin as found in the Bible for many different aspects: aspects which we no longer take cognisance of in our narrower definition of sin as any deliberate act, by thought, word or deed of a responsible individual, against the law of God. If we limit sin to an act, if we limit it to the act of the individual, and if especially we insist upon the moral responsibility of the individual, then it is vital to realise that the biblical term 'sin' has a much wider connotation than when we use the term. It is true that the fundamental meaning of *hata'*, the commonest word for 'to sin', is to miss the mark, to lose or to fail, and through all the terms used for sin there is the underlying idea of a falling short of a norm given to man by God. There is no doubt, therefore, about sin having its origin in the

---

[1] First published in *Scripture*, 1957, pp. 44–53.
[2] The Greek word *hamartia* is employed to translate fifteen different Hebrew words (and this does not include different variations of the same verbal stem); *adikia* stands for thirty-six different Hebrew words; *anomia* for twenty-four. Cf. Quell, *TWNT* I, p. 267 ff.

deliberate and conscious failure to conform to God's law; in other words, sin is fundamentally a responsible act of rebellion. The moral aspect of sin can never be lost sight of; the wider use of the term does not deny this fundamental morality. But it is precisely on the wider use of the term that we must insist, because it is here that we are most likely to fail in appreciating the teaching of holy scripture on sin. Thus the consequences of man's failure to observe the divine law loom large within the general notion of sin,[1] and those consequences are indicated by this same word. In fact, the failure to follow the norm laid down by God is often only recognised when the consequences are felt, as is shown in many of the lament psalms where the psalmist's sufferings lead him to a full realisation of his sinfulness, and of the necessity of confessing it to God: 'As long as I kept silent my bones rotted, and I moaned unceasingly; for day and night thy hand was heavy upon me; my strength ebbed as in the summer heat. I have confessed my sin to thee, and I have not concealed my wretchedness; I said: I will confess my rebellion to the Lord; and thou hast removed my wretchedness, my sin thou hast pardoned' (Ps. 32 : 3–5). We would perhaps use the word 'guilt' as a term of general reference to the consequences of sin, and the various Hebrew words which are translated by 'sin' have this meaning in those contexts where the author is not concerned with a sinful deed, but with the resulting condition and the inner state produced by this deed. The causal connection between the two is not clearly shown, since it was a most difficult question in view of the overriding sovereignty of God over all things, good and evil.[2]

Guilt is spoken of as a positive reality, in terms of a burden

---

[1] Cf. *TWNT*, I, p. 280, 29 ff.

[2] Only one Hebrew word, *'asăm*, is used to express clearly this state of guilt, and this word is found almost exclusively in ritual contexts. A man could be considered guilty, without any deliberate refusal to observe God's law; he could become guilty or impure through ignorance.

or of a disease. Thus guilt can be a burden too heavy for man
to carry (Ps. 38 : 5). It is in substance identical with sufferings
which may afflict a man, and guilt reveals itself through these
sufferings. Cain's banishment to the wilderness, to a land which
he will not be able to cultivate, is a suffering which constitutes
his 'guilt' and which, he complains, is too heavy for him to
bear (Gen. 4 : 13). Grief and regret and sorrow for sin are called
forth by grief over pain and misery and misfortunes; in practice
the grief is identical. It is particularly important for those who
wish to understand the significance of penitential practices, to
realise the close connection in the biblical theology between
guilt and bodily sickness. Thus the law (Lev. 13–14) laid down
strict regulations for various skin diseases,[1] because they were
external signs of guilt, and the result of sins (the latter word
not necessarily indicating any responsible action against God's
law on the part of the individual sufferer). These laws are not
to be adequately explained in terms of hygienic precautions,
made more effective by a religious setting; it is perfectly reasonable to suppose that such hygienic reasons as the prevention
of contagion were not ignored but their primary purpose was to
emphasise the guilt involved. Thus not only must the sufferer
keep away from others, but his clothes must be torn and his
hair unbound (Lev. 13 : 45). The priest must destroy contam-
inated clothes and houses, as well as diagnose the ailment. But
he was not simply doctor and sanitary inspector: he must offer
cultic sacrifices. For the 'leprous house' there must be a sacrifice
—for the *sin* of the house. For the sick man's cleansing there
must be a 'sacrifice for sin' which constitutes the rite of expiation
for his impurity; the Septuagint does not hesitate to speak of the
sin-offering which the priest offers as a propitiation 'concerning
the one who is being cleansed *from his sin*' (Lev. 14 : 19).
In similar fashion later Judaism taught that sickness was a

[1] Cf. L. Koehler in *Zeitschrift für die Alttestamentliche Wissenschaft*,
1955 (Heft 3/4), p. 290.

punishment for sin, and that the sick man did not get rid of his sickness until all his sins were forgiven. Death, the evil most feared by men, was the most striking consequence of sin: 'It is by woman (namely sinful Eve) that sin began, and it is because of her that we all die' (Sir. 25 : 24). 'It is by the envy of the devil that death entered the world. Those who belong to him will experience it' (Wis. 2 : 24). A similar saying among the Rabbis was 'No death without sin, and no chastisement without guilt'.

That our Lord's disciples held the same belief is clear from their question on seeing a man blind from his birth: 'Who sinned, this man or his parents, so that he should be born blind?' But our Lord's reply seems to deny the truth of their belief: 'Neither this man sinned nor his parents, but that the works of God might be shown forth in him' (Jn. 9 : 3). If the first part of this reply were taken from its context, and made to stand as an independent statement, then of course it would be a clear denial of any connection, in this case at least, between blindness and sin. But it must not be torn from its context. In examining its context, we see that something must be supplied in order to make our Lord's reply a complete sentence. There are two possibilities: 'Neither this man sinned nor his parents, *so that he should be born blind,* but in order that the works of God might be shown forth in him,' or: 'Neither this man sinned nor his parents, *but he was born blind* in order that the works of God might be shown forth in him.' The first suggestion is preferable, since it only involves repeating the words which end the disciples' question, and which therefore could reasonably be omitted as understood. In this case the sense is that in God's designs, the final purpose of sin, of which the consequence[1] had been this blindness, is the showing forth of God's works, the manifestation of his glory. Our Lord is not categorically denying the connection between blindness and sin, but is insisting rather

---

[1] 'A final *hina* corresponds here to the consecutive *hina* of the question.' Stauffer, in *TWNT* III, p. 328, 4.

on the divine purpose to be found in all human action,[1] a purpose
which is about to be made manifest here in the restoration of
sight. Our Lord is almost rebuking the disciples for asking a
question which is of lesser moment here. Had they not read in
Ben Sirach: 'You must not say: What is this? Why that? For all
has been created for a purpose' (39 : 21)? If we were to adopt
the second paraphrase, the meaning would not differ: the final
purpose of the man's blindness is the manifestation of God's
glory. Here, the statement: 'Neither this man sinned nor his
parents' seems more categorical; but it is only so in appearance,
for in what sense can we say that he was born blind in order
that the works of God might be shown forth in him, except as
an expression of the final purpose of God, whereby evil is
changed into good? Our Lord is here concerned with the final
end of all things: 'It is for judgment that I came into this world,
in order that[2] (as God's final purpose, which we can only know
from the results) those who do not see may see, and those who
see may become blind' (Jn. 9 : 39; cf. Mk. 4 : 11f.). There is a
close parallel to this text, which confirms our interpretation:
when told of Lazarus's sickness, our Lord says: 'This sickness
is not unto death, but for the glory of God, in order that the
Son of God may be glorified through it' (Jn. 11 : 4). Without
any essential change, this can be made exactly parallel to our
Lord's reply concerning the blind man: thus 'He is not sick, so
that he should die, but in order that the Son of God may be
glorified in him.' It is impossible to take the first clause as an
absolute statement, for we are told both that Lazarus was sick
and that he died (Jn. 11 : 4, 39). To understand the clause
'Neither this man sinned nor his parents that he should be
born blind' as an absolute statement, is perhaps less obviously,
but nevertheless equally, impossible.

So it would be a mistake to think that this wider use of the

[1] Ibid., pp. 327–30.
[2] Ibid., p. 328, l. 11.

term 'sin' is confined to the Old Testament. It is clear that the
one word is used in the New Testament, for three ideas which,
whilst having a common factor ultimately based, as in the Old
Testament, upon the moral act against God's law, make the
word more extensive than the modern definition of sin. The
word is used to describe an action contrary to the norm laid
down by God; it is used of the condition in which man finds
himself as a result of such sinful actions—a condition which
though not necessarily, yet generally, reveals itself in various
miseries he has to suffer; and it is used to signify the personified
power of evil which is in the world. Somewhat to our surprise,
it is in the first sense that it is used least frequently.[1] On the
other hand the word is often used in the sense of a sinful state,
i.e. the condition of a man who is separated from and at enmity
with God. Thus the Christian is dead to his sins (1 Pet. 2 : 24)
in so far as he has ceased to be in a sinful state; and yet there
are those who do not abandon (the state of) sin (2 Pet. 2 : 14—
note the singular: *hamartias*, and not the plural, which would
have been required if the sense had been: who do not cease
from doing sinful deeds). Before Baptism we walked about in
sins (Eph 2 : 2), and those who do not believe will die in their
sins (Jn. 8 : 21, 24). To the Jews our Lord said, 'Your sin
remains' (Jn. 9 : 41). Evidently they remain in the state of sin
which arises from refusing to see the light. And this condition
often brings with it the outward manifestations of sin, so that
Paul can speak of 'the body of sin' (Rom. 6 : 6) or 'the flesh of
sin' (Rom. 8 : 3) where he means the bodily weaknesses which
men suffer as a result of sin. It is because of this wider meaning
of the word that he can say that God 'made him who knew not
sin, him he made sin, for our sakes' (2 Cor. 5 : 21): Our Lord

---

[1] Out of 50 examples quoted in *TWNT* I, p. 297, 20 ff. as examples
of the word 'sin' in the sense of wicked *actions* only 11 are clearly so:
Matt. 12 : 32; Acts 7 : 60; Jas. 2 : 9; 4 : 17; 5 : 15; 1 Pet. 2 : 22; 1 Jn.
3 : 3.9; 5 : 16; 2 Cor. 11 : 7; cf. Jn. 8 : 34.

had never known what it was to sin; yet God afflicted him with sufferings and even with death, evils which may be classified under the general term 'sin'.

But the close connection between sinful deeds and the miseries which are their consequences is most clearly seen in our Lord's miracles.[1] The amount of attention given in the gospels to his works of healing is significant. The purpose behind it is not directly to show his great compassion for the sick, nor, for that matter, to represent him as a healer possessed of miraculous powers, though both are clearly true. But the precise reason is that by these miracles he shows his power over sin. The miracles of healing are a clear proof to the readers of the gospels that Jesus is the Messiah, whose victory over evil is assured; and for that reason they are the sign that God's Kingdom is truly come. The answer sent to John the Baptist is that the blind see, the lame walk, the leprous are healed, the deaf hear, the dead rise, the good news is told to the poor; Jesus, as Luke adds, was at that time healing many people suffering from diseases, infirmities, evil spirits and blindness (7 : 21 ff.). Preaching the good news and healing diseases went together (Mt. 4 : 23; 9 : 35). That the healing of diseases was external proof of our Lord's power over evil is clear from the way in which it is linked with the expulsion of evil spirits. The evil spirits themselves bore witness to the Messianic power of Jesus, for they cried out: 'Thou art the Son of God,' and he forbade them to speak because they knew he was the Christ (Lk. 4 : 40; 8 : 2; Mk. 1 : 34; 3 : 10). There is no sharp distinction to be drawn between those who were sick and those who were possessed by evil spirits, since the sickness was but the result of the power of evil. Thus we are told of the healing of a man possessed, who was blind and dumb (Mt. 12 : 22), and of the lunatic child who was healed at the moment when the demon went out of

---

[1] Beyer, *TWNT* III, pp. 129–31.

him (Mt. 17:18): Our Lord did not resort to elaborate
methods of exorcism; by a simple command the evil spirits were
expelled. Thus does he show his power, and in face of such
evidence it is constantly necessary to command that his Messiah-
ship, so clearly shown, should not yet be proclaimed; the
Messiah was to be recognised not so much by his wonderful
healing powers as by his conquest of all evil. Moreover, it was
because these miracles were not essentially manifestations of
power over nature, but of victory over evil, that our Lord gave
the same power to his disciples. Sending them to preach the
imminent coming of the kingdom, he commands them to heal
the sick, raise the dead, cleanse lepers, drive out demons
(Mt. 10:8). He gives them authority over impure spirits,
with power to expel them, and to heal any disease (Mt. 10:1).
This power was in no way magical: it could only be used success-
fully where there was faith. The disciples failed because of their
lack of it (Mt. 17:16), and our Lord himself could not do
many miracles in Nazareth because he found so little faith there
(Mk. 6:5). Throughout the Bible it is revealed that God never
conquers the evils which afflict men, without men's co-operation,
and this demands from them the belief in his power and his
willingness to rescue them. Had he not led the children of Israel
from Egypt, and yet failed to rescue those who lacked faith in the
desert? The now outmoded attack on the person of Christ used
to make great play of this need for faith in the recipients of his
healing; it gave the opening for parallels to be drawn with
cases of faith-healing, and such words as auto-suggestion,
hallucination, hysteria could then be bandied about. And some
Christian apologetes could not be wholly exonerated, for they
so stressed the miraculous nature of these works that they
obscured the true significance of this need for faith, and were
inclined to find it embarrassing. God never, throughout his
revelation of himself, worked wonders for their own sake;
they were all directed towards his redemptive purpose of saving

his people from evil. And he has never rescued anyone who freely chose not to be rescued, a choice which in practice is expressed by incredulity in face of the signs which show God as the rescuer of all who trust in him.

It is because sin has in biblical language the wider significance we have been considering that the New Testament also speaks of sins as positive realities even when, as is clear from the context, the sinful acts are a thing of the past. In this respect sins are what we would call the lasting effects of sins. St Paul speaks of the 'sufferings of sins' (*pathēmata hamartiōn*), which used to work in our limbs to bear fruit in death (Rom. 7 : 5). This expression may seem less odd when it is translated 'sinful passions', but how can we talk of 'passions' as positive active things, unless we accept the point of view which regards the injuries inflicted by sin as positive realities which remain after the sinful deeds are done? The verbs used of the action of Christ on sin—to take away, to carry, to loose, to purge—would all suggest the same thing. And it is a consequence of looking on sin as a positive and lasting reality that it is also spoken of as a personified power, which came into the world (Rom. 5 : 12) and came alive (7 : 9), seducing and killing (7 : 11) and laying siege (Heb. 12 : 1). It lives in us, bringing sufferings and desire (Rom. 7 : 17; 8 : 5, 8). In fact it is a demoniacal power, under whose tyranny man is a slave (Rom. 3 : 9; cf. 11 : 32). Sin lords it over us (Rom. 6 : 14) as a king (Rom. 5 : 21; 6 : 12), with no other reward for services rendered than death (Rom. 6 : 23). This concept of sin as a personified power is almost exclusively found in the epistle to the Romans, but we have echoes of the same idea in Jn. 8 : 34, where everyone who does sin becomes the slave of sin, and in Jas. 1 : 5 where sin is born of concupiscence, and fully formed gives birth to death.

It might well be objected that all these expressions which we have examined are simply metaphorical expressions, and that they are not to be taken literally. Sin, the objection might run, is spoken of as a positive reality *metaphorically*, it causes us physical harm metaphorically, it brings death metaphorically; when the word is used in the Bible in the sense which tallies with our definition of sin, then it is to be taken literally; in the other cases, where it goes beyond our definition, it is used metaphorically. But this is too facile altogether. When is human language *not* metaphorical in expressing the truths of faith? To define sin as an offence against God: is this any less metaphorical? To say that sin is not being, but the privation of being: is this any more direct and positive than these so-called metaphors of sin which we find in the Bible? If the expressions we have considered were few and far between, and were used for ideas which were elsewhere expressed in 'literal' terms, then we would agree with the objection. When, for instance, our Lord says, 'I am the vine', we know clearly enough already who 'I' is, not to take 'vine' literally; when we are told that the lilies of the field do not spin, we have no reason to think that lilies were thought to be capable of spinning. But sin is not spoken of in any other way than those we have examined. When we say that sin, according to its context, is regarded chiefly from the standpoint of an *act* in contravention of the divine law or, in another case, chiefly as a positive consequence of such an act producing a real state or condition or, finally, that it is a powerful force which causes certain effects, we are speaking inadequately, in human terms, about something we do not fully understand; but we are not speaking merely metaphorically, in the accepted sense of this word. If we were, then we ought to be able to go on and give the literal explanation also. These uses of the word 'sin' show us what the Biblical writers believed concerning sin; they were no more capable of expressing their belief adequately than we are, but it is rather gratuitous to dismiss their concepts as primitive. Their ideas, in the terms with which they conveyed them, are the ideas and terms which God saw fit to use in revealing the notion of sin to us. They are necessarily limited, as is the whole of God's action in human affairs; but it is important to remember that the idea of sin which we are seeking is a *revealed* idea of a truth beyond the limits of our understanding. We are quite capable of elaborating a notion of natural sin; we can develop a *philosophy* of sin; we can, moreover, offer a rational, philosophical explanation of the theological teaching on sin, in order to assist people to grasp the truths of faith in a way suited to their particular mode of thinking. But it is nevertheless important to keep before our mind the revelation of sin which we are attempting to explain: it would be unfortunate if the truth were dominated by the explanation; no one philosophical explanation has exclusive rights over any truth of faith. The definition of sin in terms of offence against God is useful for all, since all are accustomed to human relationships in which a man so frequently offends his neighbour; to explain sin as the infringement of God's law, and consequently as deserving of punishment, is almost as generally useful, since practically all men are accustomed to having their lives governed by laws, enforced by the enacting of penalties against law breakers. When, however, we speak of sin as a privation of being, we are giving an explanation which is useful to a select few: to those who have been trained to think along certain philosophical lines it is a good explanation: amongst other things, it 'exonerates' God from any positive causality with regard to sin. Even for the philosophically minded it does not, of course, satisfy all difficulties; for many it explains nothing: to speak of toothache or cancer as 'privations of being' is easier for the healthy man than for the sick; a hole in the road is positive enough for the man who falls into it.

The examination of the term 'sin', therefore, is not merely a contribution to a biblical glossary, which we have to bear in mind if we are to understand the biblical texts. It gives us the revealed teaching on sin, whether we in turn present this teaching in different terminology or not. In actual fact translation into other terms is now necessary, for we fail to realise other biblical concepts which are essential to the proper use of the biblical terminology of sin. If, for instance, we spoke of the sickness of an innocent child or the sufferings of a saintly man as sin, our hearers would be horrified, for there is no responsibility for sin in the case of these individuals. Yet according to the Bible there is such a thing as a corporate responsibility, whereby a certain group, whether a family, or a clan, or the whole of the chosen people, or even the whole of the human race, shares responsibility in certain circumstances, for good or ill. The examples of corporate punishment for sin are among the most difficult texts in the Bible for the modern reader. But they are most pertinent to our subject, and they cannot be dismissed as primitive and outmoded. It is true that there has been some development in the course of revelation, whereby the individual's rights and responsibilities were increasingly clarified; but, as J. de Fraine says, 'It is incontestable that the mention of the individual as object of the divine attention, or as subject of the religious relationship, is surpassed by far by the mention of the nation as religious object or subject.'[1] With some reason Ezechiel has been called the father of individualism (cf. Ezech. 18), but it is a mistake to think that in saying that the children's teeth will no longer be set on edge by the sour grapes their fathers ate, he removed the principle of corporate responsibility from God's scheme completely. De Fraine points out that even in Jeremiah and Ezechiel this is by no means ignored. And anyone who tries to realise the fundamental importance of St Paul's teaching on the body of Christ will refrain from dismissing the idea of a corporate responsibility as just an Old Testament idea. It is so important to emphasise this truth, though we cannot examine it here; our tendency towards an

---

[1] 'Individu et société dans la religion de l'Ancien Testament', *Biblica*, XXXIII (1952), p. 445.

exaggerated individualism causes great difficulties in theology, and perhaps especially in the theology of sin and penance. Our division of man into body and soul is another reason for the difficulty we find in accepting the biblical doctrine of sin in all its fulness. We insist so much on sin being an affair of the soul: mortal sin, for instance, causing the 'death of the soul', that bodily sickness and physical death become no more than images of sin and its effects. But this dichotomy is foreign to biblical theology, as P. Benoit has shown.[1] Yet another difficulty makes this total view of sin seem completely unreal: the forgiveness of sin fails to remove such evils. But this difficulty is only one aspect among many of the great Christian paradox: we are redeemed and yet we must still work out our salvation in fear and trembling; Christ has conquered the devil, and yet the latter goes about seeking whom he may devour (1 Pet. 5 : 8). 'We are dead to sin' (Rom. 6 : 2). But are we? Such mysterious truths as these are fully explained neither by the biblical nor the philosophical explanation of sin, and in face of the difficulties, we may prefer to retain our modern use of the term 'sin'. But we have no choice with regard to the substance of the biblical teaching which lies behind the Bible's use of this word, and in point of fact we actually retain the term in its biblical sense in the expression 'original sin'. It is here where our present definition of sin proves so inadequate that we have difficulty in showing how 'original sin' is sin. We would not refer to the sickness of the child as sin, but we must regard it as a manifestation or an effect of original sin. Every evil in biblical thought comes within that all-embracing term sin, not excluding the evils to be found in material creation, since it too awaits its redemption (Rom. 8 : 19 ff.). The taking away of sin, therefore (or, as we would say, the forgiveness, or remission of sin), means, finally at least, the taking away of all evil. A sharp

[1] See 'The accounts of the institution and what they imply', in *The Eucharist in the New Testament*, London 1964.

division between spiritual good and material good is as alien to the thought of the Bible as is a sharp division between spiritual evil and physical evil. To make such a division is to obscure the full import of the messianic hope,[1] and our Lord's fulfilment of it.

---

[1] The language in which the prophets expressed the blessings to come has too readily been taken as mere metaphor, and the Messianic hope of Israel rather too glibly labelled as materialistic. There are signs that this kind of judgment is now being modified to some extent, cf. J. Van der Ploeg, *Revue Biblique*, 1954, pp. 497 ff. Pinckaers: 'L'Espérance de l'A.T. est-elle la même que la nôtre?', *Nouvelle Revue Théologique*, LXXVII, pp. 785–99.

VIII

Sin and Repentance[1]

L. Johnston

THE great difficulty in dealing with any theme of biblical theology is the conflicting interests of theological synthesis and historical analysis. It is misguided and misleading to treat the Bible as a homogeneous block; throughout its long and complicated history we must expect that ideas will evolve and develop. Historical analysis is itself a difficult and delicate subject. But for practical purposes we may follow the accepted critical positions on the development of biblical literature, and divide it into three periods, corresponding roughly with the three strata discernible in the Pentateuch.[2] The first period runs from the beginning to about the time of the monarchy, when J and E were composed. The second is the period of the prophets, whose thought and spirit is expressed in D. The third is the exilic and post-exilic era reflected in P.

We begin, therefore, at the beginning. In fact, if we are to appreciate the origins of strictly biblical thought, we have to begin before the beginning. What idea of sin has man without revelation? We speak of the natural law—the demands of the creator known from the nature of his creation. But what idea had men at this stage of reasoning, of nature, or creation, or creator? Certainly they had some idea of God—of divinity, of something other than themselves. And man's attitude in the face of this mysterious other was one of awe, terror, recoil. It was

---

[1] First published in *Scripture*, 1961, pp. 1–12.
[2] Cf. Michael M. Winter, 'Reflections on the Sources of the Pentateuch', *Scripture*, 1960, pp. 78–89.

something he had to keep his distance from. Precisely because it was 'other', it indicated certain limitations on human existence which it was dangerous to overstep; certain spheres of interest were marked out as forbidden territory, and to trespass on that territory was 'sin'.

But even this idea of an 'other' was not clearly and specifically defined. For primitive man lived in a whole world which was to some extent 'other'; a strange and frightening place; storms, thunder, lightning—even the more benign phenomena of day and night, ordered seasons and growth of crops—all of this was utterly mysterious, beyond his comprehension and control. It made the world in which he lived a fearsome place. And this fear was not clearly distinguished from the other, namely awe of the divinity which lay beyond their sphere. Awe of the divine is not clearly distinguished from panic—terror of 'Pan', of all things, of the alien natural forces which made up their world. Mythology is an expression of that confusion—the mysterious natural forces were personified and looked on as manifestations of the divine, of the *mysterium tremendum*.

But it was not sufficient to give a theoretical explanation of the world; men had to learn also how to live in it. By a process of trial and error, coupled with the same imagination which produced the mythologies, men worked out empirical rules which enabled them to come to terms with their environment— magic, the first step in the development of the natural sciences. And here again, the rules he thus forged for himself were not clearly distinguished from the rules governing his relationship with the divine. All of them together were things 'not done', under pain of disturbing the precarious order in which we live; here too, transgression is 'sin', and the result is or may be death.

For that, at the lowest and in the concrete, is what men were —and are—most deeply concerned with: life—not merely existence, but life, health, prosperity, fertility, harmony between men, harmony with their environment, harmony with whatever it is that controls our existence. This is what men are concerned with; and 'sin' is the name given to anything which violates or endangers this vital quality. In order to ensure life and ward off 'sin', certain rules are formulated: the confused mass of convention, superstition and taboo which regulate human existence.

This is the pre-biblical concept of sin; and we do not expect revelation to make any sudden revolutionary change in this concept, bringing about a miraculous advance in clarity and precision of thought which the rest of mankind was not to achieve for centuries. We expect to find, and we do in fact find in the Bible itself, something very like what we have been talking about. We find it in the most basic Hebrew word for sin—*ḥaṭa'*; the root meaning of which is to go astray, to miss the mark: to do something which is 'not done' and in consequence to fail to achieve one's objective—just as the failure to utter the correct incantation will invalidate the spell. We find it also in the things which are called sin. Oza touched the Ark of the Covenant to prevent it falling—and he dies; for this belongs to God, and Oza has trespassed on that forbidden territory. Aaron's sons, newly consecrated and unfamiliar with the ritual, offer incense without observing the due forms—and they also die.

Sin is used to denote actions contrary to God's will where there is no question of conscious responsibility: Abraham deceives Pharoah about his relationship to Sara; but when the king takes her in good faith, he is punished and has to make amends. The Law even lays down regulations for actions which are explicitly said to be performed unwittingly: 'If anyone lets slip an oath in any of those matters in which a man may swear thoughtlessly, then, when he comes to realise it, he is responsible for it: he must then confess the sin, and offer God a sacrifice for the sin he has committed . . .' (cf. Lev. 5 : 4 ff.).[1]

---

[1] The law distinguishes between sin-offering and guilt-offering, and it is tempting to interpret this in terms with which we are more familiar, by

Even more akin to the attitude of a previous stage are those cases where sin is used of things in which there is no question of morality at all, either subjective or objective: of childbirth, for example, or menstruation. Or even more strangely, to our eyes, of dry-rot in a house—called, by analogy, leprosy: 'The priest will offer sacrifice for the sin of the house . . . and after the rite of expiation has been performed, the house will be pure' (Lev. 14 : 49–53).

Clearly, in such an indiscriminate collection there is room for many distinctions. Some of these distinctions will be indicated later. But no matter what distinction is made, the language used by the Bible points clearly to a certain attitude of mind: sin refers much more to the action done than to the intention of the doer; it is the mechanical, automatic transgression of a rule, of a standard. Even more truly one could say that sin indicates the state of disorder, of disharmony, a state of impaired vitality; and the fact that this is due to our activity, and even more whether that activity is culpable or not, is of secondary importance.

But that does not mean to say that even in this stage there is no difference at all between the biblical attitude to sin and the pre-biblical. On one vital point there is an immense step forward. We find it expressed in the Bible's account of the origin of evil. Sin covers every aspect of disorder, physical as well as moral: on this the Bible would have agreed with a pagan contemporary. But since physical disorder is a universal phenomenon, especially in its most crucial form, death, then the origin of it must be sought in some universal ancestor. This follows from the fact of corporate personality: we are all in a state of 'sin', therefore the father of us all must have put himself into a state of sin. Now, to explain how this came about, the author has before

the distinction between material and formal sin. But more probably the distinction is between offences against God and offences against the community—with the subjective consciousness a secondary element.

him various models, various theories such as those we have
outlined above. To a large extent he accepts the data of current
thought, but he reinterprets it with wonderful theological
penetration. He accepts the idea of God as 'other'; but he
realises that God is other precisely because he is not a creature.
He is creator, maker of all that is and lord of all. And if lord,
supreme controller and arbiter of its destiny—arbiter of its
good and bad, right and wrong. And man's fear in the face of
this supreme God, which for the pagan is blind panic, is for
the author of Genesis respect for God's supremacy. To trespass—
as the first man trespassed—is not merely the objective fact of
doing something which happens to displease the god; it is a
challenge to that supremacy; it is refusal to recognise the infinite
gulf between the creator and the creature; it is to arrogate to
oneself autonomy; it is to rebel—and this now is a new name for
sin which enters the biblical vocabulary: *pesha'* revolt.

Clearly, this is an immense advance, and one that makes a
decisive difference between biblical and pre-biblical thought.
But we must not over-estimate the influence of this step forward.
Sin is given a very definite religious setting; it is rebellion
against the Lord whose will is supreme. But God's supremacy
could be shown in the mere fact of a command, without regard
for which actions are commanded: the reticence of Genesis on
the exact nature of the command given to the first man is
remarkable. There is, then, not much critique at this stage of
precisely which actions are prohibited and are therefore sin.
Much of the pre-biblical material which we summed up as convention, superstition and taboo continued to be invoked in
Israel. Of course they were not now invoked as superstition.
Nor on the other hand were they rationalised (one might so
easily have expected the legislation concerning clean and unclean
animals, for example, or the laws about leprosy, to be rationalised
and presented as social legislation). They are merely incorporated
into Israel's religious life, under the rubric: 'Thus says Yahweh.'

But the fact that it *is* Yahweh's will, with all that Israel meant by Yahweh, is the great advance of this first stage of Israelite religion.

All that Israel meant by Yahweh: but it was the prophets who were mainly responsible for exploring the deeper significance of that revelation.

Israel's faith stemmed from the covenant at Sinai. A covenant is an agreement between persons—not an equal agreement, of course, but nevertheless both parties must be equally persons: you cannot have a covenant with a storm or a sun or any of the other forces which the pagans personified as gods. The God of Israel is a person as real as the Israelites themselves, as real as Moses. And the prophets realised that in the covenant and the law which embodied it God had revealed his personality. He had shown them what manner of God he was. They were not to have an image of God; no image could do other than distort and debase the notion of a transcendent God. But their God was not for that reason vague and impersonal: he was real and close to them; 'no other nation has its god so close to it as our God is to us—in commandment and precept and ceremony' (Deut. 4 : 7). The law, then, is the expression of God's will; but it is not an arbitrary will. It is the expression of his will because it is the expression of his person.

And what is God? The two words which run through the Bible as most characteristic of God are *ḥesed we'emeth* mercy and truth: charity and justice. And because these are the characteristics of God, they are the characteristics demanded of God's people Israel. Those two words are indeed a fair summing up of the whole of the prophetic teaching: their fierce indignation with social injustice, with dishonesty and luxury and wealth won by oppression, the oppression particularly of the poor and helpless. Had not God found Israel poor and oppressed, in nakedness and utter nothingness; and had he not then, out of sheer love and mercy, picked them up and clothed them and given them food and even made them rich? This is what God is; and therefore how great a distortion it is that the people who are to carry his name before the world should show no care for the fatherless, the poor and the widow.

In this way the prophets came to see which actions were sinful and why they were sinful. But they go a step further, and see also the deeper relationship between a man and his deeds. A covenant is a mutual relationship between persons. God has come to Israel in pure, unmotivated love; and he demands in return our whole selves, with equal love. Reflection on the supremacy of God led the author of Genesis to see that sin was rebellion. But reflection on the covenant gives a deeper meaning to that word rebellion: it is the rebellion of a subject against his king, of a son against a father. God is Father, and Israel is his first-born son: 'Hear, O ye heavens, and give ear, O earth! I have brought forth sons and brought them up—and they have rebelled against me. The ox knows its master, and the ass its master's stall; but Israel has not known me' (Is. 1 : 2–3). Father and son: man and wife even, prophets like Osee preach. The covenant relationship is as close as the bond of marriage, and the same love and affection and care which should be found in marriage, and which characterises God in his relationship with Israel, is demanded by God in return: 'Hear, O Israel! The Lord thy God is one God; and you will love the Lord your God with all your heart, and all your soul, and all your strength' (Deut. 6 : 4–5).

This was the implication of the Covenant. A later prophet[1] sees the same implication in the very transcendency of God.

[1] The prophet referred to is Deutero-Isaiah; this might then seem to disturb the historical development indicated at the beginning of this chapter. But in the first place it is pointed out below that this historical scheme is not to be taken in too rigid a sense; and in the second place, although this teaching is seen most characteristically in Deutero-Isaiah, it is not altogether absent from the pre-exilic prophets; cf. Is. 6 : 3, quoted below.

E

We have seen how Israel interpreted the vague intuition of an 'other' in terms of an Almighty God. Now the Hebrew word for this idea is 'holy'. The root-meaning is 'cut off': absolutely other, absolutely separate from men and our world. But this does not mean cut off in the sense of remote and uncaring. On the contrary, it means that all creation depends on him for existence, and exists for him. 'Holy, holy, holy is the Lord God of hosts—heaven and earth are full of his glory.'

This world exists for the glory of God, for his service. And it is man's function to use it in this way—to make it, like the hymn of the seraphim, a hymn of praise to the creator. This was in particular the function of Israel; that is why God had chosen them, to be a kingly priesthood and a holy nation: a nation dedicated to the service of God, and through whom the world would be dedicated to him. To fail in this function—to use creation in a way which excluded this purpose, to use it for man's own benefit without regard to the transcendent rights of the creator—was blasphemy against the holy God. And that was what made certain acts sinful, and this gave a criterion by which we could know their sinfulness.

But if dedication to the holy God means showing his dominion over creation, that dominion must extend first of all to us, to men called to his service. Total service: not merely, then, the service of our hands, but of our hearts also; not merely deeds, but deeds which express our will. Our God is a jealous God: and that means only that he will not give his glory to another—it means also that he will not allow our love to go to another; he will not accept anything less than heartfelt service.

And it is in the light of such penetrating and exalted teaching that the prophets see sin. By reflection on the covenant they see that sin is rebellion against an Almighty God, the rebellion of a son against a loving Father, the unfaithfulness of a spouse to her beloved; it is failure to reflect in our lives the God who has revealed himself to us. And by analysis of the concept of 'otherness', they see that sin is blasphemy against God's supreme and total rights. This is already a far cry from the idea of sin as simple transgression. The prophets have now been able to see exactly why certain things are wrong, and therefore to launch a pungent attack against all superstitions by showing more precisely *which* actions are wrong. But in addition they have even been able to show in what spirit these acts should be performed: the service of the heart, the giving of love for love. Jeremiah even envisages the time when this alone shall count; when there shall be a new covenant in which the law will not be written on stone, but in the hearts of the people (Jer. 31 : 31).

This is noble teaching indeed; and it would be most satisfying if we could end the Old Testament on that exalted note. But after the prophets comes that rather indeterminate body of literature called the didactic books, and, in somewhat the same spirit, the priestly author who put the finishing touches to the Pentateuch.

This seems to be the moment to take notice of an obvious objection. When we were speaking of the primitive form of biblical religion, that in which relics of the pre-biblical stage were most evident, it was to the book of Leviticus that we most naturally turned. It is here that we find all that strange legislation that attaches the word 'sin' to such things as childbirth, illness and dry-rot. And yet this book of Leviticus is normally attributed to the priestly author, who belongs to this third and latest stage of biblical development.

It is very tempting to dismiss this objection with the facile jibe that legalism is always an anachronism from the point of view of genuine morality: that to make a code of laws to regulate a personal relationship of love is bound to be a return to that mechanical, quasi-superstitious attitude which we met in peoples who are unclear on the real nature of God and on man's relationship to him. This is a temptation all the greater because there is so much truth in it, as we find from a consideration of the religion of the Pharisees.

But it is too facile to be the whole truth. In the Bible above all, we cannot admit that the ingenuity or limitation of human minds is the complete explanation of the development that takes place. It is nearer to the truth to look at it like this. We have been talking about stages of development; but we must not think of these stages as simple, clear-cut divisions, with one stage marking a complete break from the preceding. In religion above all, an immense value is attached to traditional forms and ideas; so that the characteristics of one stage persist into the following, even if it is necessary to give them a new interpretation if they are to survive. An obvious and simple example is the law of the Sabbath: by comparison with other civilisations, it seems clear that a special regard for the seventh day is connected with the idea of *dies fasti et nefasti*—days on which it was lucky or unlucky to do certain things, depending on the position of the moon: a perfect example of primitive superstition. Israel inherited this custom, but adapted it to her theology: first, through the idea of God's supremacy—all time belongs to God and one day is chosen to represent this; then the prophetical view given in Deuteronomy adds a humanitarian motive—God led Israel out of bondage into rest, and therefore on this day all should have opportunity to rest; and then the priestly author returns rather to the earlier point of view, specifying particularly the duty of refraining from work, just as God ceased work on the seventh day.

And in the same way, practices and observances which had remained current in Israel from the earliest days were reinterpreted in the exilic and post-exilic periods. This is not the place to go into the details of this reinterpretation; but in general we can say that the keeping of the law of God was made the test of true religion. The prophets had preached personal devotion to God; but this personal devotion is a meaningless phrase or empty emotionalism if it is not expressed in devotion to God's law. Of course the prophets, too, had seen this; indeed they had taught that this is what the law was—the expression of God's personality. But now the emphasis is reversed. The law now is made the touchstone of religion; this is how in practice we distinguish between good and evil: 'Blessed is the man whose will is in the law of the Lord, who has not walked with sinners. . . .' The sinner is he who has not kept the law of God; to keep the law is to put oneself on God's side. (That is the point of the self-righteous-sounding claims in some of the Psalms: 'Lord, if I have done that, if I have stained my hands with fraud or done evil to my benefactor, then rightly let me be crushed'; 'Test and search me, Lord: I have not sat with the wicked, I have hated evil-doers, I have washed my hands with the innocent.' They are not as smug as they sound: they are rather a desperate assertion of loyalty; it is taking sides—and the side that the psalmist chooses is faithfulness to the standard of God as expressed in the law.) It is above all the contrary to that practical atheism which is involved in ignoring God's law: 'The fool has said in his heart. There is no God. They are corrupt, there is not one that does good' (Ps. 13 : 1). It is an attitude we should recognise; it is the attitude of the ordinary Catholic, for whom religion is primarily a matter of keeping the commandments. We 'practise our faith', because our faith is something which has practical implications.

Religion is to be practised. It is a rule of life. In the concrete, it is the law that marks out this rule—this way, which is God's own way: *Beati immaculati in via*, God's own way, that is, his practical directions on how to reach him. It is therefore the highest wisdom—'the law of God is true, giving wisdom to little ones, enlightening the eyes and giving guidance to the feet'. Typically, then, the old term for sin is now reinterpreted: sin is *ḥaṭa'*, going astray—but not now in the sense of invalidating the ritual, but in the very concrete sense of straying from the path marked out by God. And at the same time a new word for sin now becomes popular: it is *nabal*, folly.[1]

When we come to the New Testament we find, as we would expect, that the same teaching is maintained, though it is given a wonderfully supernatural twist. We find, for example, that our Lord's practical criterion of morality is not different from that of the priestly author or the scribes: 'If you love me, keep my commandments'; 'he who claims to love God and does not keep his commandments, is a liar.' Our Lord has come to fulfil the law, not to destroy it; our justice must abound more than that of the scribes and the Pharisees. But in the New Testament even more clearly than in the Old, it is taught that it is not the act which justifies or condemns, so much as the intention: 'It is not that which enters into a man, but that which comes out of a man; for out of the heart proceed lies, murders, adulteries.'

The intention—the motive power behind the actions: above all and essentially, then, love of God. This is the centre of morality, and in the light of this, the greatest of the commandments, all other commands fade into the background: to love God and to love one's neighbour is to have kept all the law.

We return, then, to the ideal of the prophets, which we have already seen as a high-point in religious development. Our Lord himself points out that his doctrine of the primacy of charity is such an Old Testament ideal: 'What read you in the law?' But the New Testament is not a mere reaffirmation of the

[1] Clearly, there can be no question of attempting a complete theology of sin in one essay; and many valid and even important aspects have been omitted in favour of one clear line of thought. This is particularly true of the post-exilic period, in which many valuable developments took place; the increasing spiritualisation of sin, for example; the consequent suggestion of a distinction between the physical and moral elements which were up till then indiscriminately classed as 'sin'; which in turn opens the way for the theology of redemption as it will be sketched in a later section; important also is the beginining of a doctrine of Original Sin through the doctrine of man's *yeser*, his innate feebleness through which he is 'inclined to evil from his earliest youth'.

Old. It is precisely at this point that there takes place that profound deepening of the thought which gives its morality its specific character. At the very beginning of our consideration of sin, we pointed out that it should be viewed in relation to life: sin is anything which impairs or endangers this most basic quality. Even in the Old Testament there was something sacred about this quality of life—it was breathed into man from the breath of God himself. But what the Old Testament only dared hint at in impossible longings, is now in the New boldly asserted to have come true: 'I have come that they may have life, and may have it more abundantly'; 'If any man believes in me, he shall have eternal life'; 'I in them, and they in me—that they may be one, as thou, Father, and I'; 'I live now, not I, but Christ lives in me'. . . . A whole stream of texts testifies to the realisation that the Christian is living the life of God through Christ. But what is God? God is love. To share the life of God, therefore, means to share this love. God is love, and he who remains in love remains in God. God is love, and the Christian life is sharing that nature and that love. For the prophets, whole-hearted service was demanded because without it there was not total service—that which was most essential to man, his whole personality, was not involved. But the Christian demands whole-hearted service simply because it is the expression of the life that is in him. That is why St John can say that the man who claims to love God but does not keep the commandments is a liar. To sin is to deny the life that we have been given, the divine life. To sin is to return to that death from which Christ came to deliver us.

Sin, for the Old Testament, was anything which impaired the quality of life. That is why it included such things as sickness and death under the term sin. We seem to have quietly let this aspect of 'sin' drop out of sight. But in the Bible it never drops out of sight; even in the New Testament, in Matthew in particular, the attitude to our Lord's miracles makes it quite clear that our

Lord is founding the kingdom of heaven just as much in curing leprosy as in forgiving sins. But although this theology of sin still persists, on this point too, a new twist is given which lets it be seen finally, and surprisingly, as a theology of repentance. One may reconstruct the line of thought in this way.

When sin was looked on as simply transgression, the most obvious way of avoiding the harmful consequences of this transgression was sacrifice—sacrifice looked on almost as a bribe offered to God, or at the very least as a 'sweetener' or else as a recompense for the injustice of trespassing on his interests. Against this view of sacrifice the prophets reacted strongly, and stressed the internal attitude that sacrifice should express: 'What do I care about your countless sacrifices? I am sated, I am nauseated; but wash your hands, take away your evil from my sight, and then come before me. . . . Woe to those who offer sacrifice with injustice. . . . I will have charity and not sacrifice.'

At another stage, there was a clearer realisation that the impaired life that 'sin' involved was the loss of a quality which came from God. Therefore by certain symbolic acts they tried to return to union with God—by washing in water, for example: water very fittingly symbolised the living God, and by immersing himself in water a man could be symbolically united once more with God, the source of all life.

But no matter what symbolic expression was chosen, the basic attitude is summed up in the word 'return'. Sin is going astray, a step in the wrong direction; it is rebellion against God; it is a breach of personal union with God. The first thing necessary is to correct that false step, to turn away from one's sins, to turn back to God. This is true in the New Testament just as much as in the Old; the first words of the gospel are 'Repent'—*metanoeite*, change your minds.

But obviously, this change, this repentance, will involve confession: 'Repent and confess your sins' is the subject of the first Christian sermon by St Peter. It will involve admitting that we were wrong: you cannot turn back without admitting that you were going in the wrong direction. And if we admit that we were wrong, we must also admit that we deserved punishment: 'All that thou hast done to us, O Lord,' Daniel prays in the captivity after the destruction of Jerusalem, 'thou hast done justly: because we had sinned and gone astray from thee' (Dan. 3 : 28 ff.). Therefore, an important element in repentance is not merely the admission that we were wrong, and a change of direction; it is also the acceptance of suffering which our sins have deserved: we have not only to repent, but 'to bring forth fruits worthy of repentance'.

Repentance involves penance. Can penance achieve forgiveness? The Old Testament gropes towards this truth: if sacrifice can bring forgiveness, should not suffering also: 'A sacrifice to God is a contrite heart.' And the same idea, no doubt as a result of the suffering of the Exile, is even more vividly expressed by Deutero-Isaiah: 'It was our sufferings that he bore, he was crushed for our sins. And it was by his wounds that we were healed.'

And so the theology of redemption is evolved—that through the sufferings our sins deserved, our Lord expresses and effects man's return to God: atonement, reunion with God. Death is indeed conquered. Its power has been completely reversed. It was sin's most powerful partner and ally; like sin, it was the antithesis of life. But our Lord has made it the means by which sin is destroyed and the fullness of life achieved.

And from that doctrine of redemption, a doctrine of repentance too emerges in a new light. It is true that our Lord died once and for all; and it is true also that his death and resurrection are symbolically and sacramentally effected in us by Baptism, equally once and for all. But nevertheless the Christian living with the life of Christ must be continually dying to sin; we live a dying life; we die daily. Our whole Christian life is a continual turning away from sin—a continual repentance; and we do it in the same way as our Lord did it. What in Christ is redemption, in the Christian is repentance. Our Lord made suffering and death into a means of redemption; we also take them, and make them an expression of repentance. Our Lord's redemption was, in the sense that we have seen, an expression of repentance; our Christian life is a living out of the redemption, which is a living out of repentance. 'If we are dead with Christ, then we believe that we shall also live with him. . . . His death was a death to sin once and for all, and life to God. You also look on yourselves as dead to sin, and living to God in Christ Jesus' (Rom. 6 : 8–11).

IX

The Remission of Sins[1]

T. Worden

THE remission of sins is most immediately associated in the mind of a Catholic with the sacrament of Penance; for this sacrament many Catholics in England would simply use the name 'Confession', and if they reflected upon the question would probably consider it a more suitable name, since at least it refers to the most onerous part of the whole rite, whilst 'Penance' is associated with a far less essential, and certainly less onerous, complementary duty to be fulfilled, *after* forgiveness has been granted. To many the name Penance might seem something of a misnomer in present practice. And 'Confession' is evocative of the belief in the remission of sins through this sacrament, for much of the teaching concerning this is presented as an answer to the question why must we confess our sins to the priest? We are told[2] that our Lord appointed the apostles as judges, to exercise a juridical power, and that in order that this juridical power of forgiving sins may be exercised, it is necessary to reveal our sins to them, in the person of their successors. He did this after the resurrection, when he breathed upon the apostles and said: 'Receive the Holy Spirit; whose sins you shall forgive they are forgiven them and whose sins you shall retain they are retained' (Jn. 20 : 23). And the juridical nature of the apostolic authority had already been set forth in the 'binding and loosing' texts of Mt. 16 : 18 and 18 : 18.

The scriptural foundation for the belief in a juridical power

[1] First published in *Scripture*, 1957, pp. 65–79, and pp. 115–27.
[2] Cf. Council of Trent, Sess. XIV, cap. 5 (*DB* 899).

of forgiving sins seems quite clear, and it may be a matter of considerable surprise to find that the Fathers of the Church during the first three centuries failed to see this. They do not refer to these texts when dealing with the question of forgiveness of sins committed after the reception of Baptism.[1] This would not be of particular significance, if it were not for the fact that precisely during these first three centuries one of the most crucial questions which exercised the Church was whether there be any forgiveness of sins for the baptised. The penitential controversy is one of the most difficult questions in the history of theology, and there is a wide variety of opinions concerning it; but at least all would agree that a body of opinion in the Church expressed grave doubts on the possibility of any such forgiveness. In such circumstances it does seem worthy of note that those who rightly maintained the possibility of forgiveness of sins after Baptism did not have recourse to the text from John. They obviously need the support of the scriptures for their teaching; since they did not seek it here we may conjecture that they

---

[1] Origen, it is true, does refer to Jn. 20 : 23 when stating that even certain sins against God (as distinct from sins against one another) may be forgiven. To the question: When a man sins against God who will intercede for him? (cf. 1 Sam. 2 : 25), he replies: 'He upon whom Jesus has breathed, as upon the apostles, and who can be known from the fruits, as having made room for the Holy Spirit, and having become spiritual by being led by the Spirit in the manner of a son of God to each of those things to be done according to the word, remits whatever God remits, and retains the incurable sins, ministering for God who alone has power to remit, like the prophets, by speaking not their own things, but those of the divine will for God. The words for the apostles' remission run thus: "Receive . . . (Jn. 20 : 23)" ' (De Orat. 28, 9). But it is quite clear that Origen does not see in this text the conferring of a juridical power. The reception of the Spirit gives them that priestly wisdom whereby they know for whom they may intercede by prayer and sacrifice, as in the Old Law. They will not commit the monstrous error of interceding for those who have committed sins which God has no intention of forgiving—the sins unto death. Hence B. Poschmann's claim that here we have an example of interpretation *für die Vergebungsvoll macht bei der Busse* (*Handbuch der Dogmengeschichte*, IV, 3, p. 4, ftn. 4) is greatly exaggerated.

interpreted the text in a way which, to say the least, gave it a less direct reference to the forgiveness of sins after Baptism than we give to it. Thus Tertullian, arguing strongly enough for the possibility of a second repentance (namely, forgiveness of sins after Baptism) refers to such scriptural evidence as the situation of the various churches mentioned in the Apocalypse who have evidently fallen from their first fervour, and yet are all given 'general monitions to repentance—under comminations it is true; but he would not utter comminations to one *un*repentant if he did not forgive the repentant.'[1] The Spirit, he claims, has elsewhere demonstrated the profusion of his clemency, and he refers to Jer. 8 : 4 (LXX), Os. 6 : 6, Lk. 5 : 7, 10; the parables of the lost drachma, the sheep that has strayed and the prodigal son all provide excellent examples of God's willingness to forgive.[2] On the question of a juridical power exercised by God's representatives in putting into effect this forgiveness he is silent, and makes no reference to Jn. 20 : 23.[3]

The Fathers do understand this text as conferring a juridical power, but this power is exercised in the forgiving of sins by the administration of Baptism. As an example we quote St Cyprian, writing during the controversy on heretical baptism: 'But it is manifest, where and by whom remission of sins can be

---

[1] 'On Repentance', chap. VIII, in *Ante-Nicene Christian Library*, XI, Edinburgh 1869, p. 271.

[2] Ibid.

[3] Tertullian does, however, provide evidence that Mt. 16 : 16 was quoted by his adversaries to support their claim to forgive sins against chastity, committed, presumably, after the reception of Baptism: 'But, you say, the Church has the power of forgiving sins. This I acknowledge . . . I now inquire into your opinion, (to see) from what source you usurp this right to the Church. If, because the Lord has said to Peter, "Upon this rock I will build my Church", "to thee have I given the keys of the heavenly kingdom"; or, "Whatsoever thou shalt have bound or loosed in earth, shall be bound or loosed in the heavens", you therefore presume that the power of binding and loosing has derived to you, that is, to every Church akin to Peter . . .' 'On Modesty', chap. XXI, in op. cit., XVIII, Edinburgh 1870, pp. 117–18.

given, that, namely, which is given in Baptism. For to Peter
first, on whom he built the Church, and from whom he appointed
and showed that unity should spring, the Lord gave that power,
that whatsoever he should loose on earth should be loosed in
heaven. And after his resurrection also, he speaketh to the
apostles, saying, As my Father has sent me, even so send I you.
And when he had said this, he breathed on them, and saith
unto them, Receive ye the Holy Ghost: whose soever sins ye
remit . . . retained. Whence we learn that they only who are set
over the Church, and are appointed by the law of the gospel
and the ordinance of the Lord, may lawfully baptise and give
remission of sins; but, without, nothing can be bound or loosed,
where there is no one who can either bind or loose.'[1]

This interpretation of the texts is in line with the earliest
forms of the Creed where the remission of sins is linked with
Baptism: 'One Baptism unto the remission of sins.' By the time
of Hippolytus (d. 235) 'the prominence of the remission of sins
is now so great that the phrase is virtually a synonym for
Baptism itself. . . . The whole elaborate catechumenical preparation is seen to be "a vast sacramental dominated by the idea of
exorcism".'[2] On the other hand St Cyril of Alexandria, in the
fifth century, clearly states that the text of John confers the
power of forgiving sins in two ways: 'They who have the Spirit
of God remit or retain sins in two ways, as I think. For they
invite to Baptism those to whom this sacrament is already due
from the purity of their lives, and their tried adherence to the
faith; and they hinder and exclude others who are not as yet
worthy of the divine grace. And in another sense, also, they
remit and retain sins, by rebuking erring children of the Church,

---

[1] Epistle LXXIII, in *The Epistles of St Cyprian*, Oxford 1868, p. 247.
The same two texts are interpreted in exactly same way by Firmilian,
bishop of Caesarea in Cappadocia, when he writes to Cyprian complaining
that Stephen, bishop of Rome, recognises the validity of heretical baptism;
cf. Epistle LXXV in op. cit., p. 279.

[2] J. N. D. Kelly, *Early Christian Creeds*, 1950, p. 162.

and granting pardon to those who repent.'[1] The fact that the
early Fathers saw in this text a reference to the power of the
apostles to remit sins through Baptism[2] suggests that a fruitful
consideration of the sacrament of Penance should take into
consideration the relation between the two. Penance, we shall
see, is the more laborious and painful way[3] whereby the Christian
recovers the place in the Body of Christ granted to him in
Baptism, which he has forfeited by sin. We shall see how the
Holy Spirit taught the Church, largely through his inspired
word preserved in the Old Testament, to realise that those to
whom was given the power of binding and loosing, of forgiving
or retaining sins through the sacrament of Baptism, had also
been given the power of repeating such a remission of sin in
the sacrament of Penance, which an early writer calls 'the
spiritual Baptism.'[4] Considered in this way, we may understand
more clearly the place of penitential practices which constitute
the external sign of this remission of sins committed after
Baptism. But more important, we may realise more clearly that
there is no remission of sins except through Christ, the conqueror
of sin, and that Penance, therefore, remits sins as Baptism does,
by uniting us with Christ and making us one with him, so that
his victory over sin becomes ours.

1 *Remission of sins through Christ.* When we consider the
sufferings endured by the Jews during the period which immediately preceded the coming of our Lord it is not surprising that

---

[1] *Commentary on the Gospel according to St John*, II, London 1885, p. 680.

[2] From an exegetical point of view, the corresponding words in Mt.
28 : 16 ff., Mk. 16 : 16, and Lk. 24 : 47 make it likely that Jn. 20 : 23 refers
to forgiveness through Baptism; cf. J. Jeremias, in G. Kittel (editor),
Theologisches Wörterbuch zum Neuen Testament, III, 1950, p. 753, 3 ff.

[3] *Ut merito poenitentia laboriosus quidam baptismus a sanctis patribus
dicta fuerit*, Conc. Trident. Sessio XIV, Mansi, XXXIII, 92E.

[4] *De Rebaptismate*, n. 10, quoted in B. Leeming, *Principles of Sacramental Theology*, London 1956, p. 191, ftn. 31.

they had a clear realisation of their sinfulness. There had been
the bloody persecution of Antiochus Epiphanes; there had been
the humiliation of Roman rule and the indignity of the Idumean
dynasty. In such circumstances the longing for deliverance was
greatly increased; they prayed for the coming of the Messiah,
to give them the peace and prosperity, the freedom and happiness
which they could surely hope for, since they were the chosen
people of God to whom the promises had been made. The
Messiah would restore all things, there would be no longer any
grief or suffering. He would take away all this. He would take
away all sin. In the past they had won relief from God, whether
through David, or Ezechias, or the Servant, or Judas Maccabaeus,
for in the past God had forgiven them their sins when they
turned to him in sorrow and repentance. But all these partial
remedies would be perfected in the Messiah; he would 'fulfil'
them all; he would take away all evil, for he would take away all
sin. Thus they taught that the Messiah himself would be without
sin: 'Unstained by sin' (Ps. Sol. 17 : 41), 'No sin will be found
in him' (Test. Jud. 2 : 4a). All sin would be destroyed in the
Messianic kingdom, and men would be sinless: 'They will sin
no more, neither will they be chastised all the days of their life,
and they will not die because of the chastisement or the (divine)
anger; but they will complete the number of the days of their
life, and their life will go forward in peace, and the years of their
joy will be multiplied in an eternal gaiety and peace, all the
days of their life' (Hen. 5 : 8).[1]

The message of the New Testament is that Jesus is the conqueror of sin, and he is the Messiah. He came to save his people
from their sins: 'I did not come to call the just but sinners'
(Mt. 9 : 13). He is the friend of sinners (Mt. 11 : 19) and
even dines with them. Such incidents as the anointing by the
woman that was a sinner (Lk. 7 : 37 ff.), Zacchaeus (Lk. 19 : 1 ff.),

---

[1] Translated from J. Bonsirven, *La Bible Apocryphe*, Paris 1953, p. 28.

and the cure of the paralytic (Mt. 9 : 2 ff.) preach this message. John the Baptist had prepared the way for Christ by inviting the people to repent and be baptised for the remission of sins (Mk. 1 : 4), and pointing to Jesus had exclaimed: 'Behold the lamb of God, who is taking away the sin of the world' (Jn. 1 : 29). John receives proof that he was correct in thus recognising the Messiah, when it is reported to him how the blind see, the lame walk, the lepers are cleansed (Lk. 7 : 22), for Jesus' miracles of healing were proof of his power to remit sin, with which sicknesses were intimately connected.[1] This is not only shown clearly in the cure of the paralytic (Mt. 9 : 2 ff.; cf. Jn. 5 : 14), but in our Lord's own declaration in the synagogue at Nazareth: 'The spirit of the Lord is upon me, because he has anointed me to preach good news to the poor. He has sent me to proclaim release[2] to the captives, the recovering of sight to the blind, to set at liberty those who are oppressed, to proclaim the acceptable year of the Lord' (Lk. 4 : 18–19). And it is the apostolic message from the first day they preached the gospel that through Jesus, established as ruler and saviour, God gives repentance and remission of sins to Israel (Acts 5 : 31; cf. 2 : 38; 3 : 19; 3 : 26; 10 : 43; 13 : 38; 17 : 30; 26 : 20).

But it is Paul's doctrine of remission of sins through Christ which is of particular significance for our subject, for he shows so insistently the link between sin and death, that crowning evil which sums up, as it were, the sicknesses and the miseries which sinful man must endure. According to Paul sin ruled men since Adam, as can be seen from the fact that all have died (Rom. 5 : 12): death is the result of sin, it is the reward which sin gives to them, prefaced by all the misery and ailments of

---

[1] Cf. Chapter VII of this volume.

[2] *aphesis*, the word usedi n the expression '*remission* of sins'. The corresponding verb, *aphiēmi*, which is so frequently found with 'sin(s)' as its object, has a complexity of meaning which makes it very difficult to come to any firm conclusion on the exact significance of the expression *aphienai hamartias*. This text may possibly be one of the clearest indications.

which they were the victims. It is true that they did not recognise the cause of their misery until God revealed himself. But
when God made known his will to men through the law,
promising that if they would observe his commands they would
live for ever, freed from all their miseries, they realised that
their wretchedness was the result of failing to live according to
God's will, the result of sin. Time and again sin had its way
with them; when they murdered, when they committed fornication, when they stole, when they lied, they now recognised that
such actions were in opposition to God's will (Rom. 5 : 20); they
realised in the light of God's Law that they were ruled by sin,
and they never succeeded in conquering the power of sin within
them. Even the just man who observed the Law failed to conquer
sin; it still clung to him, it still brought death to him. Even
Abraham had died. The observance of the Law was the fulfilling of God's will; it did therefore bring its rewards; yet it
did not bring that complete fulfilment of God's promises for
which they hoped. He had given his promise (Rom. 4 : 13); he
therefore owed it to himself to realise all the blessing he had
pronounced over Abraham. God was supremely reliable,
faithful to his every word. But when would he prove that
fidelity finally and perfectly? When would he show forth his
'justice': when would he do full justice to his promises[1] and
save his people from the afflictions and death which were their
lot since sin had obtained its power over them? Many times in
the past he had saved them from evils which threatened; many
times he had repeated that great act of salvation whereby he
delivered them from Egypt. This deliverance had always served
as the firm foundation of their hopes. The evils which had
threatened them from the Canaanites and the Philistines, the
Assyrians and the Babylonians, the Greeks and the Syrians:
the whole of their history had been proof that God's promises

[1] Cf. S. Lyonnet, *De 'Iustitia Dei' in Epistola ad Romanos*, Romae 1947.

were not illusory, even though they had failed so frequently to co-operate in the conquest of sin which caused such evils. They had richly deserved the delay; but it remained true that however much they did co-operate, complete conquest of sin could not be achieved by anyone but God alone. Even the just man to whom the Law meant everything could do no more than await God's hour, when all sin would be dismissed, when misery, persecution, labour and that greatest horror of all, death, would be destroyed.

In his efforts to describe the change which the coming of Christ had made, Paul's comments on the Law seem so derogatory as to suggest that he did not believe the Law was the revelation of God's will. But it is impossible to describe this momentous change in human language; it is also impossible to believe that Paul actually denies the divine revelation of the Law, or the part it has played in the history of salvation. But he affirms that now, at last, that is accomplished which was never accomplished during the time of the Law: sin has been destroyed, death has been taken away. Sin had entered the world through Adam, and all men since Adam had died, even though they did not sin as Adam sinned (Rom. 5 : 14). Here was the mystery: as a result of one man's sin all suffered death. But the mystery of death as it had reigned from Adam to Moses was to some extent explained when the Law intervened, for in its light men saw their actions to be sinful, earning death. They then learned that the actions to which they were prone were actions against the will of God. 'Until the Law there was sin in the world, but sin was not imputed when there was no Law' (Rom. 5 : 13). When they had received the Law they realised that it was sin, not God, that ruled their lives. By comparison sin had been dead, previous to the Law (Rom. 7 : 8), for now so many actions previously done in ignorance were no longer to be disguised; what they might previously have taken as nothing more than the dictates of their nature was now recognised as the imperious demands of sin ruling within them. Faced with that fact they became the willing slaves of sin, for they offered their services knowing what they were about: 'Do you not know that in offering yourselves to someone to obey him as slaves, you become the slaves of the master whom you obey, either of sin unto death, or of obedience unto justice?' (Rom. 6 : 16). Death was no longer so mysterious: it was the inevitable reward of their slavery. Sin made use of God's Law to display its power and to exact a conscious service. The Law itself was certainly not sin (Rom. 7 : 7), but it revealed sin to man and thus enhanced sin's power; it became very much alive when the Law was given, and the result was that the Law, destined to give life, in reality led men to death, for sin made use of it to seduce and kill. Sin had brought death even before the Law, but it now scored the far greater triumph of bringing death in spite of men's struggles, in spite of the fact that they now knew whence death came. The Law had taught them what they wished to do, but they could not do it: 'In truth I do not understand what I do; I do not do what I wish, but do what I hate . . . in truth it is no longer I who accomplish the actions, but sin, which lives in me' (Rom 7 : 16–17). 'Wretched man that I am! Who will free me from this body which vows me to death?' (Rom. 7 : 24).

Many readers of these difficult chapters in the epistle to the Romans will consistently qualify the word 'death' with such words as 'spiritual' or 'of the soul' as they read. Was the omission of some such qualification just carelessness on Paul's part, or might he expect his readers to take it for granted? He did not mean such a qualification to be taken for granted at all. Evidently the church at Corinth did not take for granted the fact that there should be sickness and death among them so soon after becoming Christians; Paul did not take it for granted either, since he points out there is a special reason for it: they have been partaking of the Lord's Supper unworthily, and 'that is why many of you are weak and ill, and some have fallen asleep' (1 Cor. 11 : 30).

The sad fact was already emerging that even those who through
Baptism had died to sin, could fall into sin again, just as the sad
fact is with us that to this day Christians fall asleep in a manner
so similar to universal death, that when Paul asserts that death
had been conquered there are many who must make him speak
of 'spiritual death' lest he should have been proved false. Yet to
allow the great Christian paradox to influence our understanding
of Paul's teaching will not solve that paradox, for the Christian
is still in danger of 'spiritual death', in spite of Paul's insistence
that death has been swallowed up in victory. 'If we are dead to
sin, how is it possible to continue to live in it?' (Rom. 6 : 2).
When therefore Paul speaks of death it is not right to restrict
his meaning. Death is the final end,[1] the final destruction of man,
body and soul together; if it be permitted to enlarge on Paul's
meaning it is only for the sake of including within it the human
miseries and afflictions which are a foretaste of death. Paul speaks
of Abraham's old age as death (Rom. 4 : 19), and there are
other afflictions, such as blindness, lameness, leprosy, deafness,
poverty (cf. Mt. 11 : 5). Death was present in life from the
first day of a man's existence, 'For in sin my mother conceived
me' (Ps. 51 : 7; Heb. 2 : 15; Rom. 8 : 15). The very uncertainty
of life was one of the greatest triumphs of death: 'The sadness
of the world produces death' (2 Cor. 7 : 10). The hand of death
touched everything man did (cf. Heb. 9 : 14). In fact, all who
did not follow Christ were dead whilst still living (cf. Mt. 8 : 22;
1 Jn. 3 : 14; Jn. 5 : 21, 25). 'The wicked are dead, even during
their life' (Berakoth, 18b).[2] Death has a wider meaning, indeed,

---

[1] Death, as St Paul speaks of it here, is death as understood by the Jew,
before it was destroyed by Christ: it is the Old Testament idea of death:
'Death is the final separation from God. In Sheol they do not praise
Yahweh,' A.–M. Dubarle, 'La condition humaine dans l'Ancien Testament,' *Revue Biblique*, 1956, p. 235. This article is published in English
translation in A. M. Dubarle, *The Biblical Doctrine of Original Sin*,
London 1964, pp. 9–44.

[2] Quoted in C. Spicq, *L'Épitre aux Hébreux*, II, Paris 1953, p. 147.

than the end of physical existence upon this earth, and it is never a 'natural occurrence',[1] once God revealed that everlasting life was the reward which he offered, not only for his chosen people as a people, but for each chosen individual. But it never concerns the soul exclusively, since the revelation would have been speaking in riddles if it had cleaved man into a body and soul as though they were quite separate parts—belief in the resurrection of the body is no accidental or superfluous element of the Christian faith.

It is because of the intimate relation between sin and death that sin was conquered and death destroyed through the death and resurrection of Christ. In him God made the final assault, and through him the final victory was won. Christ's death bore the external resemblance of sin's usual victory: so much so that St Paul could speak of our Lord having been made sin (Cor. 5 : 21). In Christ God as it were beat sin at its own game, for sin was given every chance with Christ. Although the sinless Son of God was outside the power of sin, he nevertheless took flesh, and submitted that flesh to the treatment sin usually metes out to man: he allowed his body to be afflicted by hunger and fatigue; to be beaten with whips, and crucified. Death would seem to have triumphed. But he rose again, and Paul could exclaim: 'O death, where is thy victory?' (1 Cor. 15 : 55). God chose to redeem us in a manner which underlined the power of sin most vividly. Could there have been a more convincing way of proving to man that sin had been conquered and death destroyed? All the powers of sin and its final onslaught, death, had failed. Christ the first-born from the dead (Col. 1 : 18) is the living proof that God had finally and perfectly fulfilled his promise to free men from evil. Those promises which had fed the hope of his chosen people for hundreds of years, and of which he had on so many occasions given partial proof, were

[1] Cf. Bultmann, *TWNT* III, p. 14.

now completed. And just as sin had won its mastery over mankind through the one man, Adam, so now mankind had mastered sin through the one man, Christ.

But how could men share in the victory of Christ? They had shared in Adam's defeat by sharing in his nature, by being born of Adam, by being in a real sense so many Adams. To share in Christ's victory, then, men must become so many Christs. It now becomes true to say of man that as Adam he is doomed to death, but as Christ he has triumphed over death. To this day there is no victory over sin unless a man become Christ; only through Christ is there remission of sins. It is so easy to be part of Adam: everyone born into this world is Adam. But for the remission of sin he must be born a Christ.

2 *Remission of sins through Baptism.* 'For as many of you as were baptised into Christ have put on Christ' (Gal. 3 : 27). It is the teaching of St Paul that through Baptism we become part of the Body of Christ, and thereby die to sin (cf. Rom. 6 : 3–7). And from the beginning both the power of Christ and the reception of Baptism had been proclaimed as the means whereby sin would be destroyed. When St Peter had finished the first apostolic preaching of the gospel his hearers had asked what they must do, and he had replied: 'Repent and let each of you be baptised in the name of Jesus Christ for the remission of your sins' (Acts 2 : 38). If remission of sins is to be obtained through Christ (cf. Col. 1 : 14; Ephes. 1 : 7) then in practice we share Christ's victory over sin by Baptism, which destroys sin and gives us a new life, a sinless life. The remission of sins is therefore essentially and primarily through the sacrament of Baptism. It is impossible to treat of the nature and effects of Baptism here,[1] but it is vital to remember the part played by Baptism in the remission of sins if we are to understand the

[1] Cf. D. M. Stanley, 'Baptism in the New Testament', Chapter III above.

dilemma which faced the early Church, the doubts and the
difficulties which arose, and the way in which the Church came
to the complete realisation of the full import of the power which
Christ had given to his apostles.

The New Testament teaches that through our sharing by
Baptism in Christ's final victory, we are essentially freed from
all sin, we are new creatures, we are members of God's kingdom,
we are saved. Suffice it to wait for the coming of the Lord when
there will be the new heaven and the new earth. Since the
remission of sins is essentially through the sacrament of Baptism,
then essentially there is no call for any further remission: the
baptised are sinless. The emphasis of the New Testament is
naturally upon the final break with sin through Baptism, and
therefore the very real, but in a certain sense accidental possibility of Christians falling back into sin during their time of
waiting is less explicitly considered. There is, indeed, no question
of this possibility being either denied or wholly ignored by the
New Testament. St Paul realised that in spite of the death to sin
which is brought about by Baptism, sin is not yet wholly
destroyed, and that there is danger of sin among the saints who
form the Body of Christ; and St Peter warns his readers: 'Be
sober, be watchful. Your adversary the devil prowls around
like a roaring lion, seeking someone to devour' (1 Pet. 5 : 8).
Yet we may ask why the Church when faced with the problem
of the lapsed Christians found any difficulty in solving it. Many
would consider the teaching of St Paul to be quite explicit and
quite clear, not only on the possibility of forgiveness of sins
committed after Baptism, but also on the precise way in which
this remission is to be accomplished.

3 *Remission of sins committed after Baptism.* The degree of
clarity may, however, be questioned, and thus the doubts of
some of the earlier Christian writers viewed more indulgently.
Does St Paul explicitly deal with the situation in which the

baptised Christian has so sinned that he is cut off from the body, and does he explicitly state how such a sinner is to be readmitted to the body for the forgiveness of his sin? In 2 Thess. 3 : 14 the brethren are advised not to associate intimately[1] with anyone who does not obey Paul's instructions. They are to avoid him in order to shame him, *and* they are not to treat him as an enemy, but reprove him as a brother. In 2 Cor. 2 : 5–11, Paul speaks of someone whom they have now punished sufficiently, for an offence which is unknown to us, and whom they should now forgive and console lest he drown in grief. But these examples hardly suggest cases of such grievous sin that the offender is completely cut off from the Body, and therefore stands in need of readmission. Paul does not call their offences 'sins', and there is no clear teaching about readmission to the Body of Christ. But we have a clearer example in 2 Cor. 12 : 21, where Paul envisages the possibility that if he goes to Corinth he will grieve many[2] of those who have previously sinned and who did not repent for the impurity they had done. If, as seems certain, Paul is referring to sinners among the Christian community, then he recognises here, not only the possibility of grievous sin among Christians, but also their repentance, and the forgiveness of their sins. He does not mention, however, what means they will use in order to secure forgiveness.

In 1 Cor. 5 : 1–5, St Paul deals with a case of incest among the brethren. A member of the Church at Corinth has taken for himself the wife of his father. Whether it was a putative marriage or simply concubinage matters little; the woman was the man's stepmother, and such a union was forbidden by the Law and was punishable with stoning (Lev. 18 : 8). This was an act of impurity abhorred even by pagans, as Cicero shows when he refers to Sassia's marriage with her son-in-law Melinus, and it would lose none of its wickedness if the woman were no longer

---

[1] The same word is used of association with the impure, in 1 Cor. 5 : 9.

[2] Or 'grieve *over* many', cf. *Bible de Jérusalem, ad. vers.*

the wife of the sinner's father at the time this union took place.[1] But Paul's indignation is really directed against the Church at Corinth for allowing such a man to remain one of their number. He therefore decrees, though he cannot be actually present, that they gather together, and in union with him present in spirit, hand over the offender to Satan 'for the destruction of the flesh, that the spirit may be saved on the day of the Lord'. This is commonly interpreted to mean that the handing over of the sinner to Satan is for the destruction of the sinner's flesh, and the final salvation of the sinner's spirit. In other words Paul gives instructions for the excommunication of the incestuous man: he must be removed from the midst of the Corinthian church, and thereby cut off from the body of Christ; but this excommunication would not imply final damnation since he may be saved on the day of the Lord. Thus Paul would here teach the possibility of forgiveness of sin committed after Baptism, and the means would be the handing over to Satan for the destruction of the flesh. This latter phrase has caused great difficulty to commentators. Many understand it as the mortification of the flesh at the hand of Satan, a punishment which would last for a time, but which would leave the opportunity for reconciliation with the Church after due penance had been done. But others point out that *olethros* implies something more violent than what is implied by the word 'mortification',[2] and that it signifies not only physical affliction but complete destruction.[3] Nevertheless it is difficult to believe that Paul would envisage the salvation of a man who died outside the Body of Christ, and we must either understand 'destruction of the flesh' as a punishment which is not fatal, and which gives the sinner the opportunity of

[1] Cf. Robertson & Plummer, *Corinthians I*.

[2] 'Renan, Godet and Goudge regard the expression as meaning sentence of death by a wasting sickness.' Op. cit., p. 99., ftn.

[3] Cf. *TWNT*, *sub voce*. Other examples of the use of this word support this interpretation, cf. 1 Thess. 5 : 3; 2 Thess. 1 : 9; 1 Tim. 6 : 9.

reconciliation with the Church, or we must consider the possibility of a different interpretation of the text altogether.

There are good reasons for thinking that Paul is here concerned entirely with the good of the community, the Body of Christ, which in spite of Baptism is still in danger of corruption. It is part of Paul's general teaching that the body's weakness arises from the flesh: the body in so far as it is weak and corruptible is 'flesh',[1] whilst in its incorruptible aspect it is 'spirit'. By Baptism we die to the flesh and live to the spirit. That is the ideal; in practice the Body of Christ shows signs of still being to some extent 'flesh'. In this particular instance we have a member of the Body falling into grievous sin. He is still in the midst of the Body; he will, if left there, corrupt the whole Body. It is therefore necessary to excommunicate him, which is equivalent to handing him over to Satan, in order to destroy the 'flesh' which has again shown itself in the Body of Christ. If this is done, then the genuine Body of Christ, which is 'spirit', will be saved on the day of the Lord. This interpretation fits in well with the context, for Paul continues to speak of the corrupting influence of sin upon the Body, using the metaphor of the leaven. The terms flesh and spirit are replaced by leaven and new dough. There is only one lump of dough, that is one Body of Christians, just as there is only one loaf (1 Cor. 10 : 17). The destruction of the leaven, therefore, is for the sake of the one lump of unleavened dough, the Church, and not for the sake of the individual Christian. They are, each one of them, 'unleavened', but only as members of the one Body. The leaven which they must get rid of is the corrupting influence within the Church: in this instance the incestuous man whom they have allowed to remain in their midst. In such a context the 'flesh' to be

---

[1] But the mention of Satan as the agent of this destruction prevents us from understanding 'flesh' as the individual's sinfulness; in such an interpretation Satan would be the direct instrument of this sinner's justification.

handed over to Satan for destruction may be compared to the leaven which must be purged, and the 'spirit' to the new dough.

This interpretation supposes that Paul could speak of the Body of Christ, in its essentially incorruptible aspect, as 'the spirit', when compared with its accidentally corruptible aspect in the present world, which he calls 'the flesh'. The antithesis spirit and flesh, in the sense of the incorruptible person (both body and soul) as distinct from the corruptible, is common enough in reference to Christians. Before Baptism we were 'in the flesh'; but now we are 'in newness of spirit' (Rom 7 : 5–6), and we walk now, not according to flesh but according to spirit (Rom 8 : 4). You are not in flesh but in spirit, if God's Spirit dwells in you (8 : 8). The Spirit of him who raised up Jesus from the dead dwells in us (8 : 10). The Spirit comes to the aid of our weakness (8 : 26). We, as baptised Christians, live by the Spirit; we are guided and strengthened by him; we have the first-fruits of the Spirit; the Spirit is our essential characteristic. But the Spirit is not regarded primarily as possessed by each individual for himself; the Spirit is one. In 1 Cor. 12 : 4 ff. Paul insists that the various charisms are all due to one and the same Spirit, just as a physical body is one, though it is composed of many limbs; the Body of Christ, composed of many members, is one. In one Spirit we were baptised into one Body (1 Cor. 12 : 13); we are the Body of Christ because God has sent into our hearts the Spirit of his Son (Gal. 4 : 6). We are 'one Body, one Spirit' (Ephes. 4 : 4). Paul's use of 'the Spirit' for the Body of Christ is unusual enough, but it is called forth by the antithesis with 'flesh'. To speak of the destruction of the *flesh* in order that the *body* may be saved, would perhaps have been a paradox too jarring even for Paul. But in any case, it does seem significant that in other instances where there is question of at least the possibility of offences among the brethren, such offences are said to be against the Spirit, or in other words, to endanger the Spirit in some way. Paul urged the Ephesians to preserve the unity of the Spirit by the bond of peace: one Body and one Spirit (4 : 3). Any kind of injury to our fellow-members grieves the Holy Spirit of God by whom we have been sealed for the day of deliverance; lack of fraternal charity injures the Spirit which is the life-giving power of God, his Spirit. In 1 Thess. 5 : 12–22 Paul exhorts them not to offend one another, but to show fraternal charity in all things; and he ends by telling them not to quench the spirit, and not to depreciate prophecies. Here the spirit may perhaps be limited to the source of prophetical inspiration; yet this one spirit within the Church may be harmed, even in its prophetic manifestations, by offences against fraternal charity. Whilst therefore we admit that the actual turn of phrase is difficult, this interpretation seems preferable, mainly because of the context, and also because it offers a more acceptable meaning for the word 'destruction'. The opening verses of this pericope make it clear that Paul's preoccupation is with the community rather than the individual sinner; the verses which follow are obviously concerned with preserving the community from corruption through contact with a sinful member. But if this interpretation be correct we are deprived of the clearest example in the New Testament of how the individual sinful Christian is to be saved from the effects of his sin.

Yet this question grew more and more pressing. An increasing number of Christians who had been washed, sanctified, and justified (cf. 1 Cor. 6 : 11), and who were dead to sin, unfortunately fell into grievous sin once more. These sinners, particularly in time of persecution, fell away from the Body of Christ, and their Baptism seemed as it were annulled. But they sought readmission, they sought forgiveness of their sin and reinstatement in the Kingdom of God. Was this possible? There was ample witness in the scriptures that God willed not the death of the sinner, but rather that he should be converted and live, and God's mercy and compassionate forgiveness became increasingly emphasised. But how was the Church to dispense the mercy of God? By what means was the sinner to be read-mitted into the Body of Christ for the forgiveness of sin? Was there any way of reiterating this effect of Baptism? There was no doubt concerning the impossibility of any repetition of the sacrament of Baptism. Was then the power of forgiving sins given to the apostles when they were sent to make disciples of all nations and baptise them in the name of the Father, Son and Holy Spirit, to be frustrated by sin?

4 *Remission of sins through penitential practices.* Judging by the writings of the early fathers it seems undeniable that the question of how the grave sins committed after Baptism were to be forgiven created something of a dilemma; not, be it clearly stated, in the sense that the answer to the question was not to be found in divine revelation, but in so far as new circumstances always create dilemmas for those who have not fully penetrated the wonderful plan of God's salvation through Christ. There must have been many who long before St Augustine said much the same as he: 'Since we have to live in this world, in which life without sin is impossible, the remission of sins does not consist solely in the washing of holy Baptism.'[1] But for the early Church, so devoted to the sacred scriptures, there was clear guidance to be found in the Old Testament,[2] and they were not slow to realise it.

---

[1] Serm. 213, 8 (P.L. 38, 1064).
[2] This is an example, only one of many, of the essential part the *Old* Testament has played in the development of Christian theology. We do not mean to imply that the New Testament ignores the practice of penance, but there is no doubt that the Old Testament makes the more considerable contribution. An examination of textual readings with reference to fasting, for instance, is interesting and perhaps significant—cf. Mt. 17 : 21 (absent from *Vaticanus* and others, accepted by Merk (2nd edn. 1935) but rejected by *Bible de Jérusalem*); Mk. 9 : 29; Acts 10 : 30; 1 Cor. 7 : 5. Are these additions to be explained simply by appealing to encratite influence and not, partly at least, to the development of a penitential theology within the Church, of which the encratite heresy itself was an exaggeration?

Throughout the Old Testament we read of God's chosen people falling into sin, turning away from God and suffering the consequences. And there is the spectacle of God's continually forgiving them their sins and restoring them to their privileged position as his own personal possession among all the peoples of the earth (cf. Ex. 19 : 5). The similarity between the sinful Israelite and the sinful Christian is clear. Both were members of God's chosen people: the former because he had been incorporated through circumcision into Israel, whom God had led out from Egypt and established in Canaan, united to himself by the Covenant and enjoying the privileges of being his chosen people; the latter because he had been incorporated through Baptism into Christ, the Son of God in whom is salvation. If then the Israelites of old had been reinstated after they had sinned, then surely the new Israelites could hope for the same mercy; and the Old Testament described time and time again the way in which this reconciliation with God had been effected. Time and again the Israelites had returned to God and been restored to his favour by acknowledging their sinfuless and carrying out various penitential practices. In the Old Testament the Christians found the answer, God's own answer, to their question, 'What can we do, we who have received Baptism once and for all but have since turned away from thee? What must we do in order that we may regain our place in thy kingdom?' In order to enter the Kingdom in the first instance they had been told by John, by our Lord, by the apostles, 'Turn back[1] and be baptised for the remission of sins.' Now the answer to their question was that they must turn back, be converted, in the manner of the Israelites: a turning to God in sackcloth and ashes,

---

[1] According to Behm it is useless to seek the N.T. meaning of *metanoiein* from Greek sources (cf. *Theologisches Wörterbuch zum Neuen Testament*, IV, 976, 15). This is not to deny that a change of mind or heart is included within the N.T. significance, but it implies all that is contained within the prophetic use of *šûb*, to turn back, to return, or, as we might say, to be converted (cf. ibid. 994, 31).

a conversion accompanied by penitential practices. 'Be converted' now became synonymous with 'Do penance'.[1]

The theological significance of penitential practices is not easily demonstrated to everyone's satisfaction, and it seems worth while to re-examine the teaching of the Old Testament. But it is essential to bear in mind the biblical concept of sin,[2] which must be regarded as the foundation of a theology of penitence. According to the scriptures all evils are the effects and therefore the manifestations of sin; and there is no sharp distinction between material evils and spiritual evils. This is the implication of two fundamental articles of faith: that God created the earth and all the fulness of it, making all things good; and secondly, that Yahweh is the one and the all-powerful God, with nothing beyond his control. These two articles of faith were confronted with the fact that there were many evils in the world, such as poverty, disease, war, famine, drought and death. Only one explanation held good on the lips of a people to whom the subtleties of Greek philosophy were unknown: these evils were, as everything else, in the hand of God: they must be under his control. Yet God was supremely good. These evils then could only be the just punishment of sin, and all suffering was the result of sin, and indeed the external proof of sin. Fasting, the wearing of sackcloth, the sprinkling of ashes upon the head, the rending of garments, the shedding of tears were all practices adopted by the Israelites in times of distress when they turned to God to beg for relief. But the distress, whatever it was, was the result of sin; in turning to God for relief, therefore, they were always and inevitably turning to God for forgiveness of their sins.

There are many examples of such practices. Thus, for instance, when King Achab heard of the murder of Naboth 'he rent his

---

[1] Notice how the translation of *metanoiein* and *metanoia* fluctuates between 'repent' and 'do penance' in the various versions.

[2] Cf. Chapter VII above.

garments, put on sackcloth, even next his skin, fasted, slept on sackcloth and walked slowly' (1 Kgs. 21 : 27). The king, accustomed to wear fine linen, to dine sumptuously and to sleep in his ivory-encrusted bed, takes on the role of the poorest beggar to be seen outside his palace gate, clothed in the roughest of garments, emaciated and dragging himself along with painful steps. The evil of Naboth's murder had not actually caused him to be reduced to this physical state. Achab could have continued his regal life in such a way that the onlookers would have said no evil had befallen him. But Achab knew better; he knew that by his sin evil had really befallen him, and he wished to acknowledge and proclaim it as best he could before God and his people. The latter learned of his sin when he appeared as a penitent; God, who reads the heart, already knew, but he was waiting for that clear acknowledgment of it which would not only move him to pity, but which would provide him with the opportunity of manifesting to his people his power and his mercy. And by his penitence Achab won God's forgiveness: 'Because he has humiliated himself before me, I will bring no evil (upon his house) during his time' (1 Kgs. 21 : 29).

The consequences of sin afflict the whole community, and Israel had a vivid sense of the common responsibility. Thus, for instance, Palestine was invaded by locusts. If modern experience is a reliable guide, this was not in itself a very unusual occurrence, but it naturally brought distress and famine. Since God is Lord of all things, then he must have sent the locusts; but he could not have done this if the people had not sinned. They must therefore beg his forgiveness, and to do so they must approach him in the full display of their wretchedness: 'Lament like a virgin girded with sackcloth for the bridegroom of her youth. . . . Be confounded, O tillers of the soil; wail, O vinedressers, for the wheat and the barley, because the harvest of the field has perished. The vine withers, the fig tree languishes. . . . Gird on sackcloth and lament, O priests, wail, O ministers

F

of the altar. Go in, pass the night in sackcloth, O ministers of
my God. . . . Sanctify a fast, call a solemn assembly. Gather the
elders, and all the inhabitants of the land, to the house of
Yahweh your God, and cry to Yahweh. . . . Unto thee, Yahweh,
I cry. For fire has devoured the pastures of the wilderness, and
flame has burned all the trees of the field. Even the wild beasts
cry to thee because the water brooks are dried up and fire has
devoured the pastures of the wilderness. Blow the trumpet in
Sion; sound the alarm on my holy mountain! Let all the inhabitants of the land tremble, for the day of Yahweh is coming. . . .
Who shall endure it? Yet even now, says Yahweh, return to me
with all your heart, with fasting, with weeping, and with
mourning; and rend your hearts and not your garments'
(Joel 1 : 8–2 : 13).

Thus the people who were beginning to suffer from the effects
of the plague and already going hungry were called upon to
accentuate the signs of their distress before the Lord. When
God looked upon them in their wretchedness, hungry, weeping,
clothed like beggars, and heard their cry: 'Pity, Yahweh, for
thy people!' then he must surely have mercy. In actual fact he
once more showed mercy to them: 'Look, I am sending you
grain, wine and oil, and you will be satisfied' (2 : 19).

Again, the Jews after their return from exile sinned grievously
by marrying outside their own race. In Nehemias 9 we read of
how they begged from God forgiveness for their sins. Clothed
in sackcloth and with dirt upon their heads they gathered
together for a fast. Standing there in their misery they sang of
all the wonderful deeds God had accomplished for them in the
past. Again, when Judith sought God's help against the enemies
of her people, she fell flat upon her face, scattered ashes upon
her head, uncovered the sackcloth she was wearing, and with a
loud voice cried to the Lord (Judith 9 : 1). In the same way
Daniel, lamenting the desolation of Jerusalem, turned his face
to God, seeking him by prayer and supplications with fasting

and sackcloth and ashes (Dan. 9 : 3). The voluntary adopting of these penitential practices is the regular accompaniment to prayer in time of distress, whether an explicit acknowledgment of sin be included or not. There is no indication that by afflicting themselves with fasting, sackcloth and ashes the Israelites thought that this suffering 'satisfied' or 'placated' God, or that it was required as compensation for some abstract balance of justice. They did recognise that the evils they were suffering against their will, whether famine or war or anything else, had been justly inflicted upon them by God, and that they were a just punishment for sin. They did recognise that in order to gain an end of the evils caused by their sins they must placate God's wrath and prevail upon him to 'turn away his anger'. But this is not the same thing as saying that they thought of volun-tarily inflicted sufferings as 'satisfying' him, for the appeal was not to God's justice but to his fidelity to his promises, to his love and compassion. Their references to these penitential practices are not in terms of 'Let them placate thee: let them make satisfaction to thee' but rather, 'Look at our wretchedness and have mercy; see how we suffer and be moved to pity.' It must not be forgotten that these practices were a sincere avowal of sinfulness, and that they were the mark of repentance, for they were only adopted when the people returned to Yahweh to seek his help after having gone astray. Their purpose was to move God to pity, so that he would forgive them their sins by removing the evils that afflicted them.

Some may find this dramatic display of their miseries rather distasteful. They may ask whether there be any reason for dressing in sackcloth, for fasting, especially in those cases when famine was in any case making them go hungry. Why the need for tears and groanings? Are these things necessary to win God's compassion? Does he not already know of their misery without its being thus paraded before him? Have we here an example of primitive practice which further enlightenment has discredited? This objection is indeed a fundamental one, and is not to be answered by referring to the primitiveness of the Old Testament. Christianity, the true heir of Israel, has also its dramatic display: the element of drama is as fundamental to Christianity as are the sacraments. These penitential practices are not mere 'play-acting'. Such appearances were the outward manifestations of their real wretchedness. And they were wretched not because of murder or locusts or war or drought, but because they had offended God. If they had been wretched merely because of these 'natural' causes, they would simply have taken steps to alleviate their wretchedness as much as possible; they would have kept up appearances, they would have eaten whatever food the famine left them. It was only when they voluntarily displayed the effects of these evils, it was only when, hungry though they were they fasted, poor though they were they rent their garments and put on sackcloth, it was only then that the signs of misery became significant for their purpose. It is perfectly true that external appearances may at times be nothing more than play-acting, and the prophets warned them of this. 'Why have we fasted and thou seest it not? Why have we humbled ourselves and thou takest no knowledge of it? Behold in the day of your fast you seek your own pleasure and oppress all your workers. Behold you fast only to quarrel and to fight and to hit with wicked fist. Fasting like yours this day will not make your voice to be heard on high. Is such the fast that I choose, a day for a man to humble himself? Is it to bow down his head like a rush, and to spread sackcloth and ashes under him? Will you call this a fast, and a day acceptable to Yahweh? (Is. 58 : 3–5). The purpose of penitential practices is to come into God's presence suffering and in need; but to fast when there is no real turning away from sin makes a mockery of their protestations of dependence upon him; he who sins does not believe that God alone can free him from wretchedness' (cf. Zach. 7 : 9–10).

Penitential practices were the outward manifestations of sin
because they were the outward manifestation of the results of
sin. To the Israelites the poor man's rags, the drawn face of
the hungry, the dirt of the neglected, the tears of the mourner,
the diseases of the sick were all evils. They were therefore one
and all the result of sin. To say that the poverty was the result
of a recent war, or the hunger to the failure of last season's
rains, or the neglect to the death of parents, or the skin disease
to the lack of fresh vegetables, none of these explanations would
in any way change the Israelites' belief that the ultimate cause
was sin. They were not ignorant of these reasons: they knew
that they must till the land and conserve their water supply if
they were to have sufficient food; they knew that they must
practise hygiene to avoid the ravages of disease; they knew
that they must defend their frontiers from pillaging armies if
they were to avoid poverty and destruction. They knew and
they did all these things: they were a civilised people living in a
civilised part of the world. But they nevertheless believed, as
God himself had taught them to believe, that hunger, thirst,
disease and pain were evils, and that no evil which has ever
afflicted man has done so independently of sin.

But still we have not answered the difficulty, of the need of
such display when it was God's pity they sought. Is not this
penitential practice, calculated to move the heart, all too human
a manner of behaving when God is the one we petition? The
answer is to be found in the scriptures where the more fundamental purpose of penitence is seen. The Israelites realised
clearly that the only way whereby God can be known by men
is through his works; and so they realised the importance of
every scrap of visible, tangible evidence of God's merciful
interventions, and they consequently realised the value of
underlining that evidence. The purpose of their penitential
practices was not only to move God to pity, though this human
way of looking at things is perfectly legitimate; but more

fundamentally, it was to underline the power and the love of God displayed in his act of deliverance. To put it somewhat bluntly, their penitential practices were intended to make the setting all the more sombre, in order that God's rescue might stand out all the more clearly and convincingly, and thus strengthen their faith and confidence in his love and mercy for them. All external religion is a divine pedagogy, and this is no accidental or dispensable feature; it is essential precisely because we cannot know God except in his works among us.

That the Israelites realised this purpose is clear from another and at first sight surprising feature of their penitential practices. Their prayers on these occasions did not begin with cries for mercy but with hymns of praise for all God's wonderful deeds in the past. Thus in Neh. 9 we read how the people recalled the choosing of Abraham, the rescue from Egypt, the giving of the Law on Sinai, the manna in the desert and the giving of the promised land. It was not as though they had deserved these things; but even when they had rebelled in the past, God had not abandoned them. Whilst it was true that he had given them into the hands of their enemies when they had sinned, he had rescued them when they had cried out to him. We find the same in Judith 9 and Daniel 9. These past deeds are the guarantee that God, unchangeably faithful, will act in the same way now, since the opportunity presents itself once more. We are, perhaps, sometimes shocked at the way in which the Israelites asked God to act 'for his own sake', as though there were some suggestion that God acts from motives of vainglory. But in reality it is a request that God manifest himself to the world, and God takes away their distress explicitly for this motive: 'to make thy name known to thy adversaries, and that the nations might tremble at thy presence' (Is. 64 : 2). Judith ends her prayer: 'And make known to every nation and to every tribe that thou art Yahweh, God of all power and might, and that the people of Israel has

no other protector but him' (Judith 9 : 14). God's answer to
Israel's prayer for deliverance from the plague of locusts
emphasises the same idea: 'You shall eat in plenty and be
satisfied, and praise the name of Yahweh your God, who has
dealt wondrously with you. And my people shall never again
be put to shame. You shall know that I am in the midst of
Israel, and that I, Yahweh, am your God and there is none else.
And my people shall never again be put to shame' (Joel 2 : 26–7).
Daniel's prayer reminds God of the same motive: 'Yahweh,
give heed and act; delay not, for thy own sake, O my God,
because thy city and thy people are called by thy name' (Dan.
9 : 19). The greater the deed and the more spectacular, then the
more effective a revelation of God to man it is. And that is why
the forgiving of sin and the overcoming of evil are manifestations
of God and are to his glory. The deliverance of Israel from
Egypt, the rescuing of them from Babylon, the preservation of
the people from the locusts, the saving them from famine and
drought, these are all examples of God's power over evil; they
are object lessons and for this reason they are presented in
dramatic form. Thus their prayer, having begun with a confession of God's greatness, having continued with the confession of their own wretchedness, so often ends with the promise
that they will confess God's greatness all the more in the time
to come, when they will have a further example of his love to
which they may refer. The pedagogical purpose is only attained
when God does intervene to rescue them from their misery,
and change their grief into joy, their poverty into riches, their
famine into abundance. And the Old Testament recounts such
acts of God time and again. Penitential practices were never
considered as something complete in themselves: they were
always means to an end, an end which seems twofold: the
forgiveness of sin and the glory of God, but which is in reality
one: the glory of God made manifest in the forgiveness of sin.
And the manifestation was more brilliant when the sinfulness

to be cured by God was more vividly shown forth in penitential sufferings.

5 *Remission of sins through the sacrament of Penance.* It is necessary to understand the true significance of penitential practices because they did not lose this significance when they were adopted by the Church as the means whereby she should exercise the power given her by Christ of forgiving sins. The essential task of the Church is to impart and increase the life of Christ, and the sacraments are the seven ways in which she fulfils her task. Thus sinners who have lost the life of Christ given to them in Baptism are offered that life a second time, provided they ask for it as penitents: in sackcloth and ashes, with supplications and with fastings, provided, that is, they realise and acknowledge that they are suffering the effects of sin, and stand in need of God's merciful intervention. The sinner may, for instance, confess that he committed adultery: he is guilty of an action which took place a day or a year ago; but he can as accurately confess that he is now, at this very moment, suffering the evil effects of such an action, and this wretched condition may well be displayed by his penitential garb. When a man says that he broke his leg two days ago, he could as well say that he *has* a broken leg *now*, were this not superfluous, since the effects of his action are there for all to see. But the manifestations of sin are not so clear or so definite. It is therefore necessary to adopt certain signs of its presence, if the healing power of God's mercy is to be made plain, and his glory to be enhanced.

In the attitude of the early Christian writers towards the practice of penance we see the influence of the Old Testament (though it is clear that other factors played their part, such as Stoic philosophy and Roman jurisprudence), and the two motives of strengthening the sinner's plea for forgiveness and the pedagogical benefit to the community of the faithful are not difficult to find. Thus Tertullian writes, after having admitted that the gate of forgiveness, though shut and fastened up with the bar of Baptism, is nevertheless standing somewhat open through repentance: The narrower, then, the sphere of action of this second and only remaining repentance, the more laborious is its probation; in order that it may not be exhibited in the conscience alone, but may likewise be carried out in some external act.

'This act, which is more usually expressed and commonly spoken of under a Greek name, is *exomologesis*, whereby we confess our sins to the Lord, not indeed as if he were ignorant of them, but inasmuch as by confession satisfaction is settled; of confession repentance is born; by repentance God is appeased. And thus *exomologesis* is a discipline for man's prostration and humiliation, enjoining a demeanour calculated to move mercy. With regard also to the very dress and food, it commands the penitent to lie in sackcloth and ashes, to cover his body in mourning, to lay his spirit low in sorrows, to exchange for severe treatments the sins which he has committed; moreover, to know no food and drink but such as is plain—not for the stomach's sake, to wit, but the soul's; for the most part, however, to feed prayers on fastings, to groan, to weep and roar unto the Lord your God; to roll before the feet of the presbyters and kneel to God's dear ones; to enjoin on all the brethren to be ambassadors to bear his deprecatory supplication before God. All this *exomologesis* does, that it may enhance repentance; may honour God by its fear of the incurred danger; may, by itself pronouncing against the sinner, stand in the stead of God's indignation and by temporal mortification (I will not say frustrate, but) discharge eternal punishment.'[1]

Origen also speaks of the possible edification for the rest, when a sinner confesses his sin in the gathering of the whole

[1] *On Repentance*, ch. IX, *Ante-Nicene Christian Library*, XI, Edinburgh 1869, p. 273.

Church.[1] And the pedagogical element in penitential practice was strongly marked in the early Church, by the fact that the penitent sinner was at the door of the church for all to see. God's intervention, his forgiveness and his mercy were equally plain, for the community witnessed the reconciliation of the sinner by the bishop, the readmission into the Church and especially his readmission to the delights of the Lord's table.

Both by excluding the sinner from the life[2] of the Church and by readmitting him as a penitent, the bishop was exercising the power given by Christ to the apostles when he said: 'Whatever you may bind upon earth will be bound in heaven, and whatever you may loose upon earth will be loosed in heaven' (Matt. 18 : 18). The interpretation of this saying, which is practically identical with what had been said to Peter alone (Matt. 16 : 19), has always caused considerable difficulty. What is the meaning of 'to bind and loose'? It was a rabbinic expression, used to describe their teaching authority: they could declare certain beliefs or practices forbidden (i.e. bound) and others lawful (i.e. loosed) according to the Law. In this case, then, our Lord would be giving Peter and the rest of the apostles divine authority to support them in their teaching regarding

[1] In Ps. 37 Hom. II, 6, edition de La Rue, VIII, p. 100.
[2] It must be clearly understood that such expressions as 'expulsion from the Church,' or 'exclusion from the kingdom', or 'to cease to be a member of the Church' are all references to the living or fruitful membership. The baptised sinner *does* remain a member of the Church in so far as he retains a title to membership: he has been stamped, as it were, with an indelible mark at Baptism, and his situation in relation to the Church is not the same as that of one unbaptised. The condemnation of the practice of re-baptising heretics was a tremendous stimulus to the development of a more elaborate theology concerning the nature and effects of the Sacraments, and in particular of that most important distinction between validity and fruitfulness. Thus St Augustine taught that sinners and heretics may have a certain participation with Christ, even though it be imperfect. For this vital development in the understanding of the nature of the Sacraments cf. Bernard Leeming s.j., *Principles of Sacramental Theology*, London 1956, nn. 135–53.

what was allowed or forbidden by God. As an objection to this interpretation Büchsel[1] points to Matt. 23 : 8 where the disciples are admonished not to accept the title Rabbi, for 'you have only one teacher', and he calls attention to another possible meaning of 'to bind and loose', namely 'to put under a ban and to remove the ban, or to expel from the community and to readmit'. The evidence for such a meaning is slight and Büchsel admits that one cannot go further than to say that it is a probable interpretation of the texts in Matthew. But this may already be too much. The object of the binding and loosing is things, not people,[2] and the context of this expression in Mt. 16 : 19 where Peter is made the head of the Church favours the retaining of its normal meaning as a conferring of doctrinal authority. On the other hand, the context of Mt. 18 : 18 is precisely that of fraternal correction, of the relation between sinner and community. If a brother sin he is to be rebuked before witnesses; but if he refuse to listen the community is to be informed, and if even then he refuse to listen he is to be as a pagan or a publican, namely one excluded from the community. Here the context does seem to favour the interpretation of to bind and loose as to expel from and readmit to the community, and K. Stendhal remarks with some probability: 'It may not be taken for granted that the saying is intended to have the same function in both contexts. On the contrary, its repetition in chapter 18 is due to the fact that Matthew intends to alter its implications.'[3] But it seems possible to reconcile the two interpretations more simply. Judging by the formula used in both cases, the direct meaning is indeed that Peter and the rest of the apostles are given the authority of deciding what doctrine and what moral conduct is permitted and forbidden in

---

[1] *TWNT* II, p. 60, 8 ff.

[2] The examples Büchsel quotes, namely Jn. 7 : 39; 10 : 29; 17 : 2, 24, to show that this use of the neuter causes no difficulty are quite unconvincing.

[3] *The School of St Matthew*, Uppsala 1954, p. 28.

God's kingdom. The Scribes and Pharisees had claimed a similar authority for their interpretations of the Law, and in practice by their interpretations they had closed the kingdom of heaven to men (Mt. 23 : 13). In the same way the authority given the apostles of preaching the authentic gospel must also in practice include the authority of excluding from and readmitting to the kingdom which they preach.[1] The interpretation of this text, therefore, from the time of Tertullian[2] and Origen,[3] as a reference to the power of the bishop to exclude[4] and readmit sinners to the Church, must not be considered as alien to its original context; nor, on the other hand, as directly stated there; but rather, as an important element included in the full doctrinal authority given to the apostles by Christ. If the belief or conduct of a Christian deviate from what is taught by the apostles, then he is no longer a member of the Kingdom; if he correct this, then he regains his position in the Kingdom. But the Kingdom of God is a visible community and every aspect of life in the Kingdom has its visible side: the Kingdom is preached by the apostles, and its members are admitted by the visible sign of Baptism, which is the manifestation of their invisible belief in the gospel. So too, their deviation from that belief, and their subsequent reacceptance of it, must be made visible.

The expulsion from the Church and the later readmission of the penitent sinner is the sacramental rite whereby sins are forgiven, for the former is the external proof that the man is

[1] J. Jeremias points out that the rabbinic use of this expression ought not to lead us to ignore completely its origin as signifying the autocratic power of a judge to take prisoner and to release (cf. *TWNT* III, p. 751, 1 ff.).

[2] An interpretation he himself rejected, at least in so far as it was considered to have been handed down to the successors of Peter (cf. p. 137 above).

[3] *Comm. in Matt.* 12, 14.

[4] 'Exclusion' from the Church is not to be restricted in this context to the significance of 'excommunication' in the technical sense it now has in the Canon Law.

in the state of sin, and the latter that he is reconciled to the Body of Christ and reinstated in the Kingdom of God. The grave mistake is sometimes made of regarding expulsion from the Church and readmittance as a purely disciplinary measure, without direct reference to a man's state in relation to God. But this shows a misunderstanding of the significance of the Church as the gathering of those who are saved and who together form the one Body of Christ in whom alone is salvation. In the rite of public penitence according to the *Pontificale Romanum* the bishop said to the sinners he was expelling: 'Thus you are, today, driven from your holy mother the Church, on account of your sins and your crimes, as Adam the first man was driven from paradise on account of his sin'.[1] Their penitential garb and particularly their exclusion from the Holy Eucharist made this truth quite obvious to the community, made the penitents themselves realise their unhappy state and their need to seek forgiveness, and made their eventual reconciliation a striking proof of God's merciful intervention, a display of his love 'who willest not the death of a sinner, but rather that he be converted and live' (cf. Ezech. 33 : 11). It is in such a context that we understand the full implication of the parables of the lost sheep, the lost drachma and the prodigal son:[2] 'There will be more joy in heaven for one sinner who repents, than for ninety-nine just who need not repent' (Lk. 15 : 7).

It may well be thought that a theological consideration of the remission of sins through Penance which shows so great a dependence upon the practice of the early Church, is proved unsound by the fact that most of these practices have been abandoned by the Church, and are therefore unessential for the preservation of this sacrament. Great changes in the actual rite of Penance have taken place for various reasons which can

---

[1] Quoted by A. Villien, *Les Sacrements: Histoire et Liturgie*, 3e ed., Paris 1931, p. 167.

[2] Cf. S. Lyonnet, *Biblica*, 1954, p. 484.

only be appreciated in a careful study of liturgical history. But it is not correct to conclude that the superficial differences, great though they seem, imply that the theological significance of the sacrament, more clearly expressed in ancient practice, does not remain the same today. The absence of sackcloth and ashes, of fasting and weeping, is the reason why the name Penance seems something of a misnomer, but the name Confession draws attention to that element in the sacramental rite which plays the same part as penitential practices. The explicit confession of sins to the priest is the essential penitential practice demanded by the Church except in those circumstances in which, from the earliest days, the Church has been accustomed to dispense with penitential practices. The confession of sins is the sinner's declaration of the evils which have come upon him through sin, and it is his public humiliation. Through this humiliation the sinner moves God to pity and displays his miserable state to the Church. The confessor is the officially appointed witness on behalf of the Church, and the confession of sins, in spite of the secrecy of the confessional, still remains, essentially, a public one before the Church. But more important, the confessor is the officially appointed representative of the apostles in the sinner's reconciliation, and it is here that the drama is completed, for by this reconciliation God shows his mercy and changes the sinner's sickness into health, a wonderful work of God which is crowned before the eyes of the brethren when the sinner is once more united to them at the reception of the Holy Eucharist. A sure theological instinct joins confession and communion in the minds of the faithful, for the Holy Eucharist is the supreme proof that we are members of the Body of Christ.

The remission of sins, therefore, obtained fundamentally through union with Christ, is in practice granted through two sacraments: to those who do not already belong to the Church it is given by Baptism which makes them members of the Body of Christ; to those who have already been baptised it is given by Penance whereby they are reconciled to the Church, or in synonomous terms, readmitted into the Body of Christ. This is wonderfully expressed in the prayer at the reconciliation of penitents, which took place shortly before the Baptism of catechumens at the Paschal Vigil: 'Our number grows through those to be reborn; we increase through those who have returned. There is washing with water; there is washing with tears. From the first there is joy at the receiving of those called; from the second there is gladness at the absolution of the penitent. . . . They have eaten, as it is written, the bread of sorrow; they have watered their bed with tears, they have afflicted their heart with mourning, their body with fastings, in order that they might gain the wholeness of soul they had lost.'[1]

[1] Cf. A. Villien, op. cit., p. 169.

X

The Sacrament of Healing (Jas. 5: 14—15)[1]

Kevin Condon C.M.

THE epistle of St James, along with that of St Jude and the second of St Peter, belongs to a group of writings which, because they are independent of the great Pauline and Johannine corpus, have an importance all their own. Together with parts of the Acts of the Apostles and, to some extent, the synoptic gospels they are our chief quarry when it comes to drawing the material for a picture of the earliest church of all—the Jewish church—its organisation, its mentality, its doctrine, its prejudices. The passage with which we are dealing occurs at the end of the epistle of St James and furnishes the only allusion in the New Testament to our sacrament of last anointing. The earliest allusion to a rite of last anointing in *Christian* practice apart from the New Testament is to be found in Origen (third to fourth century).[2] Our interpretation of this passage of St James

---

[1] First published in *Scripture*, 1959, pp. 33–42.

[2] *Hom. 2 in Levit.*, *GCS* 29 295f. Origen quotes the text of St James to illustrate the seventh means of remitting sin in the N.T., 'when the sinner bathes his couch in tears . . . and when he is not ashamed to show his sin to the priest of the Lord and seek the remedy'. But it is not certain that Origen looks on the ritual as a *last* anointing prior to entry to another life, rather than as a sacrament of physical and spiritual restoration. Cf. Paul F. Palmer s.j., 'The purpose of anointing the sick', *Theological Studies*, XIX, 1958, pp. 309–44. After a detailed study of early prayer formularies and sacramentaries Father Palmer concludes that 'up to the middle of the twelfth century there is little in the documents to commend the view that extreme unction was looked upon as the preparation of the dying Christian soul for immediate entrance into heaven. The one purpose . . . was to *cure* the sick person both physically and spiritually' (art. cit., p. 342.)

will therefore derive mainly from the New Testament itself and from near-contemporary Jewish literature and practice.

After an inscription the epistle begins with a homily on patiently bearing suffering (1 : 1–18); the writer then speaks of the duty of living according to the gospel (1 : 19–29). This is followed by a warning against unjust discrimination of the poor (2 : 1–13), after which comes the well-known passage on the importance of showing one's faith by good works (2 : 14–26). There follow homilies on the control of the tongue (3 : 1–12), on true and false wisdom (3 : 13–18), on the causes of strife (4 : 1–12). In 4 : 13—5 : 6 there is a series of admonitions and proverbs directed against the traders and the rich, and in 5 : 7–20 a similar series of proverbial admonitions on patience (7–11), on swearing (12), on prayer—especially for those who are sick (13–18)—and on winning back the erring brother (19–20). All these lessons and admonitions are put together without any clear-cut principle of division; like links of a chain each passage follows on the other through an association of ideas or words. The epistle as a whole is intended to inculcate a way of life and practical wisdom pleasing to God, the dominant motives being the love of God and our neighbour and an eschatological outlook on life, its temptations and sufferings, its wealth and poverty. The style is paranetic, like that of late Jewish literature; the predominant literary form is the proverb—reminding one to some extent of the work of Jesus Sirach, or the synoptic tradition; the emphasis on practical life and wisdom gives a strong Jewish colouring to the whole work. Christian traits are few, but those which do exist are so inserted into the woof of the work as to leave little doubt that the letter is by a Jewish Christian author.[1]

---

[1] To mention the important ones: the author speaks of 'faith in the Lord Jesus Christ' (2 : 1); of 'the law of freedom' (1 : 25; 2 : 12); of being begotten to God through the 'word of truth' (1 : 18); of 'the honourable name', which in the context is the name of the Lord Jesus Christ (2 : 7); of

The writer signs himself: 'James the servant of God and of the Lord Jesus Christ' (1 : 1). In the context of New Testament history (Acts; Gal. 2; Jude) and of early Church tradition, this James can only have been the 'brother of the Lord' who was head of the Jerusalem community.[1] Along with Peter and John he was looked upon by St Paul as one of the 'pillars of the Church' (Gal. 2 : 9). This attribution has much to commend it, notably the extremely Jewish character of the work and the multiple echoes of the synoptic tradition, especially that of Matthew. On the other hand, there are difficulties against it: especially the excellent Greek style and syntax and the epistle's misunderstanding of the Pauline doctrine on faith and works (cf. 2 : 14–26), which one would hardly expect from a man who knew Paul very well (cf. Acts 15; Gal. 2). One can still speak of the 'enigma' of James.[2]

At the same time, the letter remains extremely important, since it clearly emanated from a Jewish-Christian milieu and is

the 'coming of the Lord' (5 : 7–11) and of the 'elders of the church' (5 : 14). His admonition on swearing recalls the parallel admonition in the sermon on the mount (5 : 12). The theory of A. Meyer (*Das Rätsel des Jakobsbriefes*, 1930) that the epistle was originally a Jewish writing, later re-edited and given a Christian slant by a Christian author, has not gained general acceptance. (Cf., however, B. S. Easton in *The Interpreter's Bible*, XII, 1957, who in his introduction to the epistle of James revives Meyer's hypothesis with modifications.)

[1] James, the son of Zebedee and brother of John, an apostle, had been put to death by Herod Agrippa, about A.D. 40 (Acts 12 : 2). James the son of Alphaeus, also an apostle (cf. Mk. 2 : 14; 3 : 18 and 15 : 40—'James the little'), has been identified in Church tradition with our James, the brother of the Lord. However, in view of Mk. 3 : 21, 32 f., where a clear distinction is made between the apostles and the brethren of Jesus, it is difficult to uphold this tradition.

[2] The epistle is either very early or relatively late. If very early, then it would have been written by James in the early forties, before he had yet got a clear idea of Pauline doctrine. But the present writer inclines rather to the view that the epistle is pseudonymous, probably written by a disciple of James for the hellenistic Jewish-Christian diaspora in Syria and Cilicia in the last quarter of the first century.

a witness to its faith and worship. It is addressed to the 'twelve tribes of the dispersion', namely to the Jewish-Christian diaspora outside of (and probably in the vicinity of) Palestine.

The passage on the anointing of the sick occurs in the course of an admonition about prayer at the end of the epistle. The following is a rather literal translation of the portion in which we are here interested:

> [13]Does any one among you suffer? Let him pray. Is any one cheerful? Let him sing praise. [14]Is any one sick among you? Let him call for the presbyters of the church, and let them pray over him, anointing him with oil in the name of the Lord. [15]And the prayer of faith will save the one who is infirm and the Lord will raise him up. And if he has committed sins, he will be forgiven. [16]Confess therefore your sins to one another and pray for each other, that you may be healed; for the powerful prayer of a just man has great effect.

From a warning against the wrong use of the name of God by swearing (v. 12) St James passes to its right use in prayer. By prayer the pious man can raise himself up to God, no matter what his external circumstances may be: if he suffers, then, instead of complaining, let him pray to God; if he is in good spirits, then, instead of dissipating himself, let him sing God's praise; if he is sick, then, instead of worrying or merely relying on human aid, let him call in the ministers of the Church that they may pray over him.

Is any one sick among you? Nothing in the text indicates that anything other than bodily sickness is in question, nor are we told *how* sick the person is. In the Jewish mind, it is true, sin and sickness were closely linked, somewhat as cause and punishment, or as twin evils to which our fallen flesh is heir. But it is first of all from bodily sickness, whatever the cause to which St James may have attributed it, that the sick person is to be healed. Or, perhaps, it would be better to specify that St James does not differentiate between sin and sickness in quite the same way that we do—any more than he differentiates between body and soul, in accord with ideas which we inherit more from Greek philosophy than from the Hebrew world. For St James the object of the anointing ritual is the concrete sick person— body and soul—and its effect is restoration, both bodily and spiritual.

The fundamental meaning of *asthenés* is 'without strength', 'weak'. The noun *astheneia* is the word generally used in the gospels for the many sicknesses healed by Jesus. So many were cured (*therapeuesthai*) from their sicknesses (or from 'spirits' [Lk. 8 : 2; cf. Lk. 5 : 15]) that Matthew (8 : 17) saw in Jesus the fulfilment of Is. 53 : 4: 'himself has taken our sicknesses and borne our infirmities.' The word *astheneia* does not *per se* connote a grave illness; there may, however, be a 'sickness unto death' (Jn. 11 : 4), just as there may be a 'sin unto death' (1 Jn. 5 : 16). Further on (v. 15) St James uses the word *kamnōn*, which means to be physically weary or debilitated.[1] According to the prevailing idea of the time, sickness could be brought about either by spirits (cf. Mt. 17 : 18; Lk. 13 : 11—'a spirit of sickness') or by sins (1 Cor. 11 : 30; Mk. 2 : 5).[2] Whence the treatment of sickness in the ancient world generally was not merely medicinal but often exorcistic as well (see footnote 1, p. 180).

Let him call for the presbyters of the Church. It is part of the supernatural outlook on life inculcated by St James that when sickness comes the sick person should rely first and foremost on prayer, in the present instance on the official and powerful prayer of the presbyters of the Church. Our word for presbyter

[1] Bauer, however, notes that the meaning *to be sick beyond hope, to wither away*, even *to die* (Wis. 4 : 16; 15 : 9), is not impossible.

[2] On the link between sin and sickness and on our Lord's *apparent* correction of the prevailing Jewish mentality (Jn. 9 : 2) see Chapter VII of this volume.

is priest. Yet, in ordinary Greek usage the word for a priest (meaning one deputed to offer sacrifice to the deity) is *hiereus*; it is the word used throughout the Greek Septuagint translation for the Hebrew *kohēn*. But it is very rarely used in the New Testament, except in reference to the priests of the Jewish liturgy.[1] The English word *priest* comes from the Greek *presbuteros* (presbyter) which is a comparative form meaning, primarily, 'one who is older', as opposed to one who is younger (*neōteros*). Then it can mean an 'old man' or again an 'elder', that is, one who is a member of a college of elders. In the last case it is more a title of dignity than an indication of age (like our 'Senator'). Colleges of elders were a feature of Jewish life and history. In early Hebrew history elders were the ruling authorities of tribes or clans; after the conquest of Canaan Jewish cities were ruled by elders; and in the last two centuries before Christ we find that the elders had representation on the Jewish high council along with the high-priests and the teachers of the Law. Lastly, we know from Jewish inscriptions that synagogues were administered by colleges of elders.

In the New Testament local churches were administered, at least during the early period, by colleges of elders and the analogy with the contemporary Jewish synagogues is striking. We find elders in the church at Antioch (Acts 11 : 30); we find

---

[1] This does not, of course, imply that early Christian ministers did not exercise priestly functions. Christ himself is never called an *hiereus*, except in the epistle to the Hebrews where he is depicted as a high-priest (*archiereus*) exalted to heaven, and the counterpart to the high-priest of the Jewish liturgy. Yet the priestly character of Christ's redemptive work cannot be denied. The fact is that Christianity, for all its originality, emerged as a sect of Judaism. The first Christians, while possessing their own rites (breaking of bread, Baptism) and their own identity, still participated in the cult of the Temple. The technical term 'priests' (*hiereis*) still belonged to the ministers of the Jewish liturgy.

In 1 Pet. 2 : 5,9 Christians are called a 'holy priesthood' (*hireateuma*). But the whole passage derives from Ex. 19 : 6 and has to be interpreted in the light of it.

them installed by St Paul in the churches of Lystra, Derbe and
Antioch in Pisidia (Acts 14 : 23); we find them in Jerusalem along
with the apostles, making decrees for the Church (Acts 15 : 2, 4,
6, 22 f.; 16 : 4—'apostles and elders', analogous to the Jewish
synhedrium?[1]). Together the elders form the presbyter*ion*
(1 Tim. 4 : 14), a word which almost certainly means the
'college' of elders, and not an abstract 'eldership' or 'priesthood'.
In one passage outside the pastoral epistles the presbyters are
also designated *episcopoi* (literally 'overseers'), which shows
that the use of the titles was as yet in a fluid state, the one
connoting dignity, the other a status or office (cf. Acts
20 : 18–35).[2]

In our passage the *presbyters of the Church* are clearly the
college of elders that presided over the Christian community.
The definite article sets them apart; they are not merely a
venerable body of charismatics. It is also clear that it is by

---

[1] Cf. Bornkamm *TWNT* VI 663, 15 ff.

[2] In the pastoral epistles too the office of *episcopos* might appear identical
with that of presbyter, viz. 'to preside' and 'to teach' (1 Tim. 5 : 17; 3 : 5;
Tit. 1 : 9). In Tit. 1 : 5–9, where Titus is told to establish *presbyters* in each
city, a description of the ideal *bishop* immediately follows! And yet the two
functions cannot be identified absolutely. The *episcopos* is always singular;
the presbyters always form a college and the passages about each office are
quite distinct with the exception of Tit. 1 : 5, 7–9. Even in this passage the
change of number and the special enumeration of qualities speaks against
absolute identification. The two offices, according to Bornkamm, are
envisaged from different points of view. He discerns in the pastoral epistles
a tendency towards the monarchical episcopate, growing up alongside of
the Jewish tradition of elders, a process which appears already at an earlier
stage in Acts 20 : 17,28 for the same area (Asia Minor) and in I Clement
(for Rome). The college of presbyters appear only in Jewish churches, or
in churches founded by Jews (Bornkamm, *TWNT* VI 667–8). By the
commencement of the second century the monarchical episcopate is widespread (cf. especially the letters of St Ignatius Martyr). According to
Catholic faith it was of divine institution; therefore the powers of order and
jurisdiction which belonged to the bishops must have been borne and
transmitted in the earlier period by the apostles or 'apostolic delegates' such
as Timothy and Titus.

virtue of their office as heads of the local church that they have the power of healing.[1]

The early Church knew of a charism of healing, a communication of the Holy Spirit to certain favoured Christians (cf. 1 Cor. 12 : 6, 9, 11, 28). Believers in Jesus would, according to Mk. 16 : 18, 'lay their hands on the sick and they would be well'. Such special gifts or charisms were clearly sporadic manifestations of the Spirit and not connected, so far as we can determine, with any office or rite. But the healing ritual described by St James, while it is of the same order as these charisms of healing, is not of the same kind. In St James the power of healing is connected with the *office* of the presbyters.

And let them pray over him, anointing him with oil in the name of the Lord. The presbyters are to pray *over* the man—not 'for' him. The sense is local; they gather round the sick person, who lies prostrate, and pray over him.[2] In the next verse the prayer

---

[1] With this Bornkamm is in agreement (*TWNT* VI 664). But he goes on: 'Since James 5 : 16 does not speak of confession of sins before priests but of mutual confession and prayer for one another and, especially, of the power of prayer of the just man, James 5 : 14 will not allow any deductions on the place of the presbyters as confessors or on their function as liturgists of the community.' One will agree with the first part of this statement; there is not sufficient evidence to indicate that the confession of which James speaks is sacramental confession. But the second part is open to question. If, as he himself states, the charism of healing is attached to the office of the presbyters; if, as the text would seem to indicate, the ritual has the character of a sacrament, then the presbyters are not more wise or just men praying for a sick person. The rite of anointing is one of the evidences, along with the 'laying on of hands of the priestly college' (1 Tim. 4 : 14) and the presiding over the eucharistic meal, which we must associate with the presbyters, that the office of the presbyters also included the power of order. In the very early Church the preaching of the word was, it is true, chiefly the work of charismatics. But the power of celebrating the Eucharist would have belonged solely to the presbyters. Cf. R. Bultmann, *Theology of the New Testament*, II, London 1955, pp. 103 and 109.

[2] The preposition *epi* could possibly hide an allusion to an imposition of hands, mentioned in Mk. 16 : 18 and in the rite mentioned by Origen (*Hom. in Lev.* 2, 3).

is called the 'prayer of faith', that is, prayer inspired by complete faith. In the teaching of Jesus faith is an absolute prerequisite for the performance of miracles (Mt. 21 : 21; Mk. 9 : 23; 11 : 22–4; 16 : 16 f.) and of works of healing (Mt. 9 : 22; Mk. 5 : 34; 16 : 18; Lk. 8 : 48), while St James himself says in 1 : 6: 'Let him pray in faith, in no way wavering, for he that wavers is like the billow of the sea, stirred and tossed by the wind.' This prayer of faith is accompanied by an anointing with oil, the oil being olive oil which in the ancient world was a universal therapeutic agent. When our Lord sent his disciples out into the villages and towns of Galilee to preach the kingdom we are told that 'they anointed many sick with oil and healed them' (Mk. 6 : 13), a practice which was no doubt a prelude to the rite described by St James and of the same order. In the prayer of the priest and the material anointing with oil one can detect the two elements of a sacrament.[1] 'In the New Testament

---

[1] *Aleiphō* (to anoint) in the Greek Septuagint nearly always translates the Hebrew *sûk*, used to anointing in the ordinary material or therapeutic sense. Another Hebrew verb, *mašaḥ*, is used of anointing in the sacral sense, e.g. the anointing of kings. This is usually translated by the Greek *chriō*. (The passive *masîah* [messiah] is translated *christos*, anointed one.)

Anointing texts in the N.T. fall into three categories: (1) anointing the body as an expression of joy and good spirits (Mt. 6 : 17); (2) anointing a guest to do him honour (Lk. 7 : 38, 46; Jn. 12 : 3; Mt. 26 : 7; Mk. 14 : 3) —in the last three instances the anointing is given a deeper sense: it was done in anticipation of our Lord's burial; (3) anointing the sick (Mk. 6 : 13; Jas. 5 : 14; cf. Lk. 10 : 34). Apropos of the anointing of the sick, Schlier notes that in the ancient world olive oil was used not merely for purely therapeutic or medicinal purposes (cuts, bruises, skin-diseases, etc.) but also as a *magic-medicinal* or *exorcistic* agent. The demarcation line between the two uses is never clear-cut, for all sicknesses (and especially those of a psychic character) could be traced to demonic influence. The exorcistic use of oil is testified to in Jewish writings (*Test. Sal.* 18 : 34; *Vita Adam* 36 : 40–2; *Slav. Hen.* 22 : 8 f.) and also in the Christian *Act. Thomae* (67).

Along with this exorcistic usage there also developed a sacramental practice; it was to be found among certain Gnostics in the form of a baptism of oil; it existed in the Church, in the form of an exorcism either before or after the rite of Baptism; it was practised, as a sacrament of the

anointing with oil is a medicinal-exorcistic action on the sick. In Mk. 6 : 13 the apostles, in conjunction with their preaching of penance and their casting out of demons, heal the sick and are therefore messengers and bearers of the dawning kingdom of God. In Jas. 5 : 14 the same medicinal-exorcistic ritual of anointing with oil is carried out on the sick by the officials of the Church and brings with it a healing which—corresponding to that which in Mk. 6 : 13 gives health for the Kingdom of God— here in the situation of the Church gives health to body and soul (forgiveness of sins). Jas. 5 : 14 dwells on the carrying out of the whole ritual. The anointing with oil takes place under invocation of the name of the Lord and is enclosed by prayer which, as a prayer of faith, works health and forgiveness. The oil has, in fact, the character of a sacramental material'.[1]

In the name of the Lord, that is, under invocation of the name of the Lord. The Lord could possibly mean God, in the absolute sense (as in 5 : 2), but more likely, in this rite carried out by Christian priests, it is Jesus Christ, in whose name it was promised that mighty deeds would take place (Mt. 7 : 22; Mk. 9 : 38; 16 : 17; Lk. 10 : 17; Acts 3 : 6; 4 : 10; 16 : 18).

And the prayer of faith will save the one who is infirm and the Lord will raise him up. And if he has committed sins he will be forgiven.[2] The juxtaposition in the one sentence of human prayer and effort on the one hand and divine operation on the other lead one to think that St James makes no distinction in effect between the *saving* and the *raising up*, but only in attribution. Both mean the same thing. But what *do* they mean?

St James himself uses the word *sōzein* to connote salvation in

dead, by the Mandeans and the Markosites. (The latter practice, however, is doubtful. It may have been no more than an anointing of the dead)— Schlier, *TWNT* I 230–2.

[1] Schlier, art. cit., 232.

[2] On this verse see, especially, J. Michl, *Das Regensburger Neue Testament, Band* 8, Pustet 1953, pp. 172–4.

the era to come, salvation from judgment and therefore from
eternal death—in other words salvation which consists in
'eternal life' (1 : 21; 2 : 14; 4 : 12; 5 : 20). Elsewhere in the New
Testament the word has the same meaning generally, but *not*
in contexts where there is question of sickness or death or their
danger (Mt. 9 : 21; Mk. 5 : 28, 34; 6 : 56; 10 : 52; Lk. 8 : 48
et al.). Similarly *egeirein* which occurs only here in James can
refer either to resurrection from the dead (1 Cor. 15 : 15 f.,
29, 32, 35, 42–4, 52; 2 Cor. 1 : 9; 4 : 14) or simply to raising up
from sickness, to making well and whole again (cf. Matt. 9 : 5–7,
25; Mk. 1 : 31; 2 : 9, 11 f.; 5 : 41; 9 : 27; Acts 3 : 7 *et al.*).[1] Here
in the present context the most obvious meaning of the words
seems to be that the sick man will be 'saved' from death and
'raised up' to life and health. This interpretation, which seems
to be demanded by the context, is confirmed by the fact that any
deviation from it is beset by the following difficulties:

1. If one takes it that the salvation of v. 15 means eschatological salvation, then the purpose of the ritual performed by
the priests would be to prepare the man for the 'coming of the
Lord' of which St James speaks in 5 : 7. The prayer of faith
would save the man from final judgment and give him life and salvation in the era to come. But against this one can object that
there is no reason why such a ritual should be performed for
the benefit of a *sick* man. Perhaps because he is on the point of
death? But there is no mention of a likelihood of death and, in
any case, the possibility of imminent death would have little
significance if St James in common with early Christians was
acutely conscious of the possibility of a proximate coming of
the Lord.

2. In v. 16 St James bids his readers 'confess their sins and
pray for one another in order that they may be healed'. Here the

---

[1] The Latin translation *alleviabit* stresses the idea of relief (physical or
spiritual) and may have contributed to later theological development. It
should be (with some Latin codices) *adlevabit* or *allevabit*.

'healing' he has in mind is clearly spiritual; why not also in v. 15? But it is by no means clear that the healing in v. 16 is spiritual (see below). Even if it were, the context is not the same. In v. 15a there is question solely of bodily sickness; only in v. 15b is it said 'if he should have committed sins he will be forgiven'.

3. A more difficult objection would be that St James promises this salvation without any reservation or thought of possible refusal, whence he can hardly be thinking of bodily salvation. But the same objection can be made to many other promises of the New Testament. In Mk. 16 : 18 the promise of healing is no less explicit than it is here. The early Christians cannot have been less aware than we are that, in spite of the power of healing attached to faith in Christ, sickness and death still held sway among them. Therefore in all the promises attached to faith in Christ there is implicit a tacit condition: 'If it be the will of God' (1 Jn. 5 : 14 f.). Fulfilment also depends on the faith of the prayer; if faith is wanting, the prayer cannot be heard (Jas. 1 : 6 f.).

But if the salvation in v. 15 is spiritual in nature, then in what precisely does it consist? It can hardly consist in salvation from sins which is a distinct effect of the rite, mentioned only in v. 15b. Nor can it very well consist in an increase of that divine gift which each Christian bears within him and by which he is begotten to God (1 : 18), for such an effect could hardly be described by the word 'save'. Lastly, if the effect of the anointing is spiritual salvation, then the purpose of the anointing with oil, which in the ancient world was universally therapeutic, is largely lost.

It is more in keeping with the context, then, to adhere to the simple idea of salvation from death and restoration to health. It is true that the sacrament will then be a sacrament of healing, not a sacrament of preparation for death. But this apparent inversion of purpose may well be explained as the result of a

normal development.[1] The fact is that there are two effects of
the sacrament—restoration to health and forgiveness of sins.
In the course of time the emphasis on the latter grew greater
and the idea of preparing the sick person for death grew
dominant.

If he has committed sins, he will be forgiven. It may be that
the man is sick not merely in body but also in his soul, through
sin. To the Jewish mentality the two are always closely connected. St James has in mind grievous sins, not the day-to-day
offences of which he speaks in 3 : 2. He also very probably
understands that these sins will be publicly confessed (cf. the
therefore in v. 16). And just as the miraculous healing by Jesus
in Mt. 9 : 1–8 (Mk. 2 : 1–12; Lk. 5 : 17–26) operated first on
the body and then on the soul, so here the ritual of the priests
works not only on the body but also, when necessary, on the
soul. It is in this respect especially that the rite performed by
them differs from the charisms of healing elsewhere in the New
Testament.

The admonition concludes: *Confess, therefore, your sins to one
another and pray for one another, that you may be healed.* . . . After
mention of forgiveness of sins, St James concludes ('therefore')
with a general exhortation to mutual confession. Public confes-

---

[1] That the idea of preparing the sick person for death is a later devel-
opment has been suggested by various theologians (see footnote 2 p. 172).
Also: de Letter, in *Bijdragen*, XVI 1955, pp. 258–70 (reproduced in
abstract in *Theology Digest*, IV 1956, pp. 185–8); Roguet, *The Sacraments:
Signs of Life*, London 1954; Peil, in *Handbuch der Liturgik für Katecheten
und Lehrer*, Freiburg 1955, pp. 151–5; Spaemann, in *Liturgisches Jahrbuch*,
VIII 1958, pp. 147–9; Botte, in *La Maison-Dieu*, XV 1948, pp. 91–107;
Meurant, in *La Vie Spirituelle*, March 1955, pp. 242–51. For an excellent
commentary on all these works—and others in a contrary vein—see
Charles Davis, in *The Clergy Review*, XVIII, 1958, pp. 726–46. On the
uncertainty or lack of fixity of form in the sacrament of Extreme Unction
up to the Middle Ages, see Bernard Leeming s.j. in *The Principles of
Sacramental Theology*, 1956, p. 421 f. On the Canons of the Council of
Trent and the deliberations preceding them, see Palmer, art. cit.

sion of sins in sorrow and repentance was known to the Jews (Dan. 9 : 4 ff.; Neh. 9 : 2 ff.; Mt. 3 : 6; Mk. 1 : 5) and was made by newly converted Christians at Ephesus (Acts 19 : 18); 1 Jn. 1 : 9 speaks of its salutary effects and the *Didache* (14 : 1) bids Christians celebrate the Eucharist on Sundays 'after you have publicly made known your sins'. So too James probably speaks of mutual confession of sins in the course of liturgical service of God, such as still persists in the *Confiteor*. But there is no adequate ground for thinking that a confession before priests is envisaged, or that it is followed by sacramental absolution. The readers are bid to confess their sins and pray for one another, that they may be *healed*. Healed from spiritual need and sin? Or from bodily infirmity? In view of the association in Jewish minds between sin and bodily infirmity, it seems more probable that the 'healing' St James has in mind embraces both. St Paul could say that because there were some among the Corinthians who received the Eucharist unworthily 'therefore there are among you many sick and infirm and some die' (1 Cor. 11 : 30).

For the powerful prayer of a just man has great effect—as had that of the wonder-working Elias (vv. 17–18). The 'just man' could be an allusion to the presbyters of whom he has been speaking, but in this later and broader context more probably means Christians generally.

So concludes St James's account of the ritual of healing by the presbyters of the early Church. Catholic commentators in general are not unaware of a certain deviation between the text of St James and the theology of the sacrament which has become current since the Middle Ages.[1] It needs but little reflection, however, to realise that the original motif of the sacrament of anointing is more in keeping with the character of the sacraments as a whole. The sacraments envisage not directly the final end

[1] The true motif of the sacrament (now to be called 'the anointing of the sick') has been restored by the *Constitution on the Sacred Liturgy*, no. 73.

of man but his condition as a *viator* here on earth. The true sacrament of the dying is the *viaticum*; the first end of the sacrament of anointing is to *heal*—both physically and spiritually. And from a pastoral point of view, what a consolation it would be for the priest to be able to assure the sick or the dying that the anointing is not a summons to the next world but rather—first and foremost—an antidote to death, a powerful remedy for life.

XI

Priestly Virtues in the New Testament[1]

C. Spicq O.P.

UNDER the title of this essay you would expect a whole book, if one were to give exhaustive treatment to the subject. However, we intend rather to extract from the inspired writings the key qualities demanded from priests, by Christ our Lord or the Holy Ghost. Since we can mention only briefly each of these virtues, it will be the reader's task to meditate further on the texts quoted and plumb their meaning.

These priestly virtues are drawn from three passages of major theological importance: 1. The 'Conference after the Last Supper', namely chapters 13 to 18 of the fourth gospel, in which Jesus, after making his chosen disciples priests, gave them instructions on the spirit in which they should exercise their new powers. 2. The epistle to the Hebrews, which defines the virtues proper to the high priest of the new covenant, virtues which consequently all those who have received the sacrament of the priesthood should possess. 3. The epistles to Timothy and Titus, in which St Paul delineates for the shepherds of the churches of Ephesus and Crete qualities that are indispensable for carrying out their duties.

We are talking of 'priests', where the gospels and St Paul speak mainly of disciples and apostles. But this last term certainly denotes the priesthood, such as we understand it today. Actually, the New Testament term 'apostle' by no means stands for messenger or missionary in the way its etymology suggests. It

[1] First published in *Scripture*, 1958, pp. 10–17 and pp. 84–93.

corresponds to the Hebrew *šeliaḥ*, denoting the plenipotentiary, the *chargé d'affaires*, the legal representative of an elector (Mt. 10 : 40; Mk. 9 : 37). Of course, the apostle is an 'envoy', speaking and acting in the name of another person, but he takes the place of that person so much that the acts of the *šeliaḥ* are binding on the sender. The Talmud declares expressly: 'A man's *šeliaḥ* is the same as the man himself.'

It is in this sense that Christ is the apostle and high priest of the Father (Heb. 3 : 1; cf. Jn. 17 : 8; 1 Jn. 4 : 9–10). He represents God and acts in his name: 'God was in Christ, reconciling the world to himself' (2 Cor. 5 : 19); whoever sees Christ, sees the Father (Jn. 14 : 9–10). Similarly the apostles represent Christ, they speak and act in his name, to such a point that their words and actions are 'Christ-done deeds': 'As the Father has sent me, I also send you' (Jn. 20 : 21). They can claim: 'God appeals to you through us' (2 Cor. 5 : 20); 'You welcomed me . . . as Christ Jesus in person' (Gal. 4 : 14).

In fact, by the almighty words that consecrated them (Jn. 17 : 17–19), the apostles are God's plenipotentiaries and mediators. Endowed with the same power as Jesus (Mt. 28 : 16–20; Jn. 14 : 12), they continue to do what Christ did. Not only have they the supreme prerogative of priesthood— that of blessing the eucharistic cup of the new covenant (Mt. 26 : 20 seq.; 1 Cor. 11 : 24); but they carry on the sacred ministry of the Gospel: 'I have written to you . . . in virtue of the grace which God has given me to be a sacred minister of Jesus Christ for the Gentiles, with God's gospel for my priestly charge (*hierourgounta*), to make the Gentiles' offering worthy of his acceptance, consecrated by the Holy Spirit' (Rom. 15 : 15–16).

If then the word 'apostle' indicates that the ministers of the Church have the same 'mission' as our Saviour, the word 'priest' emphasises the fact that they control the same power. Very soon, the passing-on of this power of communication of the Holy Ghost will be performed by the imposition of hands (Acts

14 : 23). It is in virtue of this rite that priests will be ordained to be pastors of a specific community (Acts 20 : 28), as shepherds and teachers (Eph. 4 : 11), pilots (1 Cor. 12 : 28), rulers (I Thess. 5 : 12; Rom. 12 : 8).

Faith. The fundamental virtue required of these apostle-priests is faith. The priest as such is first and foremost a soul full of faith. If eternal life is to know the one true God and to instruct souls in the doctrine of Christ, then it goes without saying that the priest must declare himself—echoing the incarnate word himself—to be God's witness, and must speak with conviction of what he has seen and heard (Jn. 15 : 27). The only Son, who was in the bosom of the Father, 'has unfolded God's story' (Jn. 1 : 18). He was the authorised witness of the mysteries of the divine life (Jn. 3 : 11–12; 31–2), and as such the light of the world. Now he confided his secrets to the Twelve (Jn. 15 : 15), and thenceforward it is they who are to be the light of the world (Mt. 5 : 14). Trustees of the mysteries of God (1 Cor. 4 : 1), their mission is to disburse 'the unfathomable riches of Christ's knowledge' (Eph. 3 : 8). The conclusion is inevitable that a priestly soul possesses outstandingly that grasp of the unseen which is the spirit of faith (Heb. 11 : 1). The priest's soul has become so familiar with the heavenly world and realises so keenly its beauty, that it cannot stop itself from proclaiming aloud its faith and conviction: 'We believe, that is why we speak' (2 Cor. 14 : 13). In a word, when we see and hear a priest, we should have the impression that we are seeing and hearing Jesus Christ.

In fact, our Lord devoted himself first of all to the intellectual and religious formation of his chosen disciples. It is to them that he reveals the secrets of the Kingdom of Heaven (Mt. 13 : 11). He disperses their doubts, clears away their misunderstandings, strives to initiate them into the relationship between the Father and the Son—and it is only on the final day of this patient

G

course of instructions that Jesus is able to declare: 'At last, you have come to believe' (Jn. 16 : 31). With what emotion the Master must have said this! He goes on to bless the Father for this enthusiastically: 'I have made thee known to these men, whom thou hast taken out of this world to give me. Now they have learned that all thou hast given me comes from thee. . . . They have recognised it for truth that I came from thee and they have found faith to believe that thou art the one who sent me' (Jn. 17 : 6–8).

No doubt the new priests will have to undergo severe trials; persecutions and the apparent triumph of evil will be violent shocks that will bowl them over and stun them (Jn. 16 : 32). But Peter—whose name means: a solid block that juts out and offers a shelter—will have the grace to uphold their convictions unwaveringly: 'Look now, Satan has claimed power over you all, so that he can sift you like wheat. But I have prayed for thee, that thy faith may not fail; when, after a while, thou hast come back to the right road, thy task is to hold up thy brethren' (Lk. 22 : 31–2). A priest's faith is not different in kind from that of the faithful; but it has a special quality: the solidity of a rock. As a man chosen to bear witness and to preach, the priest's characteristics are steadfastness and stability. These words, in biblical language, are the exact equivalent of the word generally translated as 'truth': *amen, 'emûnah.*

Hope. On the day of his ordination the priest hears our Lord say to him: 'Without me, you can do nothing' (Jn. 15 : 5). Hence he cannot count on his own strength for success in his mission of saving souls. He knows that he 'can do all things in him who strengthens' him (Phil. 4 : 13; cf . 2 Cor. 12 : 9–10). So he is never put off or scandalised by trials that are inherent in the ministry (Jn. 16 : 1). If he is surrounded by a world that is evil and often hostile (Jn. 15 : 18–25), yet he is helped by an almighty defender, the Paraclete (Jn. 14 : 17, 25–6; 16 : 7–15), and ringing in his ears is the last word of our Lord, encouraging him to an invincible confidence: 'In the world, you will have tribulation; but, take courage! I myself am the conqueror of the world' (Jn. 16 : 33; cf. 14 : 1).

It follows that God's help far exceeds the difficulties to be met. St Paul speaks of a superabundance of power (2 Cor. 4 : 7). The priest's hope is born of this triumph won by Christ crucified and risen from the dead. His death became the source of life. Now this same mystery unfolds in the day-to-day apostolate. Under the most unpromising circumstances, the priest not only benefits from this victory by our Lord over Satan and sin; he repeats it and completes it (1 Jn. 5 : 4–5). He too will raise the dead to life, because the power of the risen Jesus goes on working through his lips and through his hands. A priest who did not live by joyful hope would no longer have any reason for existence; he would be like a soldier who had enlisted in an army, but who set out for battle certain of defeat and taking it for granted beforehand that he would be beaten, having no confidence either in the genius or the capability of his commander-in-chief. But 'believe me when I tell you this: The man who has confidence in me will himself be able to do the things that I do, and even greater things still, because I am going away to be with my Father' (Jn. 14 : 12).

To this unshakable confidence belong the repeated encouragements of the prayer in the discourse after the Last Supper. After promising his apostle-priests that their ministry will be magnificently fruitful, Jesus immediately adds: 'Everything you ask in my name I will grant, that through the Son the Father may be glorified. If you ask anything from me in my own name I will do it' (Jn. 14 : 13–14). Actually, our Lord had just granted his disciples the highest power and authority, the immeasurable task of converting the world, of speaking and acting in his name. How will they be able to 'bear fruit in abundance and so prove themselves his disciples'? By prayer. A man of flesh and blood can do divine work only with this effective means, by harnessing God's own power to the task. Now it is intercession that will guarantee heavenly co-operation and unfailing fruitfulness. Hence: 'As long as you live in me and my words live in you, you can ask what you like and you will obtain it' (Jn. 15 : 7); 'I have appointed you to go forth and bear fruit, fruit which will endure, so the Father will give you anything you ask for in my name' (15 : 16); 'In very truth, I tell you: Whatever you ask the Father for, he will give it you in my name. So far you have not asked for anything in my name; ask and you will receive, so that you may be filled with joy' (16 : 23–4); 'When that day comes, you will make your requests in my name, and I do not say that I will ask them from the Father for you. For the Father himself loves you, because you have loved me and have come to believe that I came forth from God' (16 : 26–7).

The duty of making intercession is therefore an integral part of the priest-apostle's vocation. In fact, when our Lord chose the twelve, it was so that *they should be with him* and go out preaching at his command' (Mk. 3 : 14). The apostles are more essentially disciples than all the others, they follow the master more closely (Mk. 1 : 17). There is no apostolate worthy of the name unless it stems from a permanent union with our Lord. It is prayer that keeps this contact alive and active.

Charity. The fundamental lesson of the parable of the vine (Jn. 15 : 1–10) bears on the union of charity between Christ and his priests. For a vine-branch, the sole law of life is to remain attached to the vinestock; for a priest, the whole of his spiritual life is to love Christ exclusively, or rather to cleave fervently to the love of predilection with which Christ envelops him. Priestly spirituality is summed up in this word of command: Abide in my love. To be sure, to love God is the sole law imposed on all the faithful in the old and new covenants alike. But from priests, who are chosen out of the world and set apart for the work of bearing the fruits of grace to other souls (Jn. 15 : 16), our Lord requires a total surrender of the heart (Jn. 16 : 27; cf. Mt. 6 : 24). From each of them he expects priority of attachment: Lovest thou me more than these? (Jn. 21 : 15–17). In fact, authority to feed the sheep belonging to the supreme shepherd is given only on condition that the recipient be dedicated body and soul to his chief, in the same way as our saviour consecrated himself to the will of his Father to the point of total immolation (Jn. 17 : 16–19). Priestly charity, according to St John, is on the one hand a union of real love towards the person of Christ, an attachment of the whole being, a vital allegiance; on the other hand, it means what today we call the virtue of religion, worship and total reverence towards God, flowering into 'devotion', that is to say into unqualified obedience and devotedness: 'The man who has my commandments and keeps them, he is the one who loves me' (Jn. 14 : 21).

It is into this union of wills and hearts that a priest's love and zeal for souls is grafted: 'This is how we can be sure that we love God's children: it is when we love God and keep his commandments; since loving God means keeping his commandments' (1 Jn. 5 : 2–3). Love achieves a harmony of wills: *idem velle, idem nolle*. The heart of a priest, locked in the embrace of Christ's love (2 Cor. 5 : 14), will therefore love souls as Christ loves them and because he loves them (Jn. 15 : 12). It is not a case of human sympathy or of some kind of sublimation of the paternal instinct. Just as Jesus received those converted to him as a gift from his Father (Jn. 6 : 37–40; 15 : 9), so the priest carries over and extends to men that divine love of which he is the official channel. Following our saviour's example, his mission is to enkindle men's hearts with this heavenly fire (Lk. 12 : 49); he spreads its flame. This refers to the inexhaustible funds of zeal and energy in priestly charity, 'which great waters cannot extinguish, nor can the waves submerge it' (Cant. 8 : 7). Christians in the world may be allowed to have a divided heart, attached simultaneously to their Saviour and their husband or wife (1 Cor. 7 : 25–35); but this division is impossible for the priest. His charity is so intense that it must be exclusive; it leaves no room for any other object than this one: 'It is by this that we have known God's love of charity for us: he gave his life for us. We too must give our life for our brethren' (1 Jn. 3 : 16). The only thing for the priest is to possess, by vocation, a charity strictly parallel to that of the incarnate Son of God. It is a religious love, springing from the gift of self and from a consecration which, through union with God, devotes itself in life and death to the work of saving souls.

On these lines our Lord defined the spirit of the ministry which he was about to entrust to his first priests, in the scene of washing their feet. At this moment, as it happened, a dispute had arisen between the disciples: 'Which of them would be the greatest? He said to them: Kings, among their peoples, give them orders as masters, and it is those who use their authority over them who are praised as benefactors. For you, it will not be like that; but the oldest among you will act as if he were the littlest, and the one who is in command as if he were the servant. Who, in fact, is the greater: the one who sits at table or the one who serves at table? Is it not the one who sits at table? Now I, among you, am like the one who serves' (Lk. 22 : 24–7). Adding example to his teaching, the Master takes off his outer garments, ties a napkin to his girdle, sets down the basin of water before the apostles and, like a slave, washes and dries the feet of each in turn.

It seems as if Jesus feared nothing so much for his Church as a place-hunting hierarchy. The disciples knew that their master was establishing a kingdom, and this one word awakened ideas of domination in the earthly sense. So Jesus corrects this pagan notion and demonstrates for them the paradox that, in the spiritual kingdom, the way to climb high is to come down, and that to attain the first place you must choose the last: 'When you speak to me, you give me the title of master and Lord. That is the simple truth, I am'—Jesus is fully conscious of his position; authority and humility are by no means mutually exclusive. 'If then I, being your Lord and master, have washed your feet, how much more are you bound to wash one another's feet?' (Jn. 13 : 13–14). My example teaches you the dignity and duty of serving one another (cf. 12 : 26). This has the force of a command (cf. Mt. 11 : 29–30): 'What I have done, you likewise ought to do.'

What is the point of this example? It does not seem to lie simply in bodily purification, which has the force of a symbolic act. Symbolic of what? First of humility; but this is only an accidental and secondary aspect of the psychology which Jesus wants to drive home. There is certainly a lesson in mutual love (Jn. 13 : 1) and even something more complex. Humility is in it, together with fraternal charity, but then something much deeper: the gift of oneself. The washing of feet is the sacrament of apostolic authority; it signifies the humble service of love which the disciples owe to one another. For St John, this act is a synthesis of all the lowly service of love in which the whole life of the word incarnate was spent for men: this is the religious psychology which the master wants to instil into the leaders of his church. He chooses an example that is homely and menial, precisely because it best conveys love's humble service of souls which a priest's life is meant to be, after the pattern of his own. Just as Christ, out of love, lowered himself in the service of his own so as to save them, so the apostles in their turn, in spite of their position—nowadays we should call it their eminence in the hierarchy—will devote themselves in the ministry to the humble service of souls, out of love.

This is suggested by verses 16 and 17, which emphasise the real dignity of service, and therefore the whole idea of the apostolate: 'In very truth I tell you: There is no servant who is greater than his master, and no apostle greater than him who

sent him. Knowing this, blessed are you if you act in this way.'
That is a priest's blessedness! It is easy to see the beauty of serving
the brethren; it is more difficult to put it into practice. Jesus
knows this, and that is why he adds a blessing to the injunction
of duty and even to his own example. But the man who can
humiliate himself in practice like a slave, will be blessed from
then on in the present life, and in the future dispensation he will
have a real superiority. One is never so great in the eyes of
Jesus and never more closely united to him than when one agrees
to lower oneself further, like him (Phil. 2 : 3), to serve one's
neighbour.

ST PAUL'S TEACHING

The epistle to the Hebrews singles out two virtues proper to
the priest of the new covenant, *compassion* and *fidelity*: It was
fitting, indeed, that God—for whom and by whom all things
exist—while guiding a host of his sons to glory, should raise
the author of their salvation to the peak of perfection by the
path of suffering. In this way the Son who sanctifies and the sons
who are sanctified have a common origin. That is why he is not
ashamed to call them his brethren. . . . Since these children are
akin in having flesh and blood, he too came to share this common
bond with them. In this way he was able by his death to annihilate
the prince of death, that is the devil, and to liberate those multi-
tudes who lived as slaves under the fearful bondage of death all
their lives. It was certainly not angels that he came to rescue;
no, he came to rescue the sons of Abraham (Heb. 2 : 10–16).

We could not give too much consideration to the implications of the primary theological concept in this passage: Christ
being perfected by suffering in his mission as saviour. The

purpose of the Incarnation and the form it took would not have
been the same if Jesus had been obliged to ransom pure spirits.
In this case, by all the evidence, he would have been spared from
taking human nature and undergoing death and the passion.
But since it is men whom he intends to save and sanctify, he has
to share their state. He takes upon him their nature, that is to
say he becomes like them, not just in a limited or superficial
way but by a real and complete identification with these human
beings. Hence they truly become his brethren, notably in
suffering and in the doom of death. Now it is precisely because
by the Incarnation Jesus became capable of feeling pain and of
experiencing the pangs of death that he is set up as 'the perfect
priest'. He is the ideal saviour, if one may say so, in the sense
that he has been fitted to share the same sufferings and trials
as those whom he represents before God and to whom he brings
pardon and grace. In other words, by the Incarnation and the
crucifixion the high priest of the new covenant, having shared
the wretched state of his brethren in human nature, was able to
learn compassion. Therein lies his priestly perfection.

'Because of that, he had to make himself like his brethren in
everything, so that he might become a high priest who was both
merciful and faithful in the service of God, to make atonement
for the sins of the people. It is, in fact, because he himself has
suffered and been schooled in trials that he is able to help those
who are suffering' (Heb. 2 : 17–18). The adjective 'merciful' is
found only here and in Mt. 5 : 7 in the whole of the New
Testament. It does not mean mercy in the strict sense of forgiving the guilty, so much as compassion in the face of others'
misery. It is a real revelation! For Philo forbade the high priest
to weep at the death of his parents, the better to prove by this
insensibility that he belonged exclusively to God. The epistle
to the Hebrews, on the contrary, envisages compassion as the
first of priestly virtues; it is even the explanation it gives for the
mystery of *why God became man and suffered!*

The epistle presses the point home. It is precisely because Christ has suffered that he can bring help to men. The verb *paschō* in the perfect tense indicates not so much the historic fact of the Passion as the permanent characteristic it has left in Christ, together with its enduring validity and effectiveness. First and foremost it indicates the ever-present mercy which suffering arouses in the high priest. For he, one might translate, is 'a perpetual sufferer'. The nature of this ordeal is pin-pointed by the aorist participle *peirastheis*. It was a temptation. It refers to the ordeal of the cross and the temptation to escape it at Gethsemane (Heb. 5 : 7; cf. Mk. 14 : 16). Having experienced human weakness in the face of death, knowing the violence of moral fear and of bodily pain, our saving hero is ever ready literally to 'run to the help' of those who cry out to him when they are in the throes and are tempted to give way. In fact, our high priest has not only suffered for us, but like us. But sharing the same ordeals makes one compassionate and devoted to companions in misfortune.

This subject is so important, and this qualification for the priest of the New Testament so unexpected that our author returns to it in a new section, 4 : 14—5 : 10: 'Since we have in Jesus, the Son of God, a great high priest who is perfect, who has penetrated into heaven, let us stand fast in professing our faith. For ours is not a high priest who is incapable of feeling for us in our weaknesses; no, to be like us he suffered every weakness, except sin. Let us draw near to the throne of grace, therefore, with confidence' (4 : 14–15).

Our profession of faith centres on Jesus as the sovereign pontiff of God's people. The faithful in the new covenant have been given an authorised mediator. Their pontiff stands at God's right hand, crowned with honour and glory, so placed that his intercession is effective. Now our confidence in his help has a unique foundation from the fact that this priest is one of us by his human nature and because he knows by experience what our weakness is. *Sumpatheō*, literally, 'to suffer with another', can mean 'to share his sufferings' or 'to experience the same feelings' as the other. God, for example, as our Father, 'sympathises' with men, in the sense in which love, and even a sharing of nature, gives the power to understand and share another's affections. But sympathy also springs from a shared experience: anyone who has undergone a certain kind of suffering or tasted a certain kind of joy has a spontaneous fellow-feeling for anyone else who has done so. It was for this very reason that the Son of God sought to experience our weaknesses in his human nature. His 'weakness' is pre-eminently that of human nature subject to weariness, sorrow and death. It encompasses all the deficiencies and limitations of a created being, its natural frailty, its disconcerting mutability; everything, in fact, which in the moral order comes under the capacity of being 'tempted'.

The Bible uses the word 'trials' for the means by which God sounds man's reins and heart and makes proof of his fidelity, but which may also put him in danger. Hence the ecclesiastical sense of the word 'temptation' and the humble plea in the *Our Father*: 'Lead us not into temptation' . . . which could be fatal to us, given our weakness. Temptation (*peirasmos*) is a fundamental factor in man's religious life, a 'trial' of his faith and his love. Now Christ, Son of God though he was, had temptations. He too was put to the trial, not only in the desert and at Gethsemane—when he had to be strengthened by an angel that he might continue the struggle (*agōnia*)—but throughout his whole life, during which, apart from the material difficulties of hunger and thirst and fatigue, he endured condemnation by the Synagogue, the hatred of the Pharisees, desertion by his first converts, the fruitlessness of his preaching. He himself could describe his whole life as overshadowed by the stigma of 'temptation', in which his apostles were included: 'You are the ones who have remained faithfully by my side in my trials' (Lk. 22 : 28). If the saviour and the saved belong to the same race and enjoy the same grace (Heb. 2 : 11), they also share the same tribulations; their union and their family likeness are perfect.

This conformity of the Son of God to our state and our misery is so marked that the writer has to add a saving note: 'Except for sin.' This means not only that Christ at his weakest did not yield to temptation, but also that he never knew those enticements to evil or inclinations to sin which come from a corrupt nature. But this inherent innocence in no way lessens our Lord's abiding compassion. On the contrary, we know what a wealth of tenderness and forgiveness the saints extend to sinners; whereas sinners themselves often adopt a rigorous and harsh attitude towards the faults of their neighbours. The fact is that every sin shuts up the heart upon itself and lessens its sympathy for others. True love does the opposite, it opens wide the soul and makes it welcome all human wretchedness. In this way Christ's holiness enlarged the power of his mercy and his devotedness to 'poor sinners'.

Such is the exact measure of the greatness and misery of the priesthood of Jesus Christ. Following the pattern of the supreme high priest, every priest—set apart and dedicated to God's service—shares the weakness of those whom he has to save. If God did not appoint angels but men to intercede on behalf of sinners, it is because these mediators had to know by experience the depths of misery in the human heart and had to be capable of 'fellow-feeling'. It follows that a priest who is 'un-feeling', without the gift of sympathy, unable to be moved, has not the spirit of his priesthood. On the other hand, how closely St Paul became a faithful reproduction of his model: 'Who is weak, without my sharing his weakness? Who is tempted, without the same fire burning me and setting me on fire?' (2 Cor. 11: 29).

Faithfulness. Faithfulness is the quality required from all those who are entrusted with a responsible task (Neh. 13 : 13) or a mission, as were Abraham (Neh. 9 : 8), Moses (Heb. 3 : 2, 5), St Paul (1 Tim. 1 : 12); likewise from those appointed as steward or administrator (Lk. 14 : 42; 16 : 10; 1 Cor. 4 : 2). Under the command and at the disposal of a master, their duty is to conform to his will at every point. They are to combine therefore precision and perseverance in the fulfilment of their task in the most practical sense. These were the qualities Yahweh sought in Sadoc: 'I shall raise up to myself a faithful priest who will act according to my heart and soul' (1 Sam. 2 : 35). Now the high priest of the new covenant shows outstanding faithfulness both in his intercession before God and in his devotedness to men (Heb. 3 : 2–6). Did he not himself bear witness on the cross that he had carried out completely the work which the Father had entrusted to him? He would not give up his last breath until he had proclaimed: 'All is accomplished.' Therefore his priests will be expected to imitate his fidelity. As servants who are vigilant and zealous in fulfilling their ministry, they will never be dilettante dreamers or idle amateurs. Their meat must be 'to do the will of him that sent them and to bring his work to its conclusion' (Jn. 4 : 34), to sacrifice themselves unto death in this obedience: 'Consecrate them in faithfulness' (Jn. 17 : 17).

It is in this spirit that, for example, they will hasten to the bedside of a sick man at the first call, to pray for him (Jas. 5 : 14) and will keep most vigilant watch over the flock for whom they are responsible before God. In Heb. 13 : 17 we see the leaders of the community keeping anxious vigil for the good of souls. The verb *agrupneō*, 'to stay awake, to suffer from insomnia', well describes the depth of this apostolic care—it involves losing sleep! No-one felt this solicitude more keenly than St Paul who, after recalling the scourgings, imprisonments, shipwrecks—all the severe trials he had undergone in his endeavours to preach the gospel—adds as the supreme burden: 'This strain which daily weighs upon me: anxiety for all the Churches' (2 Cor. 11 : 28).

The grace of the priesthood. In the pastoral epistles the priest-hood is considered as a charism. Granted by God, it is trans-mitted by the imposition of hands from the presbyters and bestows all the graces that the minister of the Church needs for his personal life and for his ministry.

On several occasions St Paul exhorts Timothy not to neglect 'the gift of God which is in thee' (1 Tim. 4 : 14), since its original creation at his ordination. This grace, then, is both immanent and permanent. It is exercised in external signs: prayers, pro-phecies, etc., and is efficacious; so that to hoard it fruitlessly would be to incur a grave sin of omission. The man who receives grace must not neglect it, but is bound to bear fruit from it. The servant who hides his lord's money in the earth is punished for negligence. When one is enriched with grace by God and deputed to represent him before men, indolence is sinful. The more talents we have been given, the greater our obligations to draw profit from them (cf. Lk. 12 : 48). Our Lord expressly declared to his apostles that he had chosen them and established them that they might bring forth much fruit (cf. Jn 15 : 8, 10). St Paul singles out the grace of the priesthood itself as the power that should be set to work to produce this fruit by whole-hearted fidelity.

'I remind you again: Rouse up the gift of God which was put into you when I laid hands on you' (2 Tim. 1 : 6). The Greek verb *anazōpurein* is sometimes translated 're-animate', as Jacob was re-animated when he heard the good news about Joseph (Gen. 45 : 27), or 'revive', as when the Sunamite's child was brought to life by Eliseus (2 Kgs. 8 : 1, 5); but it means literally 'influence' (1 Macc. 13 : 7), 're-kindle,' 'fan into flame'. It is frequently used in the metaphorical sense of stirring up or re-starting; and this seems to be the shade of meaning intended here, where it is not a question of re-lighting a fire that has gone out, but rather of using the bellows to make the hearth blaze with bright flames. We must not merely refrain from extinguishing the Spirit (1 Thess. 5 : 19), but must even stir it up to increase its manifestations. This metaphor of fire applied to the action of the Holy Ghost (cf. Acts 2 : 3) in the sacrament of Holy Orders is as apt as that of water to signify his activity in the sacrament of Baptism (Tit. 3 : 6). It is no longer a question of purification, but of the light of faith and the burning zeal of charity. The priestly ministry, like that of John the Baptist, is to be a burning and a shining light (cf. Jn. 5 : 35).

Furthermore St Paul defines what he means by this gift: 'Revive the gift of God that is in you. . . . For it is not a cowardly spirit that God has given us, but a strong spirit of charity and solid good sense' (1 Tim. 1 : 6–7). For the apostle, *courage and energy, boldness and strength* are the prime qualities in a priest. This is because on the one hand they are a direct sharing in that 'power' which sums up the action of the Holy Ghost (1 Thess. 1 : 5; Gal. 3 : 5); on the other hand because he sees the ministry as uphill work and even as a battle. Weaklings could never take part in it. Hence: 'Jesus Christ made me strong when he set me up in the priesthood' (cf. 1 Tim. 1 : 12); 'Take strength from the grace which dwells in Christ Jesus' (2 Tim. 2 : 1); 'This charge, then, I give into thy hands, my son Timothy, in virtue of the prophecies that singled thee out, long ago, to support thee in fighting the good fight' (1 Tim. 1 : 18). This metaphor brings out the seriousness, the obligations, the trials and the difficulty of the apostolate in which, for soldiers in the field as St John Chrysostom says, the struggle with the enemy, the night-watches, 'fatigues' and work is continuous. But our fight is in the service of the noblest of causes and will end in victory, so long as the priest mistrusts his own strength and 'leans' on the grace of his priesthood, that is to say on the Holy Ghost, who continually works and lives in him. 'Human indeed we are, but it is in no human strength that we fight our battles. The weapons we fight with are not human weapons; they are divinely powerful, ready to pull down strongholds.

Yes, we can pull down the conceits of men, every barrier of pride which sets itself up against the true knowledge of God; we make every mind surrender to Christ's command' (2 Cor. 10 : 3–5), like a garrison that capitulates but finds salvation in surrender, because it is truth which gives freedom (Jn. 8 : 32).

Charity. Together with this power, the priest received on the day of his ordination 'a spirit of charity' in the service of his neighbour. This is to be the key inspiration of his ministry, whatever form that may take. 'As for thee, O man of God, aim at charity' (1 Tim. 6 : 11; 2 Tim. 2 : 22). 'Be a model to the faithful, in word and deed, by your charity and faith' (1 Tim. 4 : 12). The priest should appear as a revelation of divine love. In his own person he teaches souls what it is to love. Has he to rule and command? In this his fundamental intention must always be to promote an increase of charity in the Church: 'The aim of all commandments is charity' (1 Tim. 1 : 5). This assumes that the priest lives intensely by this love, and St Paul is surely revealing the innermost depths of his apostolic heart when he confesses: *Caritas Christi urget nos* (2 Cor. 5 : 4). This might well be translated, 'The love which Christ has for us and we for him locks us in its embrace.' It is a holdfast, a pressure which is also a spur. It exerts a kind of internal violence which will not allow the apostle to be self-reflexive or to consider his own tastes and comfort, still less to remain inert. It is an over-mastering power that drives him to sacrifice himself without measure, to make himself all things to all men. As Christ's deputy, his plans, his words, his actions, his fears and hopes and joys are governed by an ardent charity that does not seek his own interest but solely the good of his neighbour.

Prudence also is clearly indispensable to the head of a community. St Paul thinks of it as the spirit of moderation or of self-discipline (cf. 1 Tim. 1 : 7), which combines with charity to control the exercise of authority. It is as foreign to harshness as it is to weakness, avoiding equally bitter bigotry and reckless enthusiasm. Prudence enjoys clear-sighted judgment—'the Lord will give you understanding in all things' (2 Tim. 2 : 7) —and takes into account the differences between individual subjects, in age, sex or social standing (1 Tim. 5 : 1–3; Tit. 2 : 1–10). It gives its decisions firmly and clearly and always knows how to make itself respected (1 Tim. 4 : 12; Tit. 2 : 15).

According to 1 Tim. 3 : 2 this spirit of moderation and thoughtfulness is a criterion for a vocation. Without good sense and sound judgment a man should not be admitted to Orders. The priest has to stand out from the crowd by the rightness of his ideas combined with well-balanced behaviour and marked self-control. For this reason prudence must be partnered by *temperance*, which in the first place requires an equable temperament. With a horror of violence or of raising a storm by his intervention, the pastor of souls should never display bad temper. Considerate and polite, he takes no notice of hostile or hurtful remarks. In his role of peacemaker his business is to reconcile enmity: 'a servant of God must not give battle; but be gentle towards all' (2 Tim. 2 : 24). Faced with enemies, his meekness is literally disarming.

The *purity* of his life is bound up with the good name of the Church: 'We commend ourselves as God's ministers . . . by purity' (2 Cor. 6 : 6). Men who have been married more than once are not to be admitted to the priesthood (1 Tim. 3 : 2). The Christian who, having lost his wife, has not re-married, has given proof of sufficient control of his heart and senses and of his appreciation of the religious freedom of his state, 'how he may best attend the Lord without distraction' (1 Cor. 7 : 35). He has shown himself capable of dedicating himself without hindrance to the service of all. It is a case, then, of a religious consecration: 'Keep thyself chaste' (1 Tim. 5 : 22), without defilement, like a temple consecrated to God. It was in this spirit that the first clerics began very soon and spontaneously to vow themselves to celibacy: 'How many in holy orders remain continent and have chosen God as the spouse of their souls' (Tertullian, *Exhortation to chastity*, 12).

Preaching the word. Christ came to preach (Mk. 1 : 35) and people expected him to teach them all things (Jn. 4 : 25). The apostles gave themselves up to 'the service of the word' (Acts 6 : 4), since 'faith comes by hearing' (Rom. 10 : 14–17; cf. 2 Cor. 5 : 18–20). If this preaching promulgates the mystery of salvation (1 Tim. 3 : 16; Tit. 1 : 3), then the preachers are exercising a truly priestly function: they are transmitting sacred realities. For this purpose they have received the spirit of truth (Jn. 15 : 26; cf. Acts 1 : 8; 1 Pet. 1 : 12) and their aim is to offer those they have converted as a holy oblation to God (Rom. 12 : 1; 15 : 15–16; Phil. 2 : 17; 4 : 18).

In the pastoral epistles, St Paul insists most particularly on the necessity of this doctrinal instruction. When he introduces Timothy and Titus into the hierarchy of the Church it is primarily for the work of preaching: 'You must speak' (Tit. 2 : 15); 'Preach the word' (2 Tim. 4 : 2); 'Attend to reading, to exhortation, to teaching' (1 Tim. 4 : 13). In his turn Timothy will lay hands on new ministers who are capable of instructing the faithful: 'What you have learned from me or from many who can witness to it, give to the keeping of men you can trust; men who will know how to teach it to others' (2 Tim. 2 : 2; cf. 1 Tim. 5 : 22). It is not necessary for the preacher to be naturally eloquent, still less for him to have degrees. But he must possess a minimum of intellectual capacity and an interest in things of the mind, with an understanding that is alive to doctrinal problems and capable of forming a personal opinion. He must be able to make a decision on disputed points, to define and promulgate the truth, to refute error and, should occasion arise, to refute those who deny the truth (1 Tim. 3 : 2; Tit. 1 : 9; 2 Tim. 2 : 24). In effect, since 'God wills all men to be saved and to come to the knowledge of the truth' (1 Tim. 2 : 4; cf. Tit. 1 : 1), so the candidate for the priesthood should be ready to put forward 'the word of God' (Tit. 2 : 5; 2 Tim. 2 : 9, 4 : 2) or 'the word of truth' (2 Tim. 2 : 15), 'the sound principles of our Lord Jesus Christ' (1 Tim. 6 : 3; Tit. 2 : 8; 2 Tim. 1 : 13), 'the words of faith' (1 Tim. 4 : 6). He should be prompt to reiterate the traditional teaching (2 Tim. 2 : 14) and to give unshakable witness (Tit. 3 : 8). Just as 'Christ has given light to life' (2 Tim. 1 : 10), so the priest throws light on the doctrine of salvation and makes it shine out. This is one of the points by which the priest's fidelity to his vocation is best realised: 'By instructing thy brethren thou wilt show thyself a true servant of Jesus Christ, thriving on the principles of that faith whose wholesome doctrine thou hast followed' (1 Tim. 4 : 6).

We can see that preaching means the handing on of a tradition, of a teaching already determined; but first of all it involves the explanation of sacred scripture. 'It is for thee to hold fast by the doctrine handed on to thee, the charge committed to thee; thou knowest well from whom that commission came; thou canst remember the holy learning thou hast been taught from childhood upwards. This will train thee up for salvation, through the faith which rests in Christ Jesus. Everything in the scripture has been divinely inspired, and has its uses: to instruct us, to expose our errors, to correct our faults, to educate us in holy living; so God's servant will become a master of his craft, and each noble task that comes will find him ready for it' (2 Tim. 3 : 14–17).

The Bible, the foundation of the faith, is the source-book for preaching and even for the whole ministry: 'All the words written long ago were written for our instruction; we were to derive hope from that message of endurance and courage which the scriptures bring us' (Rom. 15 : 4). These sacred documents, in fact, are inspired by God, whence comes their universal efficaciousness. They have the abiding power of communicating God's wisdom, that is to say of nourishing and educating Christian life. If the priest—another Christ—is the instrument for saving the world, then by definition he must be the man of the Bible and thereby 'equipped for every good work'. He has, so to speak, only to act as a sounding-board for this divine word, to proclaim it like a herald, so that it may come to the knowledge of each generation of mankind.

For this purpose he studies it, makes it part of himself, explains its meaning and uses it for all occasions. He uses it both for teaching in church and in private conversations in which he consoles the afflicted, encourages the faint-hearted and spurs devout souls towards perfection. But his first duty is to 'dispense correctly the word of truth' (2 Tim. 2 : 15). He has no right to substitute his own ideas for the divine thought enshrined in the texts. If he has to explain and adapt them to everyone's understanding, he must take care while doing so to safeguard 'sound doctrine in the life of faith' (Tit. 1 : 13). This means that, as 'teacher in faith and truth' (1 Tim. 2 : 7), the priest should maintain strict orthodoxy (1 Tim. 1 : 5; 2 Tim. 1 : 5) and his integrity should be above suspicion. Is he not the mouthpiece of a church which is the pillar and support of truth? (1 Tim 3 : 15). He will therefore be concerned to 'shun foolish novelties and stand fast in the doctrine thou hast learned' (1 Tim. 4 : 6–15; 6 : 20; 2 Tim. 3 : 14), to preserve the 'sound deposit' (2 Tim. 1 : 14).

This preservation of pure faith against all contamination from error will be all the more called for as we draw nearer to the final period of time, which will be characterised by the reign of falsehood: 'The time will surely come, when men will grow tired of sound doctrine, always itching to hear something fresh; and so they will provide themselves with a continuous succession of new teachers, as the whim takes them, turning a deaf ear to the truth, bestowing their attention on fables instead' (2 Tim. 4 : 3–4). For minds that are infected with an itch for novelties the traditional truth seems insipid, as manna did of old to the children of Israel, and they are only too ready to make shipwreck of the faith (1 Tim. 1 : 19).

Whether in dispensing grace or in preaching the faith, the priest-apostle, according to the New Testament, comes forth as God's ambassador, a saviour from sin and error, another Christ. That is why he must reproduce in himself the features of the incarnate word. 'As thou hast sent me into the world, I in my turn have sent them into the world; and I dedicate myself for their sakes, that they too may be dedicated through the truth' (Jn. 17 : 18–19).

XII

Love and Marriage in the Old Testament[1]

Jean-Paul Audet O.P.

BY WAY of introduction a few words of warning seem necessary since the subject is so much less simple than might appear at first sight. To begin with it is not easy to avoid anachronism. There is the danger of projecting our own ideas into our sources. It is obvious to everybody that we are widely separated from the patriarchs, from Moses and the Prophets, both in time and space. The difficulty of accurately assessing the consequences of this obvious fact cannot be exaggerated. It is not merely institutions which have changed, but also habits of thought.

Now it is always an extremely delicate manœuvre to pass from one habit of thought to another, whether it be in the temporal or the spatial sense. In fact we are bound to fail to some extent; a certain degree of misapprehension concerning the past is inevitable. My task will be to prevent in the first place this misapprehension from distorting the essential truth of the matter.

Then again, one might easily give way to another temptation: it is easier to give a kind of global interpretation of the texts, as if everything read in the Bible about love and marriage was, without more ado, to be called 'biblical', and thereby be regarded as unchangeable. Actually it is the intention of the authors or editors which is decisive here. The limits within which each of them confined his attention cannot lightly be exceeded. Indeed these limits stand as a warning that outside of

---

[1] First published in *Scripture*, 1958, pp. 65–83.

them the field of inspiration has already been left behind. The weight, crushing at times, of the problems connected with our existing Christian consciousness is no excuse for us to search at random in the Bible for support which it was not God's intention to give us therein. The Bible is not our only resort. We cannot misuse it to cover our own liabilities. Whatever its value be, the bearing which the Bible has on the problem of marriage does not amount to the same thing as supplying us with a ready-made solution from every point of view. We shall far better lay hold of the real enrichment it is capable of providing, by a correctly adjusted attitude towards it.

Thus it is to the point to emphasise right from the beginning that it would be profitless, for instance, to seek from the Bible any reply other than an indirect one, to the many varied problems which follow from the appreciable raising of the average age at which young people enter marriage. The Bible is not familiar with our long-drawn-out period of adolescence, but it must immediately be said that this was above all a matter of a particular civilisation and culture, and not of a privileged position in God's eyes. Hence we must not be too hasty to give the name 'biblical' to everything which perhaps in a very ordinary way is found 'in the Bible'. A host of misunderstandings still arise from day to day, both in the theological and pastoral spheres, as a result of not observing this modest distinction.

Moreover it must be acknowledged, in fairness to everybody, that whilst it is apparently elementary as an abstract formula, such discrimination proves much less simple in individual cases. To confine ourselves to the basic elements of our subject, nothing is more difficult than to separate, in the view of love presented in the Bible, the truly lasting qualities, capable of being smoothly assimilated into the Christian sacrament, and the merely circumstantial qualities which are consequently more or less ephemeral. The eternal emotion which is love has none the less a whole history behind it, a history which is very far from being a mere repetition of the same attitudes, actions and words from generation to generation.[1]

On the other hand it is also possible that the full significance of a teaching, of a fact or of a certain state of affairs implied in the Bible should for us, at the present time, really go beyond the narrower perspective to which the sacred author confined himself. We can look back on the past and draw on the profound experience which centuries of existence have given to the Church, and this is in certain cases a positive advantage allowing us to judge the true proportions of what existed in the past. Some fundamental elements of the family system then existing will thus come under our consideration, in spite of the fact that the sacred authors do not appear to have explicitly given them their attention.

Even thus abridged, the subject is still vast. Without going into too many details, we shall have dealt with what is essential if, after an important preliminary observation on the triple relationship of individual, family and people in Jewish antiquity, we afterwards sift out, from our own standpoint, whatever may be gathered from the first two narratives of Genesis relating to the creation of man and woman; then from the great prophetical image of the love of Yahweh and Israel (cf. Osee), and finally from the general meaning of the Canticle of Canticles, which reflects betrothal, and other customs connected in various ways with marriage, before the post-exilic Sages made of this song, then falling into oblivion, a text which was henceforth almost completely severed from the concrete circumstances which had given it birth.

Individual, family and people The tenth chapter of Genesis is doubtless one of the least read in the Bible. The specialists with professional interest have given it the title 'Table of the

[1] We are given a glimpse of this history, for the period relatively close to us, by D. de Rougemont, *L'amour et l'Occident* (Présences), Paris 1939.

Nations'. They examine it from different points of view: historical, ethnological, topographical and so on. It is clear, however, that the editor's final intention was quite different, and that it is a grave error from the theological point of view to rate this passage as an unimportant curiosity. I do not wish to exaggerate, but I find it hard to believe that we can really understand Genesis without giving close attention to this long genealogy of Noah's three sons. It is hardly necessary to add that if the Book of Genesis is badly interpreted, it is our understanding of the remainder (including certain essential parts of the new Testament) which suffers.

In effect, the genealogy of the tenth chapter of Genesis is inseparable in the mind of the editor (priestly tradition), not only from all the documents which are of the same kind or related, and which are met with in abundance in the Pentateuch, but also from the two accounts of creation and original blessing themselves (Gen. 1–3). Now what is it that begins to take shape here? It is the whole structure of the story of salvation, and hence the whole internal order and unity of God's plan, as understood by the faith of Israel and inherited by Christianity.

In fact it is no mere chance nor simple literary convenience which produced immediately prior to the chronicles of Abraham's lineage an account of the creation of man and woman integrated on the one hand in an account of the beginnings of the world which is their home and accompanied on the other hand by an explanation of the existence of good and evil in human destiny by the first blessing and curse.[1] In this vision the first couple (Gen. 1 : 1–2, 4a), or Adam and Eve (2 : 4b–3 : 24),

[1] 'Curse' is a word to be understood with reserve and in a relative sense, allowing for the well-known tendency of the Jewish mind towards violent contrasts. In Hebrew strong convictions are vigorously expressed. There is no grey, but black and white without any intermediate shades. Thus the 'curse' boils down to what is in fact a more or less attenuated blessing: see, for example, the 'curse' pronounced against Cain (Gen. 4 : 11–16); and the 'blessing' of Esau which follows that of Jacob (Gen. 27 : 27–9, 39–40).

form the one and only genealogical root of mankind. Hence their descendants constitute a single family within which, subject to unending variations of quality and extent, the original blessing and curse are passed on as an inheritance.

Now the first blessing, as effective in the thought of the editor as the creative word itself, is that of fruitfulness: 'And God created man to his own image; to the image of God he created him. Male and female he created them. And God blessed them, saying: increase, and multiply, and fill the earth . . .' (Gen. 1 : 27–8). At this point we can understand the profound reason which led the editors of Genesis to develop their accounts within a genealogical framework. It is their pondered faith and hope which spontaneously develop within the conviction of the unity of origin of the great human family.

So the genealogy of Noah's sons in Gen. 10 is far from being a merely accessory curiosity which the reader might leave on one side. On the contrary, it emphasises the primary thing to be understood. It is, if you wish, the point where the framework of the building has been left exposed to view. Moreover, with this in mind, you need do no more than read any chronicle in the Old Testament prior to the period of the monarchy to realise the persistence of this phenomenon. The frame is always a genealogical one. It may be more obvious in those accounts in Genesis which precede the history of the patriarchs (ch. 1–11). This is natural. But it is never lost sight of in what follows. Its ultimate meaning likewise remains always the same.

In point of fact it is only after the setting up of the monarchy that a dynastic framework, comparable to that found in all the chronicles of the ancient East, becomes possible in Israel.[1] It is common knowledge that this plan was adopted in particular by the editor of the book of Kings. However, it is relevant to notice the fact that the relatively late adoption of the dynastic

[1] Cf. P. van der Meer, *The Chronology of Ancient Western Asia and Egypt*, Leiden 1955, passim.

framework had a purpose, theological or literary, far more restricted than had been that of the ancient genealogical framework. Actually the latter was never ousted by the former.

I add, in order to put everything in its proper place, that this genealogical framework within which the faith of Israel pictured the basic history of mankind, is still not rendered void in every respect by the chronological (sidereal) framework, more or less definite and all embracing, which we can now superimpose on it. From the theological point of view, the only plan which is truly connatural to the story of salvation as the sacred authors understood it, remains the genealogical one of which Genesis gives us the essential outlines.

This is seen clearly in the New Testament also. It is the ancient genealogical framework which is everywhere presupposed, deep down, in the elaboration and continuation of God's plan. Jesus, who is of 'the house of David', announces to the 'house of Israel' the 'good news' of God's kingdom. Now the house of Israel obviously means the descendants of Jacob, as a long history of faith, suffering, mercy, grace and hope had modelled them. But the descendants of the patriarchs from generation to generation evoked the passing on of the inheritance of blessings and promises. The genealogical framework is evident.

It shows itself even more clearly in several particular places. The genealogy which Luke gives after his account of the Baptism of Jesus (Lk. 3 : 23–38) is an imposing résumé of the whole of ancient history, considered as a long preparation for the gospel. It is, again, quite remarkable how the ascending genealogy of the third gospel, contrary to the genealogy by descent of Matthew which begins at Abraham (Mt. 1 : 1–16), goes right back to the first man and woman, and from them to God himself. We are thus at one stroke brought back to the creation accounts in the very first pages of Genesis. It would be impossible to underline in a more striking manner the fact that the 'good news' announced by Jesus was the continuation of the original blessing, beyond the privileges of Abraham's descendants.

The thought of Paul himself also, every time it comes up against the problem of the universality of the gospel, moves within the genealogical framework familiar to the whole of ancient tradition. This fact stands out particularly in the epistle to the Romans and in the epistles of the captivity (Eph., Phil., Col.). I shall quote one text only, which I think is perfectly clear: 'Remember that of old, you the Gentiles in the flesh (a reference to circumcision) . . . you were at that time without Christ (without a Messiah), shut out from the community of Israel (the 'house of Israel'), not belonging to the alliance of the promise, and having neither hope nor God in this world! Well now, at the present time, in Christ (the Messiah) Jesus, you who were formerly afar off, you have been brought near, thanks to the blood of Christ. For it is he who is our peace, he who out of these two (Jews and Gentiles) has made one people, destroying the barrier which was separating them, doing away, in his flesh, with the enmity (fostered by) the law of precepts with its decrees (the law of Moses, the precepts of which singled out the Jewish people and separated it from other peoples), in order to mould (*lit.* create) the two into a single new man (the second Adam) and to bring about peace between them and reconcile them with God. He came to proclaim peace, peace for yourselves who were afar off, and peace too for those who were near. . . . In this way, then, you are no longer foreigners nor visitors; you are fellow citizens of the saints (Israel), you are of the House of God' (Eph. 2 : 11–19).

This extraordinary vision of the fulfilment of God's plan could not, from our point of view, have ended with more characteristic expressions. It is no longer merely Israel, but also the peoples scattered from the beginning (Gen. 11) and hence excluded from the inheritance and the promise (Gen. 12 ff.), who are now reconciled and, so to speak, gathered together, 'thanks to the blood of Christ', in the one and only 'House of God'. All is restored. There is now but one God and Father of all, a single 'house' of the saints, in which there are neither foreigners nor guests, a single new blessing, a single inheritance promised to the offspring of this humanity now re-created in Christ. The name 'church' is not mentioned, but it is quite clear that it is there. It is itself the new 'people of God'.[1]

In spite of appearances I have not forgotten my subject. We are at the heart of the matter. That is in no way a paradox: it is a question of distinguishing various points of view. When we say 'family' we think of marriage, father, mother, children, education and so on. The human group towards which our attention is spontaneously attracted is one which is reduced to its ultimate limit: a limit which, as a matter of fact, is the next thing to the individual. For us, what a marriage does is to 'found' a home, to give birth to a family. Before one has gone far from the latter, moreover, the ties of relationship begin to be strained, and soon snap completely. Thus family problems are in our eyes immediately connected with individual problems: to a large extent they are reciprocal. Beyond the family unit whose limits are precisely defined by the fruitfulness of the marriage in the first generation (or near enough to it), the assimilation of the individual into higher groupings ordinarily comes about for us along lines other than those resulting from birth, such as school, trade, profession, nationality, international association or religion.

But it is to our world that these factors belong, not, generally

---

[1] 'People' should be taken here in the sense it generally has in the Bible, especially when it is a question of Israel. The first implication of the term is that of a common ancestor. A 'people' has first a 'father', then an 'inheritance': land, customs, laws, institutions, traditions, etc. But it is descent from one single ancestor which is the deciding factor among all the rest. These ideas, it must be admitted, have become somewhat foreign to our way of thinking.

speaking, to the world of the ancients, and in particular to that of Israel.[1] There have been in the meantime enormous changes in the forms of civilisation, and culture and habit of thought. The convergence of these has gradually led the individual to take upon himself an increasingly greater measure of autonomy. This autonomy has brought with it his present state, which could be defined as one of freedom in individual isolation. Numerous links have thus been broken. The family could not escape this evolution and it has followed suit. Many and varied historical circumstances have progressively brought it nearer to the kind of existence proper to the individual, or perhaps rather to the kind of existence proper to those individuals who were its own children, now emancipated at an increasingly tender age, certainly in their own minds, if not always in the mind of the law. This is the stage at which we have now arrived. But a fact which must be recognised is that this evolution has brought us a long way; in fact, we have moved from a time in history when the opposite seemed the natural thing, namely that the family should develop into a people, and when, inversely, it was hardly intelligible that a people should have no father to whom it could appeal.

It is above all from this point of view, and not from ours, that the faith and reason of Israel regarded the institution of marriage. We cannot forget this if we are intent on properly assimilating what they have to offer us. It is against this background of the family becoming a people that Israel's faith and reason most effectively prepared for the Church. In the course of the evolution which led towards the latter there were in fact discovered, little by little, some of the precious things on which Christian hope will continue to nourish itself: the fatherhood of God, the adoption, the new and eternal alliance, the rights of the first-born

[1] It goes without saying that I am speaking here of an antiquity to which we are more directly indebted for what we have become: that of the Middle and Near East, Greek and Roman antiquity.

Christ (Rom. 8 : 28–30; Col. 1 : 15, 18), the promise which cannot fail, the blessing and the inheritance. In order to understand ourselves and sustain our fidelity we could do no better here than 'bear in mind the rock from which we have been hewn'.

Nevertheless there exists, even in Jewish antiquity, a counterpoise which assures the balance. The family which, at one extreme, tends to take to itself the kind of existence proper to the people, is nevertheless not absorbed by the people: it becomes integrated therein. More precisely, the counterweight is provided by that aspect of the family under which it appears as the common life and mutual love of a man and woman. It is understandable, furthermore, that in this respect marriage should have been conducive, after a fashion, to a reversal of the first tendency. For if the family, by the extension of its fruitfulness, tends in certain circumstances to form a people, it is nonetheless manifest that through the inevitable renewal of conjugal relations in each generation, it tends at the same time to create and keep in being more circumscribed units: first of all in the union of husband and wife, then in that of father, mother, and their immediate descendants.

In this respect I think it is a remarkable fact that the faith of Israel, so expansive over the first factor (the people), should have had so little to tell us about the second (married partners). This difference is a good indication of where attention was principally focused. The family is first and foremost the people, and in a very special way the people *par excellence*, namely the posterity of Abraham, Isaac and Jacob, of which, in a sense, Yahweh is the real father.

However it is probably not less significant that on the rare occasions when ancient Jewish tradition felt the need to express its basic concept of marriage, it should have chosen to do so in its two accounts of creation and original blessing (Gen. 1–3). This displays the universality and grandeur of this concept to the full. In the genealogical framework of Genesis it is obviously not by chance that marriage is brought to the fore at the same time as the very act which, on God's side, gives birth to the great human family. The two aspects are on a par.

The creation of man and woman Nevertheless it is important to take a closer look at these facts. Genesis begins with two accounts of the creation. It is quite permissible to present them in the aggregate if one's purpose is limited. But the proceeding carries with it a great risk of confusion. It is much better for our subject to distinguish what really is distinct. The two accounts do in fact belong to literary traditions which are more or less independent, and whose individual characters are now fairly well defined. Each of these traditions has its distinctive preferences, manner, style and above all its own points of view. The first account of creation (Gen. 1 : 1–2, 4a) is worked out within the framework of the six days of the week and a seventh day, the sabbath, as a day of rest. The second account (Gen. 2 : 4b–25) is composed within a framework which is no longer temporal, but 'geographical', that of the 'earthly paradise', and it is interwoven with an explanation of the general distribution of good and evil, blessing and curse, in the human condition (Gen. 3 : 1–24).

For our particular purpose here we must notice the very definite difference of intention in both editors. The first treats at some length of the creation of heaven and earth, and passes quite quickly over the creation of man. The second, on the contrary, treats at length of the creation of man, and is content with a few schematic references to the origin of the rest of the world. But there is one point which is perhaps even more typical of the difference of intention in the work of each editor, and this is the creation of man and woman, conjoined in the first and separated in the second.

The texts are well known, but perhaps it will not be amiss to examine them once again. The first account reads as follows: '(On the sixth day) God said: let us make man to our image, in our likeness, and let him be master of the fish in the sea, of the birds of the heavens, of the domestic animals, and of the whole earth, and of all the reptiles which crawl upon the earth. And God created man to his own image: to the image of God he created him: he created them male and female. Then God blessed them and said to them: be fruitful, multiply, fill the earth and bring it into subjection; rule over the fish in the sea, the birds of the heavens, and over all the beasts which crawl upon the earth. . . . Now God saw all that he had made, and lo! it was very good' (Gen. 1 : 26–31).

You will have noticed the choice of words and the gradual unfolding of the main idea. In the first part of the text the subject is 'man' only, without any explicit distinction of sex. It is 'man' thus regarded who is created 'to the image of God'.[1] The underlying conception would be best expressed, perhaps, along this line of argumentation: God, inasmuch as he is the creator of everything, is obviously also its master. But 'man' created by God has received from him a share in his sovereignty as it were; he is, in fact, to some extent master of the earth, his dwelling-place. This obvious and explicitly stated quality: 'Man' is master in his own dwelling-place, leads further to the mention of that more mysterious quality which explains it: if 'man' is master in his own dwelling-place as God is master of the universe, it is because he must have in him, from his very

---

[1] 'In our likeness' is an emphatic repetition with apparently no special meaning beyond a reinforcement of the first formula 'to our image'. The expression does not aim at evoking anything with a precise ontological structure: body, soul, intellect, will, liberty, etc. Rather it tends to bring into relief the features of human beings as a whole, compared with the lower creatures of which 'man' is master, and compared with God who is their creator. It defines a situation rather than an essence. An analogous expression may be found in Ps. 8 : 6. Moreover the idea is the same.

H

origin, some 'likeness' to his creator. Hence the words: 'man'
was created 'to the image of God'. Moreover, from our present
point of view, it is important to note that no further determination is expressed by the narrator: it is 'man', in the organic
unity of the two sexes, inasmuch as both exercise a joint sovereignty over the earth on which they live, who is created 'to the
image of God'. As regards this divine likeness, then, the body
is not excluded from it or simply left on one side, as perhaps
one might be inclined to think. In the writer's intention, what
has been made in the image of God is the total being of man and
woman, as static individuals, no doubt, but also and still more
in that active union through which both exercise as stewards
what the author calls their rule over the earth, regarded, in a
sense, as their inheritance.

Such at least is the natural sense of the expressions used, due
regard being had to the literary form of the account as a whole.
Moreover in this way an explanation is found without any
difficulty, for a transition which otherwise comes as much more
of a shock: 'God created man in his own image: in the image of
God he created him; he created *them male and female*'.[1] It is
quite clear that the narrator found nothing incongruous in the
connection he established. We must therefore assume that the
perspective in his thought did not change as it developed. 'Man'
created 'in the image of God' was then, in actual fact, as we have
suggested, *man and woman*, to whom the account later gives an
assurance of the double blessing of fruitfulness and domination.
'Then God blessed them and said to them: be fruitful, multiply,
fill the earth, and bring it into subjection.' All this is perfectly
worked out and forms one whole.

There is a shade of meaning here which should not escape
our attention. Idiomatically, the phrase which we translate

---

[1] In Hebrew the etymology of the terms, which was possibly still
influencing linguistic usage, has reference to the sexually morphological
differences between man and woman.

'God blessed them and said to them' should be understood as
'God blessed them in the following words'. Hence what follows
is not strictly speaking a command, as it is usually taken to be.
It is above all a blessing, which is something quite different.
This idea finds more ready acceptance with the realisation that
a similar blessing of fruitfulness (but without mention of
'domination') has already been imparted to fish, birds and
reptiles (Gen. 1 : 22). In fact, in the mind of the narrator the
'blessings' are exactly parallel to the creative words: 'Let there
be light . . . Let there be a firmament . . .', and produce a like
effect; or if you wish, the blessings carry on the creation, passing
from the plane of being to that of action. The relation of cause
and effect remains the same, only its modality is changed, from
the human standpoint. Having created the first man and woman
in his own image, God by blessing them proclaims, equivalently,
his intention of carrying on the work begun, both in them and
in their descendants. This work will go on in this way, following
the same lines, without alteration or interruption. The word of
blessing is not less than the creative word: the image of God
which was present at the beginning will also be present at the
end.

It must also be emphasised that the blessing of the first man
and woman is not solely a blessing of fruitfulness. This is
doubtless to the fore, and it is natural in the context. But there
is something more and it should not pass unnoticed: 'Bring
(the earth) into subjection, and rule over the fish in the sea, the
birds of the heavens and over all the beasts which crawl upon
the earth.' The meaning the narrator wished to give these words
of subjection imposed on the earth and of rule over the animal
world certainly bears upon human activity insofar as this carries
on the creation. The perspective is vast and one may suppose
that the expressions chosen by the narrator are deliberately
vague. The man and woman are blessed not only in that fruitful
union by which they are to fill the earth and which will give

birth to the human family, but also in that union, fruitful too in its own way, by which they will *together* make the earth minister to their needs. Thus in every respect the blessing is not an individual but a common one. It is a man and woman, *by their joint activity*, who will be masters of the 'house' bestowed by God on their race. In this way too the blessing appears once more as a correlative of the creation. What has been made in the image of God to occupy the earth and bring it into subjection is a man and a woman not isolated from one another but together. The context of the thought here, for creation as for blessing, is that of marriage and the home.

The second account, for its part, far from abandoning this perspective, seems rather to accentuate it by giving the creation a more domestic and intimate atmosphere. The majestic 'geography' of Eden with its spring and its four rivers does not prevent it being a garden of human proportions; we have the impression that we could make the round of all the trees in a single day. Such a 'geography' is obviously not descriptive. It might well be attributed to the poetic impressionism of the East. Nevertheless it goes without saying that it has a purpose, namely that of suggesting the ideal state of affairs within the limits of the human condition which, in the narrator's mind, is the most evident sign of God's favour. It was in this flawless garden that Yahweh put 'man' to cultivate and preserve it. You remember what follows: the reflection of Yahweh that 'It is not good that man should be alone; I must make him a helper who will be suited to him'; the survey of the animals by their master, who imposes names on them and yet finds no suitable helper; the man's sleep during which Yahweh takes from him a 'rib', out of which he shapes woman; the introduction of this woman to the man by Yahweh, and the exclamation: 'Here is the one, this time, who is bone of my bones, and flesh of my flesh. She will be called woman ('*iššah*) because she has been taken out of man ('*iš*),' with the editor's final comment: 'This is why man leaves his father and his mother, to join himself to his wife, and the two become one single flesh.'

The object of the account is so complex that in part it falls outside our subject. It cannot, moreover, be studied except through images and symbols whose associations now partly escape us. Nevertheless one thing seems certain, and starting from this we can reach a suitable explanation of the rest. What we have here is the account of a beginning: man and woman have been created by God. But the ways they have been made are thought of as distinct and separate in virtue of various circumstances, of which the principal is that man is taken from the 'dust' of the earth whereas woman is taken from a 'rib' of the man.[1] Hence it is clear that if the basic intention of the account

---

[1] To us, a 'rib' is very simply a lateral bone. Consequently, in our representation, 'ribs' go by pairs. Moreover, the function of the 'ribs', as we see them, is essentially to protect vital organs in the body. But we must refrain from thinking, at the outset, that such a representation was also that of the ancient cultures of the Near East in general, and of the culture of ancient Israel in particular. Research in historical anthropology shows, I believe, that many ancient cultures actually saw the 'rib' as a circular bone: that is, they saw the 'rib' as an anatomically and physiologically complex structure which included *both* lateral bones, tying up at the back with the vertebra as part of the spine, and tying up again in front with the sternum as counterpart of the backbone. Accordingly, these cultures counted seven, and apparently sometimes eight 'ribs' in the human body, not twenty-four, as we do. Further, from a functional point of view, the same cultures saw the 'rib' as directly and intimately connected with both phenomena of respiration and generation: that is, they saw the 'rib' not only as playing a vital role of protection of the breath-soul (the Hebrew *nepheš*) whose seat and centre of diffusion were thought to be in the chest, but also as playing an even more important part, through the vertebra, in the transmission of the life-soul (the Hebrew *rûah*) from generation to generation, the seat and source of the life-soul fluid (the 'seed') being located in the brain of the male head. Thus, in this view, far from being a rather insignificant bone, the 'rib' was, on the contrary, the one fundamental bone of the human body. Hence the quite natural idea of the woman being 'built', as it were, upon the foundation of the man's 'rib'. Again, underlying this last idea is, of course, the more familiar conception of the woman as an 'auxiliary' to man, dominated by him both in the specific function of the transmission of

is directed towards the origin of man and woman, its secondary object must be to render an account, through this origin, of their mutual relations in the context of domestic life.

But what special associations were, in the editor's mind, connected with man being created before woman on the one hand, and on the other with woman's being taken out of the man? It is hard to tell with certainty. The total effect of the account suggests, however, that the editor's main idea was to ascribe to God, as to its first origin, the mysterious attraction which draws man and woman towards each other; at the same time, following contemporary ideas, he regards it as more or less established that woman is to a certain extent dependent upon man within the circle of domestic life. Love, anyway, could not be surrounded by a more exalted yet calm atmosphere. In order to gain a balanced appreciation of this faith and give it its due, it may perhaps be well to recall that at the time when the Genesis account was drawn up the oriental pantheon abounded in erotic legends, and that of all the nations of antiquity Israel alone did not deify love. Indeed Israel does not seem even to have personified it, as, for example, she did in the case of 'Wisdom'. It was one of her noblest traits to regard love soberly as a good which man and woman held from God by their common origin.

To a great extent then the two accounts of the creation of man and woman overlap each other, although each has in part a distinct objective. Their common context is that of conjugal and domestic life. In actual fact Jewish tradition did not consider here, properly speaking, a creation of 'man', understood as

'life' from the individual to his lineage, and in the general structure of domestic and social life.—In connection with Gen. 2: 21, V. Scheil, S. N. Kramer and others have already pointed out that the same ideogram *T I* is used, in Sumerian, to represent both 'life' and the 'rib'. I would suggest, further, that the well-known Egyptian *ankh*, the 'sign of life' (the so-called 'ansated cross') is nothing else than a stylised representation of a human 'rib', seen as the fundamental 'bone of life'.

'human being', with the implications which our western culture might give to this expression. Jewish tradition, very organic and very concrete, was not disposed to split up man into isolated components. In its eyes 'man' was not abstractly a 'rational being', but in a much more comprehensive way a man and woman together, in those conditions of existence determined by the complementary nature of their sex and by their effective union inside the family circle. It is 'man' thus understood whom the first account shows to us as created in the image of God, and whose love is hallowed by the second account. But in the minds of both narrators 'creation' is the inauguration of destiny. Hence in the first account, that blessing imparted by God to the first man and woman, and in the second account, in continuity with creation, that division between man and woman of responsibility for the whole field of human activity on this earth which is their common inheritance and their common abode. Hence finally the assurance, discernible everywhere but more obvious in certain places, that such a destiny has received in its very origin a goodness against which nothing will prevail, not even the Fall: 'God saw all that he had made, and lo! it was very good' (Gen. 1 : 31).

The love of Yahweh and Israel. It is clear that the prophets from Osee onward had inherited from the past a deep and spontaneous conviction of this original goodness.[1] Consequently, they felt no real difficulty in introducing the image of a love relationship between Yahweh and Israel. It was an impressive reappearance, though not intentional, of the representation, in the first creation account, of man and woman created in the

[1] This 'goodness' is not to be taken in a vaguely moral sense, as if there were question of a simple 'rightness' of things, understood in terms of human freedom. That which is 'good' in the sense of the first creation account, is whatever is beautiful to see, well ordered, permanent, regular, useful and pleasant. It is a cumulative quality which reflects a 'totalising' experience of God's creatures.

image of God (Gen. 1 : 27). This time, as a matter of fact, it is as if man and woman were reflecting upon God the intense light of their being, a being so often at once united and torn apart, to catch a glimpse of something of his own goodness.

Many questions have been asked about the origin of this prophetical theme.[1] But they cannot be answered with certainty, for explanations are not always forthcoming. What may in a general manner be said, is that Israel, like all the ancient peoples of the East, had inherited the ways of thought which the men of prehistory had slowly drawn from domestic experience. During thousands of years man and woman, in their most intimate relations, had been the two poles of this thought. Their mutual relations within the privileged sphere of generation had little by little shaped in their minds the first traces of the notion of causality, on the admittedly limited plane of beginning and end. As the oldest legends which have come down to us bear witness, it was with this still very elementary intellectual equipment, even in historical times, that the first paths towards the idea of God were opened up. The total result of this prolonged effort reaches us in the shape of cosmogonies, most often polytheist, and almost always comprising as a principal feature an anthropogony under divers forms.

Such was the normal approach. It would not be difficult to show the active part played by this way of thought in Israel's religious consciousness until a comparatively late period; although certainly some elements of the ancient scheme became gradually fossilised in the language, in proportion as monotheism was more and more strongly established (thus, for example, the survival in Hebrew of *ba'al*: master-spouse, as a divine title, Os. 2 : 18). One may add to this the proximity felt to exist between the two realities, analogous in several respects, of

---

[1] The main texts to which from this point onwards I should like to refer the reader are: Os. 2 : 4–25; 11 : 1–9; Jer. 2 : 1–4, 4; 31 : 1–22; Is. 54 : 1–10; 62 : 1–12; Ez. 16 and 23.

alliance and marriage.[1] It no longer comes as a surprise then to find in prophetical tradition, and no longer merely germinating but in full flower, the image of a (conjugal) love between Yahweh and Israel.

For us at least, seeing these things at a distance, it is in Osee that the theme appears for the first time (*c.* 750 B.C). If this circumstance alone does not allow us to say that Osee was its originator, it is nevertheless an easy matter to see that those who took it up again after him (Jeremiah, Deutero-Isaiah, Ezechiel) have scarcely done anything but follow his example. Besides, the pattern was complete in Osee so that for our own particular point of view we may limit our remarks to him alone.

To avoid confusion, it will perhaps not be amiss to stress first of all that this image of the love of Yahweh and Israel is at once loftier and more restricted than the reality of marriage on which it is based. It is in fact obvious that the prophet did not develop this theme to cast new light upon marriage, but to trace out a path, through marriage—and a marriage seriously threatened if not broken[2]—towards an understanding of God's plans, which show in spite of all human erring an indestructible love. Nevertheless marriage itself was indirectly enhanced in some fashion, as if the glimpse of something of God through the sensuous medium of the flesh had in return conferred on it a certain divine grandeur. The creature is no longer the same when once God has been glimpsed through it, even if this were but in a sudden

---

[1] Cf. the form of marriage contract employed at Elephantine (fifth century B.C.): 'She is my wife and I am her husband from today, henceforth and for ever', and the phraseology of the new alliance in Jer. 31 : 33, 'Then I shall be their God and they shall be my people' (cf. Jer. 30 : 22; Lev. 26 : 12; Os. 2 : 21). With regard to the marriage contracts of Elephantine, see R. Yaron. 'Aramaic Marriage Contracts from Elephantine', *Journal of Semitic Studies* III 1958, pp. 2–4; 30–2.

[2] An excellent review of current opinions on this point will be found in H. H. Rowley, 'The Marriage of Hosea', in *Bulletin of the John Rylands Library* XXXIX (1956–7), pp. 200–33.

H*

illumination of thought and consciousness. This mediatory quality lifts it once for all above itself; or rather, restores it to its true dimensions, when once it has been viewed in such a wide perspective. It is not for nothing that sometimes those things which are nearest and most familiar to us have a share in revealing our ultimate hopes. Thus marriage first served in the mind of the prophet as a help in the difficult search for God's plan for erring men; as a result it became a ready-made path which others, individually or collectively, could follow him in using.

Moreover it is important to be exact about the aspect of marriage which serves as the implicit theme in Osee's image of the love between Yahweh and Israel. It is not that of fruitfulness or generation, but an aspect which is in a sense much more radical, and which is more specifically human, namely that of love. Outside of this the image would even lose all significance. It is marriage insofar as it is love, and thus it is the yearning, in itself unlimited, of a man and a woman for each other, over and above any consideration of fruitfulness, which is spontaneously borrowed by the prophet as a means of access to the most mysterious part of Yahweh's plan for his people: that which maintains fidelity to the promise and its fulfilment in spite of the widespread flourishing of evil.

In actual fact it is not of the sterility of his marriage that Osee complains. It appears that Gomer, his wife, had given him within a few years two sons and a daughter (Os. 1 : 3–9). The genius of the prophet on the contrary lay precisely in this, that he had left aside that aspect of marriage in which from the beginning of time, according to the tradition of his people, a sign of God's blessing had invariably been seen. It is rather insatiable love as such, disappointed in spite of fruitfulness, which shows him the tremendous spiritual drama of the idolatry to which his nation has become addicted. This is so true that when the prophet, spurning despair, resolves to restore his wounded affection, it is the memory of the *espousals* which comes back to his mind, and which he sets up as an indestructible ideal for the future (2 : 16–22).

The Canticle of Canticles. Osee had acquired a unique awareness of his union with Gomer, the daughter of Diblaïm. But in this awareness what was the essential element? It was the espousals, above and beyond the drama itself and the fruitfulness of the marriage, because they stood for love alone. Now Jewish antiquity has handed down to us a remarkable witness of the unique force to be found in betrothal, as being love unadorned. This witness, of extraordinary charm and beauty, is the Canticle of Canticles. Moreover if we now turn our attention to it as we draw towards the end of this investigation we are doing no more than taking a hint from Osee himself. For it seems probable that in Osee 2 : 17 there is an allusion to betrothal songs parallel with, if not identical to, those we have in the Canticle: 'There, she will *reply* as in the days of her youth.' This 'reply' could not take a more apt form than that in which the Canticle clothes the expression of the betrothed girl's feelings.

For the critics the general interpretation of the poem remains doubtful. It is of course unnecessary to add that we are only concerned here with the general interpretation of the songs; it would be impossible to go into the details of the text. A few years ago I proposed a simple solution to this supposedly abstruse problem. I was not so ingenuous as to think that everybody would be immediately convinced of its truth, and I venture to go back, very briefly, over a point which seems to me decisive even apart from any other consideration.

In the article just referred to[1] I distinguished a 'pre-literary' stage of the Canticle, corresponding to the period during which its actual use was widespread, and its original purpose, a matter

---

[1] 'Le sens du Cantique des Cantiques', *Revue biblique*, LXII (1955), pp. 197–221.

of common knowledge (approximately the period of the monarchy down to the exile), from a 'literary' stage, corresponding to the subsequent period. By this time the Canticle had become quite simply (thanks to the Wisdom writers who had first collected and then edited it) a text like other texts, having from now on an existence which was much diminished by comparison with that which it had had before. I suggested at the same time that the gradual transition from Hebrew to Aramaic as the spoken language of Palestine in the Persian era had something to do with this change. At any rate, if the main premise was correct, it became sufficiently evident, so it seemed to me, that the meaning of the Canticle should be sought first and foremost at its pre-literary stage, not, as many suppose, at the literary stage. In short, the meaning of the Canticle should be above all that which derives from its use as a song, rather than that which results from reading it as a text.

This was the starting-point of my interpretation. It remained to decide what could have been the purpose which the Canticle originally fulfilled. At this point two methods of analysis seemed possible: one internal, the other external. In actual fact both converged upon the same conclusion: the original purpose of the Canticle had been to serve various forms of social encounter eventually leading up to betrothal and marriage. Thus, one could say that it was essentially, though not exclusively, a betrothal song. With its warm lyrical form, it compensated, so to speak, psychologically and socially, for the business-like nature of the marriage-contract,[1] and when used at betrothal or marriage feasts, it took on quite naturally the more specific meaning of an exchange of love between the betrothed, equivalent to a mutual promise of fidelity.

Such then must have been the general sense of the Canticle when it was taken up and edited by the Wisdom writers some

---

[1] Cf. R. Yaron, art. cit., pp. 1–39.

time after the exile. For there is no indication—rather the contrary—that the Wisdom writers wished to modify this primitive meaning, and this is made sufficiently clear by what they added to it (8 : 6b–7). But if this is so it is clear that we ought to read the Canticle now, in the same way as did the Sages then, mainly as a betrothal song.

This has not been the usual attitude, for interpreters, by force of circumstances and because of certain basic assumptions, have generally read it in a prophetical setting, as an allegory or parable of the love (eschatological or otherwise) between Yahweh and Israel.[1] To read it in a sapiential setting is simply to return to the more ancient Jewish tradition, at least up to about the

---

[1] M. Feuillet, in a note attached to one of his recent articles ('L'universalisme et l'alliance dans la religion d'Osée,' in *Bible et vie chrétienne*, XVIII (1957), p. 32, note 6), puts the question: 'Does the Canticle make use of prophetical ideas or does it not?' As far as I am concerned, the answer is: No! The Canticle is confined to the betrothal theme; it shows no knowledge of the idea of the betrothal or marriage of Yahweh and Israel, which could be the prophetical idea. This is a fact, and it is easily provable if silence means anything. The onus of proof falls upon those who claim the opposite, making the dumb to speak. For it is my supposition that in Jewish antiquity you could think of betrothal without straightway implying, by allegory or parable, the transference of this universal and fundamental idea to the special case of the relation between Yahweh and Israel. The writer adds: 'Nothing that has been said to the contrary has, in my opinion, advanced by one step the understanding of the Canticle, because people have restricted themselves to general considerations without troubling to go into a detailed discussion of the text.' There must be some misunderstanding here. In any problem the most detailed solution is not necessarily the most accurate. I would even go so far as to say that in the present case, any temptation to enter too soon into detailed examination may very easily conceal a retreat from the much more serious problem raised by the text as a whole. For in such a situation detailed analysis is only possible on a basis of assumptions, and in the nature of things, with every move it sinks deeper into erroneous details. So it is with the assumptions themselves that one must quarrel. The detail will fill itself in later quite naturally, without any need for force to make it fit a system. As regards seeing in love 'an essentially sacred character', this was always foreign to the thought of the prophets as it was to that of the Canticle of Canticles. Religious ethnology, moreover, proves abundantly that each

first century A.D., as well as to return to the original function of
the poem as a betrothal song, or more precisely, as a collection
of betrothal songs more or less closely connected together by
unity of theme, style and purpose. In fact, the prophetical
reading of the Canticle, as a figure of the love between Yahweh
and Israel, does not appear in tradition until a relatively late
date (the second century A.D.), when, because of the remoteness
from its original purpose, the Canticle had become actually no
more than a text, handed over defenceless to the imagination
and preconceived ideas of the erudite. In this way it was finally
separated, both among Jews and Christians, from that sapiential
tradition which had ensured its survival in the first place. This
could happen because by the second century A.D the sapiential
tradition was practically dead The only thing remaining, and
that in a predominantly Pharisaic form, was the tradition of the
Law and the Prophets. This tradition, by the familiar procedure
of allegory, took to itself the whole interpretation of the Canticle.
But it was a misinterpretation, and it is fairly easy to see how this
misinterpretation was accepted. This line of reasoning, after
further time to consider it, still seems to me to be sound. For the
moment I should merely like to support it by making an observation which as far as I know has not previously been expressed
by anybody else.

I refer to the title 'Canticle of Canticles' (Hebrew: *šir
ha-šîrîm*), to which insufficient attention has been paid. This
title can hardly be the one under which the poem was composed.
It is an appreciative title: 'The most beautiful of songs,' which
one hesitates to attribute to an author, but which, on the contrary, it would not be hard to imagine coming from the pen of

time the sacred has been grafted on to love, it has risked degeneration into
superstition (religious prostitution, innumerable fecundity rites, etc.). The
prophets of Israel were well aware of this because they had examples of it
before their very eyes. And what they knew did not exactly incline them to
find in love 'an essentially sacred character'. It was enough for them that
love was 'blessed' by its connection with creation.

an editor. The latter could, without vanity or presumption, write over the poem: Canticle of Canticles. It was a name which bore witness to the recognised merit of the composition, and to the affection for it, bred of long use or a long tradition. Canticle of Canticles is not the author's name for it, but that given it by an editor.[1]

But if Canticle of Canticles is the editor's name for it, the question immediately arises as to what the poem was previously called. If an original name could be found, it goes without saying that it would be of exceptional value in establishing the general meaning which the song must have had in its original context. Now this pre-literary title of the poem, in my opinion, is still in existence. Since in fact it is a song which is under discussion, it is natural to suppose that this song must have been known by a name which indicated the theme both of the music and the words. But in any literature or folklore in the world, such titles are only conceivable as being borrowed in some way from the very songs to which they are applied. Normally the first line or hemistich of the composition (a verse or refrain) is chosen. We ourselves retain this same practice, and examples of it are far too numerous to choose from. This practice of naming pieces according to melody or theme was, needless to say, perfectly well known to Jewish antiquity. The Psalter still contains some examples: Ps. 22, 'Concerning: The doe at early dawn'; 56, 'Concerning: The dumb dove of far-off gods'; 57–9, 75, 'Do not destroy', to quote only the most certain cases of this.[2]

If we bear this in mind, it suffices to look at the beginning of the Canticle to recognise there a literary form similar to that

[1] Within these limits this fact is recognised by a fair number of exegetes: cf. a recent work, R. Gordis, *The Song of Songs*, New York 1954, p. 78.

[2] Cf. R. Tournay, *Les Psaumes* (*Bible de Jérusalem*), Paris 1950, pp. 9–10; E. Gerson-Kiwi, 'Musique', in *Dictionnaire de la Bible* (*Suppl.*), V, coll. 1437–8.

which one might have expected. Everybody has noticed that the first hemistich, whilst being in harmony with the general tone of the poem, nevertheless has no close textual connection with what follows. After 'May he kiss me with the kisses of his mouth', the second hemistich carries on in the second person without any transition. The temptation for critics has naturally been, after supposing every possible meaning for this isolated hemistich, to suggest textual emendations, all equally unsatisfactory.[1]

But is it in fact necessary to make any correction? The most natural supposition in such a case is rather that we have here the designation under which a certain melody was known in antiquity, this designation having been preserved by the Wisdom writers who edited the ancient betrothal song after the exile. Thus Canticle of Canticles would be the name given to it by the editors simply to express their esteem when, belatedly, it became part of that literary treasure we know as the Wisdom writings. And so 'May he kiss me with the kisses of his mouth' is, on this supposition, a name given to both music and words, in short, a name by which the songs were called as long as they remained in current use, and as long as they accompanied ancient Jewish betrothal and marriage celebrations, to say nothing of many other forms of social encounter, where the younger people found an opportunity to express their mutual preferences. This hypothesis has in its favour the fact that it is quite obvious when once it is considered, and that, without strain, it accounts for all the elements of the problem.[2]

---

[1] Cf. the review of the main opinions in P. Jouon, *Le Cantique des Cantiques* (*La Sainte Bible* VI), pp. 297–8; the apparatus of *Biblia Hebraica* (Kittel-Kahle), 3rd ed., *in loc.*

[2] The initial *kî* of the second hemistich (1, 2) does not offer any real difficulty for this explanation. The syntactical value of this *kî* is reduced to the minimum in any hypothesis which does not arbitrarily correct the text of the first hemistich. It is a usage which may be likened to the recitative *kî*, to introduce the whole of the succeeding development. The particle is,

It may, as I believe, become accepted, and if so it supplies at the same time a perfectly plain indication of the general sense of the Canticle as it was originally used. This wonderful song which the Wisdom writers have preserved for us with the literary title of Canticle of Canticles was first of all, if you like, a 'Kissing song for the betrothed'.

So by a new and more direct way we arrive at a general interpretation of the poem which already seems to commend itself sufficiently on other grounds. The Canticle is, in a wide sense, a nuptial song whose appropriate religious values must be looked for within the implied framework, namely the very profound regard which Israel had for the union of man and woman.

Thus we come once more to our starting-point, the creation stories. What has already been said about these will suffice to give us an understanding of the greatness of the Canticle of Canticles. It must have been virtually the equal of the exaltation which, in the mind of the editor of the Genesis account, had marked *for ever* the first meeting of the first man and woman: 'Yahweh God fashioned into woman the rib which he had taken from the man. He brought her before the man, and the man

however, a little stronger than our colon; it is a reinforced colon, which may quite well be translated as 'Yes, . . .' (cf. 8, 6b for another usage of the same sort to introduce a reflection of the editor: 'For (yes) love is as strong as death,' etc.). It is, moreover, probable that this *kî* is proper to the 'literary' period of the Canticle, and must have been added for purposes of 'reading'; without doubt it had less reason for appearing in the song. This observation finds support too in the obvious fact that parallelism only becomes evident from the second hemistich onwards. During the period of the pre-literary use of the songs, the first hemistich would serve all the related poems as both a musical and thematic archetype. The musical import of this archetype, it goes without saying, is irretrievably lost, but its thematic value remains. It fixes the general sense of the poem as we now have it. This sense excludes any parabolic or allegorical purpose. With its melody and (principal) theme thus determined by its original title, the Canticle appears to move entirely in a 'nuptial' atmosphere. It is the 'Song of the kiss of the betrothed'.

cried out: this time, it is bone of my bones, and flesh of my flesh. This one shall be called woman, because she has been taken from man! This is why man leaves his mother and father and joins himself to his wife, and they become one single flesh' (Gen. 2 : 23–4). Someone else, who had doubtless understood, was to add later after quoting part of the text, and taking up once more the profound inspiration of Osee for the benefit of the gospel: 'This mystery is great: I mean with regard to Christ and the Church' (Eph. 5 : 32).

XIII

The Mystery of Marriage[1]

L. Johnston

THE most effective symbol of the relationship between God and his people in the Old Testament was that of marriage. The messianic era, then, when this relationship would reach fulfilment, was spoken of in terms of a wedding feast; and there are echoes of this idea in the gospels—in the parables, for instance, or when our Lord refers to himself as the bridegroom: 'Can the bridegroom's friends fast when the bridegroom is still with them?' (Mk. 2 : 19). But it is in St Paul that the marriage figure is taken up again and explicitly applied to Christ and the Church. Indeed, so real is the relationship to St Paul that he can even reverse the figure; instead of comparing the Church to matrimony, he can use the mystical Body to clarify and illustrate his teaching on marriage. That is what he is doing in Eph. 5 : 22 ff. His subject is family relationships; and in order to drive home the obligations of married persons he points to the relationship between Christ and the Church which their marriage symbolises. Wives are to be subject to their husbands as the Church is subject to Christ; and husbands are to care for their wives as Christ does for the Church. And he sums it all up with the words: 'This is a great mystery—the relationship, that is, of Christ and the Church.'

The Mystery

It is unfortunate that the Latin uses here the word *sacramentum*, which has such technical connotations for most of us. Certainly,

[1] First published in *Scripture*, 1959, pp. 1–6.

St Paul has a theology about the sacred character of matrimony; but this is not necessarily identical with the development which it receives in scholastic theology. The Council of Trent uses this text indeed in its treatment of marriage; but it is careful to point out that it does not prove the sacramental nature of marriage, but merely suggests it: *Innuit Paulus* . . . The correct meaning of the word 'mystery', is one which is well known to Pauline theology, and central to it.[1]

The term belongs to the language of Jewish apocalyptic literature. It is the word used in Daniel, for example, to describe the secret revelation given in a dream which only Daniel could interpret. The Qumran literature uses it in the same way—the hidden wisdom of the divine plan and of its execution, revealed to the Prophets in part, and now to the sect of the new covenant.[2] It is used in the gospels in much the same way—the deeper truth of the Kingdom which was confided to the apostles.[3]

For St Paul, it includes the whole mystery of salvation which is the sum of his gospel. At the beginning of this same epistle to the Ephesians, Paul shows how all-embracing it is (1 : 3–14). It begins with God: it is in fact essentially Trinitarian—it depends on the good-will of the Father, it is effected by the Son, and it is sealed in the Holy Spirit. It is part of the idea of 'mystery' that it is progressive—not just a secret body of information, but God's hidden plan which unfolds in time; and in a sense this progressive movement begins in the procession of the Trinity. From there it moves outwards to creation, and encounters the fact of the fall. And it is then that the mystery

---

[1] There is practically no limit to the bibliography which might be given on this subject; the article by John T. Trinidad s.j., in *Biblica*, 1950, pp. 1–26, gives, besides a fair treatment of the subject, an extensive bibliography. See also P. Benoit, 'Corps, tête et plérome dans les Epîtres de la captivité', *Revue Biblique*, 1956, pp. 5–44.

[2] Cf. *Biblica*, 1956, pp. 247–57.

[3] Mt. 13 : 11: 'To you it is given to know the mysteries of the kingdom . . .'

properly so-called comes into play, God's secret wisdom by which he plans to bring the world back to him. It is prepared throughout the ages, it is foretold in the Prophets; and it is finally realised when God becomes man in the person of Christ. It includes our redemption through Christ's death and resurrection, our adoption as sons, our sanctification in the Spirit; it includes the mystery of the rejection of the Jews and the choice of the Gentiles; it includes the summing up of all things, visible and invisible, in Christ. And it ends with the final return of all this, which is the fulness of Christ, to God who fills everything. And Christ then returns to the bosom of the Trinity, so that we end where we began, with God who is all in all—and the whole is for the praise of his glory.

Christ, then, is the heart and centre and sum of the whole mystery: Christ who contains in himself all the fulness of the godhead, and who unites himself in one body with man in the Church. It is here, in the mystical Body of Christ, that the mystery is fulfilled; for it is in the mystical Body that the 'restoring of all things', 'the fulness of God', is initially completed. It is in the union of Christ with his Church that the union of God with creation is effected.

Matrimony

And now, in Eph. 5 : 32, matrimony is associated with this great mystery of Christ and the Church. In the previous verses, the symbol of Christ and the Church has been used as a basis for exhorting husband and wife in their relationship with each other; but now we see that it is not just a comparison, with a homiletic value, but a real analogy with a theological value. The relationship of husband and wife is not just like the great mystery of Christ and the Church, but a part of it.

How is this so? In the first place, we should notice that it is not the individual man and woman who are spoken of, but the state of matrimony. As individuals both husband and wife are equally members of the Church, the bride of Christ. It is their union in matrimony which is the term of the comparison. We should notice also that the point of comparison is not the mutual love of husband and wife; from this point of view they are equal—each is bound to love the other, for Christ's sake, as every Christian is bound to do. Nor can we say that there is a specific quality in marital love which makes it a fitting symbol of the love of Christ for the Church; there is indeed a specific quality to marital love, but this quality is the result of the marital relationship, not the cause of it. Just as there is a specific quality in the love of parents which differentiates it from ordinary charity—but this quality is the result of the filial relationship, not the cause of it. Thus it is not accurate to say that the man represents Christ and the woman represents the Church. It is the man, in his specific character as husband, who represents Christ; and the woman, as a wife, who represents the Church; and the matrimony which represents the mystical Body.

That is the point of Eph. 5 : 26: 'Husbands, love your wives —as Christ also loved the Church, and gave himself up for it, so as to sanctify it and prepare for himself a Church that was spotless and without stain.' The point is not merely that Christ loved the Church enough to die for it; but that in dying for it he made it fit for union with himself. The stress of the sentence falls on the words: 'to sanctify it and prepare it for himself'.

And so it is too with marriage. The husband is not merely exhorted to love his wife; he is exhorted to love his wife because she is part of him, and no man ever hates his own flesh.

'For this cause . . .'

This point is brought out finally and most definitely in a text which has caused some difficulty—St Paul's reference to Gen. 2 : 23 f. in this context: 'For this reason shall a man leave father and mother and cleave to his wife, and they shall be two in one flesh.' What is the reason? In Genesis it is because woman was fitted by creation from Adam's rib to be united in one flesh with him. But for St Paul the reason is that we are members of his body, flesh of his flesh and bone of his bone (he uses of the mystical Body the same phrase as Genesis uses of the relationship between Eve and Adam). Christ and the Church are one thing just as really as man and wife are one thing. And not only that but—'for this reason . . .'—the union of man and wife is in fact directed to this union of the mystical Body; it was, so to speak, the reason why God invented it. Marriage is not merely a symbol of the mystical Body; the mystical is the prototype which marriage was intended to portray.

This, however, causes a difficulty. The text of Genesis refers to the natural contract of matrimony, as it existed before our Lord. Its symbolic relationship with the mystical Body then can hardly be the mark of the sacrament, the Christian reality. This is true; but there is no reason why an Old Testament reality, which in the Old Testament was purely symbolic, should not be raised to a higher status after the coming of our Lord. The sacrifices of the old law were preparatory, foreshadowing; but they did have a certain value in so far as they symbolised the supreme sacrifice in which they were fulfilled. Circumcision had a certain value in so far as it was a mark of that covenant which was fulfilled in the New Testament and into which we are initiated by Baptism. Now, it is not absolutely impossible that baptism should have been used in the Old Testament as the mark of initiation into the covenant; or conversely, that circumcision should have been retained in the New, to signify our union with Christ. One can see good reason why a new symbol was chosen to convey the new and greater reality; but there is no intrinsic reason why the old symbol should not have been retained. And if it had been retained it would still have had the sacramental efficacy which baptism now has in fact. And if that had happened, if God had chosen to act in that way, we would have had the same symbol referring to the same thing in different ways—the one, the Old Testament rite, preparing for the reality which was to come; the other, in the New Testament, looking back to that reality and sacramentally renewing it. So, in the same way, there is no reason why the same institution of matrimony should not refer to the same thing in the Old Testament and in the New, but in two different ways—in the Old, as prefiguring the great reality which was to come, in the New sacramentally repeating it.

'Filling up'

Christian marriage, then, does not merely symbolise the union of Christ and the Church; in some sense it re-creates it. It is something like the sacrifice of the Mass, which re-enacts daily the single sacrifice of Calvary. It is something analogous to what St Paul teaches concerning our sufferings—that they 'fill up the things that are wanting to the body of Christ'. Our Lord suffered for us—and that suffering was 'once and for all'. Yet that suffering in his physical body in some mysterious way receives a complement from the sufferings of his mystical Body. And that mystical Body is the real Christ—it is the concrete, almost physical reality of that truth that gives marriage its place in the 'mystery' of salvation. When God became man he bound himself by the conditions of humanity; and the essential condition of humanity is contingency—to exist only at a particular moment in time. We say that our Lord became 'man'; but it would be more accurate to say that he became *a* man; there is no universal, generalised man, no abstract human nature that he took, containing thus in some way all other men. Christ, now, is the church, which is flesh of his flesh and bone of his bone.[1] This re-incarnation of Christ has to be realised

---

[1] Eph. 5, 22; the phrase is omitted by some Greek MSS, but those which have it are of sufficient weight to make the reading at least probable.

anew in every generation; and it is in marriage that this union is realised. By Baptism, Christ is united with the individual soul; by marriage he is united with a new being, one who is 'two-in-one-flesh'; and in that new union he takes on a new mode of being—the mode of being which in fact we call the mystical Body. It is sometimes said that the family is a microcosm of the state; it is even truer to say that by the sacrament of marriage the Church in microcosm is produced.

Sacrament

Here, however, we must exercise caution. The union of matrimony certainly portrays and gives a concrete expression to the realism of the Church's union with Christ. But for the technical definition of a sacrament in the modern sense it is demanded that the symbol should be efficacious—that it should produce that which it symbolises. Now this does not seem to be true of marriage, at least from this point of view. It is certainly true that the sacramental contract of marriage produces the graces which that contract symbolises, the graces necessary to make the union a living supernatural reality in Christ. It is true also that the union symbolises most vividly the union of Christ and the Church. But it is very difficult to see that it produces this union. That is to say, the union of a husband with his wife does not actually produce Christ in his union with the Church—that relationship is a fact prior to and independent of the sacrament of marriage.[1]

One can indeed see that all that later sacramental theology looks for in marriage does stem from this its most essential function of portraying the union of the mystical Body: the charity that makes this union supernatural, and the fruitfulness of that union in charity which produces offspring who are to be sons of God. But St Paul is content to dwell on that essential

[1] Cf. *Summa*, III (supp.), q.42, a.I, ad 4um.

aspect: that the sacred character of marriage is due to the part it plays in the great mystery of salvation; this mystery is centred on the Incarnation, where God and man became one person; it is continued in Christ's mystical Body, where God and men become one being; and it is in marriage that this union is re-enacted and continued.

XIV

Christ on Divorce[1]

H. J. Richards

'WHY is your Church so strict about divorce? If a marriage has turned out a failure, why not dissolve it? Surely you will do more harm than good otherwise. People are human, and if they have made a mistake they ought to be given a second chance. What right have you to be stricter than Christ, who admitted that unfaithfulness could be a ground for divorce?'

The objection may not be put in so many words, but it is implicit in the minds of many people, who are frankly puzzled and even shocked by the Catholic Church's attitude to divorce, and who cannot see in Christ's words, as St Matthew reports them,[2] anything other than a permission at least for the innocent party in a divorce to remarry.

In actual fact the meaning of the phrase *except it be for fornication* is not nearly as obvious as people think. That it should have given rise to a great variety of interpretations is sufficient indication that it is an ambiguous phrase. About the only thing that scholars agree on is that it cannot be taken to mean that Christ gave any sort of permission for divorce and remarriage: it simply will not fit the context or the rest of the New Testament teaching on marriage.

[1] We are grateful to the Catholic Truth Society for permission to print with slight alterations this fuller text, which the Society published as a pamphlet. A shorter text of the same first appeared in *Scripture*, 1959, pp. 22–32.

[2] Matt. 19 : 9 'Whosoever shall put away his wife, *except it be for fornication*, and shall marry another, committeth adultery.' (Douay version). The saying is repeated in a slightly different form in Mt. 5 : 32.

It will be useful to look into that general New Testament teaching before discussing the possible meaning of the words which St Matthew has put on Christ's lips. It forms the necessary background for the understanding of that enigmatic phrase.

ST PAUL ON MARRIAGE

It may seem odd to approach the teaching of Christ by way of the occasional letters written by St Paul to his converts twenty or thirty years later. It will seem less odd when it is remembered that these letters introduce us into the life of communities who were practising the teaching of Christ long before it was ever written down in the gospels. If we wish to know what Christ taught, we can have no safer guide than the practice of the first Christian churches.

About the year 55 A.D St Paul wrote his first letter to Corinth, a church which he had founded on his second missionary journey five years earlier. In common with the rest of the first generation of Christians, his converts there lived in the fixed hope that they would remain alive to see Christ's second coming, and they had written to ask whether, in view of this transportation into heaven, 'where there will be no more marrying or being married' (Mt. 22 : 30), it might not be better to remain celibates; whether in fact it might not even be advisable to break up existing marriages. Paul wrote: In reply to the questions you asked me to answer: (1) Yes, you are quite right in supposing that celibacy is a good thing. But that does not mean that marriage is something evil. In fact, in an atmosphere like that of Corinth, where there is such constant danger of immorality, it is better for a man to have a wife, and for a woman to have a husband.

(2) No, you are wrong in supposing that husband and wife

should live as brother and sister. In fact, by the marriage contract the wife has given over to her husband the right to her body, as the husband has to his wife, and you have no business to deny this right to each other. You may both agree to abstain from the use of marriage for some spiritual reason, but this should only be for a short period at a time. To refuse to come together again would leave both of you wide open to temptation. (What I have said here about the advisability of marriage is of course not to be taken as a command. As far as my own preferences in the matter go, I would personally advise anyone to follow the greater perfection of the celibate life I lead myself. But this demands a gift from God, and if God has not given you this gift, then celibacy is not for you. For you he has a different gift in store. So, I repeat, any unmarried person, widow or widower would do well to remain celibate as I do, but only if they can exercise self control. If they are constantly being overcome by the flames of passion, they should marry.)

(3) You are equally wrong in suggesting that existing marriages should be broken up. And here it is not merely a question of my own personal preferences: Christ himself has forbidden wives to leave their husbands, and husbands to divorce their wives. Consequently, if they have separated from each other, they must either remain single or else be reconciled. (cf. 1 Cor. 7 : 1–11).

This page of St Paul has been paraphrased in order to suggest the answer to some of the objections which it has aroused. What sort of a view of marriage is this, people ask, which makes it a poor second-best to celibacy, a concession allowed to those who cannot exercise self control? The objection is fair enough, if it is presumed that St Paul set out in this letter to present the full Christian doctrine on marriage. But he did not. He set out to answer the twisted questions of some very twisted people.

The Corinthians had moulded their newly found Christianity

on the Greek model, with the Greek assumption that religion concerned the soul alone. Salvation was a matter of intellectual appreciation in which the body played no part, to which in fact the body could only be a hindrance. The mentality can be read between every line of the letter which St Paul wrote to counteract it, from the first chapter's castigation of Corinth's intellectual cliques, to the last chapter's impassioned appeal to the Corinthians to understand that Christianity involves a bodily resurrection, not a merely spiritual one. It is this mentality that has coloured the chapter on marriage too, and allowance must be made for it if St Paul's thought is not to be misrepresented. It is in answer to the soulless asceticism of the Corinthians that he admits the superiority of Christian celibacy, only to express his doubts about whether they are spiritually mature enough to practise it. It is in answer to the suggestion that marriage is intrinsically evil that he insists on its sacred character and he is not afraid to call it, in v. 7, a *charisma* on the same title as the 'spiritual gifts' that are to be outlined in chapters 12–14. It is on the command of Christ (who gave it this sacred character) and not on Paul's preference that Christian marriage is to be regarded as unbreakable. As far as the teaching of Christ went, the first generation of Christians knew of no exception to the indissolubility of Christian marriage.

If we want a more balanced and a more complete picture of St Paul's teaching on marriage, we will go to the epistles he wrote later in life, when the heat of controversy was over, when the heresies which threatened to corrupt Christianity from within—Greek intellectualism on the one hand (cf. Thess. and Cor.) and Jewish legalism on the other (cf. Gal., Rom. and Phil.)—had been finally defeated, and when he could set forth his concept of Christianity *ex professo* instead of merely using it to illustrate a debating point.

From his prison in Rome, about the year 62, Paul wrote a letter to the Christian communities which he and his fellow

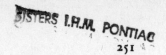

missionaries had founded from Ephesus, the headquarters of his third journey eight or nine years earlier. The epistle is known to us as 'Ephesians', but with its lack of the usual personal greetings it was probably designed as an encyclical letter to all the Churches in the Roman province of Asia of which Ephesus was the capital. It is the calmest of all Paul's writings. Not that he had no errors to deal with: between the lines of this epistle he is clearly referring to an incipient form of the Gnosticism which was to give so much trouble to the Christian writers of the second century. But Paul does not write with any of his former anxiety. He is content here to put forward, quite positively, a synthesis of the Christian mystery as it has matured in his mind, convinced that this will satisfy all the searchings of Asia for a philosophy of life. And the sum content of this mystery is Christ, a Christ who possesses from eternity all the fulness of the Godhead, a Christ in whose incarnation God has become present to us, a Christ who has already returned to the earth in the Church, which is his Body, filled at every moment with his fulness. In the Church the Christian is 'in Christ' (the phrase is repeated again and again) and has already entered heaven.

For St Paul, this sublime concept of Christianity is not simply the concern of the speculative theologian. It is the guiding principle which must govern the attitude of each Christian to such everyday matters as honesty, patience, humility and purity. It is the reality which must form the background to the everyday relationship between a slave and his master, between a child and his parents . . . and between a wife and her husband:

'The wife should be subject to her husband as if to Christ, since he is her head, just as Christ is the head and saviour of his Body, the Church. Just as the Church is subject to Christ, so should the wife be subject in all things to her husband.

'The husband, for his part, should love his wife in the way

that Christ loved the Church. It was for the Church that he gave himself up in order to bring it to God. . . . It is in this way that the husband should love his wife, as if she were his own body . . . which he takes such care to keep fed and free from harm. For this is precisely how Christ loves us, the limbs that make up his Body, the Church. Genesis spoke of a man leaving his father and mother in order to be united to his wife in one flesh. Those words contain a great mystery, a mystery which has now been revealed in the union between Christ and his Church' (cf. Eph. 5 : 22–32).

The text again needs to be opened out to reveal the depth of its meaning. The use of the marriage metaphor to describe the union between Christ and the Church is not new. The Old Testament had frequently referred to the covenant between God and his people in these terms (Deut. 4 : 24; Is. 1 : 21–6; 50 : 1; 54 : 6–7; Jer. 2 : 2; 3 : 1–12; Ez. 16 and 23; Os. 1–2; Ps. 44; Cant. *passim*, etc.), and Christ in his teaching had already appropriated the metaphor to himself (Mt. 9 : 15; 22 : 1–14; 25 : 1–13). What is new is the light that St Paul has thrown on it by turning it back to front. It is not God's union with man that is something like human marriage. It is human marriage that is the metaphor, an imperfect copy of that other union which is the true reality. And that union between God and man, first echoed in the union between Adam and Eve, and echoed down the ages by the union into one flesh of every human marriage, has received its final seal in the incarnation, where God has become one flesh with mankind. The marriage of which Genesis spoke, itself already an image of God's marriage with man, was, in St Paul's mind, a mystical foreshadowing of a more sublime reality still, the marriage between Christ and his Church. And this in its turn becomes the model for Christian marriage, in which two Christians present a replica of that action of Christ and make real again his presence upon the earth. It is, in the last analysis, this sacramental nature of Christian marriage which makes it absolutely indissoluble. It can no more be broken than can the new and eternal covenant into which Christ has entered with his Church.

There are not many other references to marriage in the rest of the New Testament epistles. What references there are all reflect this same conviction that Christian marriage is something more than a merely human contract, because Christ's coming has raised the world to a superhuman level, and marriage with it. Writing to his converts in Salonika, St Paul is anxious to point the contrast between the pagan attitude to marriage and that which must inspire the Christian who is a member of Christ's Body and a temple of Christ's Spirit (1 Thess. 4 : 4–8). In his epistle to the disciple who is to take over his work in Ephesus, he returns to the Greek heresy against which he had to battle in Corinth ten years earlier, which would maintain that the body is irredeemably evil and the marriage act hopelessly sinful. He insists that everything that God created is good (1 Tim. 4 : 1–11), and that in fact it is in the very relationship of marriage that the wife is to win her salvation (2 : 15). The epistle to the Hebrews similarly stresses the sacred character of marriage (Heb. 13 : 4).

Perhaps the closest parallel to the sublime ideal outlined in Eph. 5 is to be found in the encyclical letter written by St Peter only a year or two later. With the ease and confidence which marks the first Christian exegesis of the Old Testament, St Peter finds the model of the Christian wife in Sarah, who addressed Abraham as her 'Lord' (Gen. 18 : 12, Septuagint), as every wife is to see the figure of Christ the Lord in her husband. It is because Christian marriage has this sacramental character that St Peter can point to it as the means by which husband and wife inherit eternal life (1 Pet. 3 : 1–7).

These quotations from the writings of the apostles are sufficient to give some indication of the light in which Christian marriage was seen by the first generation of Christians. If they do not

I

at first seem to have much relevance to the subject under discussion, the teaching of Christ on divorce, they form its essential
background and express something of the spirit in which we
must approach the words of Christ as the gospels have recorded
them.

CHRIST ON MARRIAGE

The gospels mention only one occasion on which Christ made
any pronouncement on marriage. It is to be found in all the
three synoptics (Matthew, Mark and Luke). Luke is content to
report the operative sentence which contains Christ's teaching
on the matter, and has included it (16 : 18) haphazardly in the
middle of the long collection he has made of Christ's sayings
(Lk. 9 : 51—19 : 27). Matthew has also included the sentence
(5 : 32) in the middle of his more compact collection of Christ's
sayings, known to us as the Sermon on the Mount (Mt. 5–7).
Mark has been more careful to report the circumstances which
gave rise to the saying (Mk. 10 : 1–12), and these are reproduced, with slight variation, in a later chapter of St Matthew's
gospel.

'Some Pharisees came up to him and put him to the proof by
asking him, Is it right for a man to divorce his wife for any
reason whatsoever? He answered them, Have you not read that
the creator made them, from the beginning, male and female,
and said to them, "For this reason shall a man leave his father
and mother in order to be united to his wife, so that the two
become one flesh"? A man and his wife are no longer two but
one, and no one has the right to separate what God has thus
joined together. Why then did Moses, they asked, make pro-
vision for separation by means of a certificate of divorce? It
was, he replied, because of your moral immaturity that Moses
allowed divorce; but that was not God's original plan. And so

I repeat that original plan to you: Whoever divorces his wife ("*Except it be for fornication*") and marries another woman, commits adultery; and whoever marries a woman who has been divorced by her husband, also commits adultery.' (cf. Mt. 19 : 3–9).

It will be useful to look a little more closely at the context here provided by Matthew. It will give us some indication of the way in which Christ's final words are to be understood. Mark and Luke omit the phrase in italics. For the time being we may do the same. Whatever its meaning might be, it will appear more clearly in the full light of this context.

Christ's pronouncement on divorce was not given out of the blue. It was given in answer to one of the many 'trick questions' by which his adversaries hoped to catch him out in argument. St Matthew gives several examples of these questions—on the poll-tax, on the general resurrection, on the greatest commandment, on the Messiah—in this section of his gospel. On each of these occasions Christ had carved clean through the controversy, and had forced his questioners to re-examine their own principles. The question of the Roman tax was based on the assumption that he must either pronounce for it (and antagonise the crowd) or against it (and cause trouble with the authorities). Christ did neither. He simply declared the supreme principle that the obedience owed to God does not prejudice the obedience owed to Caesar. The question of the resurrection of the dead was based on the assumption that the limitations of this life would be carried over into the next. Christ took away the whole foundation of the objection by pointing to the spiritual nature of the life of heaven. The question on the Law hoped to embroil him in the fruitless dispute about the relative importance of the 623 commandments which the scribes had discovered in the Old Testament. Christ disposed of the whole argument by returning to the one fundamental—the commandment of love. And on the ancestry of the Messiah, it was he himself who asked the awkward question, and forced his critics to think again about the relationship between the first David and the second (Mt. 22 : 15–45).

On the occasion that here concerns us, the trick question was asked in the hope that it would force Christ to declare for one side or the other of a dispute famous in his day, and so split his following. The dispute revolved around the precise meaning of the phrase in Jewish law which specified the grounds for which a divorce might be granted. The Code of Deuteronomy had allowed a husband to dismiss his wife, by the formality of giving her a certificate of divorce, if he discovered in her the shamefulness of a thing', that is to say, something shameful or indecent (Deut. 24 : 1). For many, these words could refer only to the ultimate indecency of adultery, which consequently alone gave a man the right to divorce his wife. This strict interpretation was upheld, in the time of Christ, by the great rabbi Shammai. But the phrase was obscure enough to allow of a very liberal interpretation too, and indeed the rabbi Hillel had gone on record as ruling that a spoilt dinner or a wife's fading good looks constituted sufficient 'shamefulness of a thing' to allow the husband to demand a divorce. The phrase continued to provide a subject of bitter argument and disagreement, and its overtones are clear in the question which is put to Christ in Mt. 19: 'Is it right for a man to divorce his wife for *any* reason whatsoever?' In effect he is being asked: 'Are your sympathies with the stricter view of Shammai, or do you side with Hillel who holds that divorce may be granted even for the *slightest* reason?'

The questioners hoped to force Christ into one of the two camps. He does neither. He bypasses the whole dispute in order to return to the fundamental unity and indissolubility of marriage as it was created by God. The marriage tie, as instituted by God, is stronger even than the natural bond between parent and child, because it has made 'one flesh' of the two partners, who can no more be divided again into two than can a living body. The same text of Genesis, of which St Paul is later to make such effective use, is appealed to as witness of this God-designed unity. Christ refuses to declare for either Hillel or Shammai. Both are wrong. No man, neither Shammai nor Hillel, has the right to separate again two beings whom God has made so indissolubly one.

If any doubt should remain that Christ has not merely sided with the stricter view of Shammai, but has excluded divorce in any circumstances, that doubt disappears when even Shammai's followers have to appeal against Christ's interpretation of Genesis by quoting Deuteronomy. Christ does not reply: 'Of course, in certain restricted cases that interpretation of Genesis does not apply.' He merely repeats it and points out that the prescription of Deuteronomy, far from being a divine command, was a temporary concession to the immature moral stage of Israel. His own mind is that from now marriage should return to its original and absolute indissolubility. In short, his reply is entirely in keeping with his reply to the other trick questions. He refuses the alternative presented to him: 'Does this provide sufficient grounds for divorce or not?' The whole foundation of the question is wrong. Nothing provides sufficient grounds for divorce. It is the reply we should have expected once we had read the rest of the New Testament teaching on divorce, for the one depends on the other. Neither Paul nor Peter nor any of the early Christian communities knew of any grounds for divorce. The reason was that Christ had absolutely excluded it.

'EXCEPT IT BE FOR FORNICATION'

There is not a scholar who questions the fact that Christ's words, as reported in Mk. 10, Lk. 16 and Mt. 5 and 19, exclude divorce and remarriage. The whole context of Mt. 19 makes it so clear that there can be no possible doubt on the matter. If scholars continue to disagree, it is not on that fundamental fact. They may argue about the meaning of the phrase *except it be for fornication*, but none of them imagines that by it Christ made any exception to his repudiation of divorce. It would make nonsense of the whole scene. Even the apostles who close the scene bear witness, by their shocked attitude, that Christ's ruling is uncompromisingly stricter than Shammai's: 'If that is your decision about the relationship between a man and his wife,' they say, 'better not to marry at all!' (Mt. 19 : 10).

This, it must be repeated, is so clear that those scholars who still think that the words *except it be for fornication* are really meant to provide an exception to Christ's ruling, conclude that they cannot be Christ's own words (they are such a blatant contradiction of all that he has said), but must have been interpolated by some Christian community which found itself unable to live up to the high standard set by Christ. But this is the easy way out. Is there no other possible meaning of the phrase?

Scholars of all times have returned again to struggle with this phrase. On the one hand it does seem at first sight to qualify in some way Christ's general repudiation of divorce. On the other hand the context makes it clear that Christ considered a divorced person still bound by the marriage bond: to attempt marriage with another would be 'adultery'. If there is to be any solution to the dilemma, some alternative translation must be found for one or other of the three words which appear in our text as 'divorce', 'except' and 'fornication'.

Some scholars (by far the majority) have suggested that it is the word 'divorce' which has been mistranslated. Since Christ explicitly excludes remarriage, the word might be better translated as 'separation'. In this case his ruling could be paraphrased: *If anyone separates from his wife (and this he may do for 'fornica-*

tion') then he may not marry again. Christ would be making a real exception, not indeed to his repudiation of remarriage, but to his repudiation of 'divorce' (i.e. separation). It is a possible solution.

Others have queried the word 'except', especially in view of the forceful word used in the Greek original of Mt. 5 : 32, and suggested that it might be better translated 'leaving aside' so that Christ would be saying: *If any one divorces his wife (and I am not considering the question of 'fornication', which makes no difference one way or the other) he may not marry again.* Christ would be bypassing the whole dispute about what constitutes sufficient grounds for divorce, as irrelevant. It is a possible solution.

But it is the third word, 'fornication', that perhaps provides the most satisfying solution to the problem. The solutions based on the other two words unconsciously make this word equivalent to 'adultery', without allowing for the fact that when the text speaks of the adultery of the divorced husband or wife, it uses an entirely different word. It would seem that 'fornication' refers to something else. Can we discover its exact meaning by looking to see how it is used elsewhere in the New Testament?

The Greek word *porneia* that is used in Mt. 5 and 19 is in fact both more general and more specific in meaning than the English word 'fornication'. In itself it means simply 'impurity' (the English word 'pornography' which is taken from it has a similarly wide meaning) and the context must decide what precise impurity is being referred to. Such a context is provided, for instance, by St Paul in his first letter to Corinth, where he condemns the illicit union between a Christian and his dead father's wife. This he calls *porneia* (1 Cor. 5 : 1). The Council of Jerusalem in Acts 15 uses the word in exactly the same sense when it directs Christians of Gentile origin to respect the susceptibilities of their brethren of Jewish origin by complying, where necessary, with Jewish custom in the matter of *porneia*. The Council had made it clear that, in principle, the Christian is no longer bound by the ritual laws of the Old Testament (Acts 15 : 7–19). But charity demanded that where converts from Judaism were in a majority and continued to live according to these ancestral laws, the Gentile Christians among them should make a communal life possible by respecting their social taboos in the matter of 'idolothytes' (food which had been offered in pagan sacrifices), 'porneia' (marriage within forbidden degrees), 'blood' and 'things strangled' (non-kosher meat) (Acts 15 : 20). Exactly the same four concessions had for centuries been demanded of any stranger who wished to make his home in Israel (Lev. 17 : 8—18 : 26).

These two examples make it possible, if not likely, that *porneia*, as well as bearing the generic meaning of impurity, had in certain circumstances the technical meaning of marriage within the degrees of kinship forbidden by Jewish law. Among the Gentiles there was no restriction on the matter, and marriage between near relatives was not unusual. But it was the Jewish custom which was eventually taken over by the Church, where a marriage of this kind was regarded as being one in name only, and in reality as illicit a union as plain fornication. The use of the same word *porneia* in the context of a dispute about marriage makes it at least possible (more and more scholars today think that it is certain) that the text of Mt. 5 : 32 and 19 : 9 refers to such illicit unions, and so makes an exception from the general law of indissolubility for those 'marriages' which were already null and void through forbidden degrees of kinship. The text could then be paraphrased: *If any one divorces his wife, he may not marry again, except when his marriage was not a real one at all, but had only the appearance of one.*

It will be asked whether it is likely that Christ would have gone out of his way to mention anything as obvious as this. If the union between two people is only an apparent marriage and not a real one at all, then anyone of the meanest intelligence could conclude that it does not fall under Christ's ruling on marriage, without explicit mention of the fact having to be made. It would be rather as if Christ said: 'Blessed are the merciful for they shall obtain mercy (unless they are not really merciful, but only appear to be)'. On the other hand, if the word *porneia* was meant to refer only to the case of marriages which were invalid because of the technical law on kinship (and this admittedly would be less obvious), then one could still ask whether it is likely that Christ would bother to insert a parenthesis referring to something so remote. After all, it was not as if the case would crop up in every other marriage or so. As well expect him to say: 'If anyone divorces his wife he may not marry again (except where his marriage to the woman has been a case of mistaken identity).' It is too rare a thing to mention in a general ruling about the indissolubility of marriage. Is it even likely that the word *porneia* was understood by the first Christians to refer to those forbidden degrees of kinship, when they found it necessary to legislate for the matter themselves in the Council of Jerusalem? Perhaps this fact provides the clue to the final solution of the problem. It is indeed unlikely that Christ should have legislated for such an obscure case. But it is not unlikely that St Matthew should have inserted a reference to it into Christ's words.

It is significant that when St Mark, St Luke and St Paul refer to Christ's teaching on the indissolubility of marriage, they make no mention of any exception to the rule. The phrase *except it be for fornication* is to be found in St Matthew alone. Now Matthew, far more than the other Synoptics, has a habit of adding his own explanation to the words of Christ. Where Luke reports Christ as saying, 'Blessed are the poor' (Lk. 6 : 20), Matthew reads, 'Blessed are the poor *in spirit*' (Mt. 5 : 3) in order to ensure that the words are understood of the spirit of poverty, and not of merely material destitution, in which there is no particular virtue. The very next verse of Luke 'Blessed are they who hunger and thirst' has similarly become in Matthew 'those who hunger and thirst for righteousness' (Mt. 5 : 6), to emphasise again the spiritual nature of these qualifications for entry into the Kingdom.

These examples are well known, but many others could be quoted: St Peter's 'Thou art the Christ' (Mark and Luke) becomes in Mt. 16 : 16 'Thou art the Christ, the Son of God', to express the full meaning behind this profession of faith: in 9 : 13; 11 : 14; 12 : 7; 12 : 40; 13 : 14; 21 : 2; 24 : 30, Matthew has put the words of the Old Testament prophets Osee, Malachi, Jonah, Isaiah, Zachariah, and Daniel into the mouth of Christ (they are missing from the parallel places in Mark and Luke) in order to emphasise the element of fulfilment that is to be seen in these examples of Christ's teaching;[1] the questions asked by Christ in Mk. 5 : 9; 5 : 30; 6 : 38; 7 : 12; 8 : 23; 9 : 16; 9 : 33; 11 : 21; 14 : 14 have all been omitted by Matthew lest they should seem to imply ignorance on the part of Christ; and so on.[2] Nor should it worry us to discover that Matthew has added his own commentary to Christ's teaching in this way. His purpose, as that of the other Evangelists, is not to provide us with a tape-recording of Christ's words, but to tell us their meaning. And it is only those who do not believe in the inspiration of the gospels who will find in this any cause for anxiety, lest perhaps the Evangelists have falsified or misrepresented Christ's intentions.

If then Matthew frequently inserts his own explanation into the words of Christ, and if he alone has included the phrase about *porneia* in Christ's teaching on divorce, it is highly

---

[1] In 16 : 27; 18 : 16 and 19 : 19 the books of Psalms, Deuteronomy and Leviticus are quoted in the same way by Matthew alone.

[2] Other examples of explanatory words to be found in Matthew alone may be seen in 7 : 24–26; 9 : 4; 13 : 12; 13 : 19; 13 : 23; 19 : 17; 19 : 21; 19 : 28–29; 22 : 10; 26 : 28.

probable that we should understand it as his commentary rather than as part of the actual teaching of Christ, who, as we have seen, would have had no reason to make any reference to it. It is Matthew who has to teach Christ's legislation on marriage to Christians who have already experienced the controversy which led to the Council of Jerusalem and are living by its decree (Acts 15, A.D. 50—60). And it is Matthew who has to make it clear to them that Christ's words on the indissolubility of marriage are not to be taken to mean that the kinship marriage mentioned in that decree is indissoluble. It is not. It is *porneia*, and does not come under Christ's words about divorce.

This solution to the long disputed phrase seems to be the most satisfactory of those that are offered. If we have taken a long time in reaching it, it is only because we are so far removed from the circumstances in which Christ's words were uttered and St Matthew's Gospel was written. In itself the solution is simple. In view of the legislation made at Jerusalem about the time he was writing, St Matthew has added a clause to Christ's teaching on divorce in order to tell his readers that this has no bearing on marriages contracted contrary to the Jerusalem decree. His original readers would have understood the reference without any difficulty. The parenthesis is indeed a short one, but the use of the word *porneia* would have recalled the Jerusalem decree to their minds immediately, and shown them the purpose of the clause. A modern author would obtain the same effect by relegating the clause to a footnote and adding a cross reference to Acts 15 : 20.

The solution remains only one among several. This means that it is not certain. Let us repeat for the last time that it does *not* mean that Christ's teaching on divorce is uncertain. However the phrase *except it be for fornication* is translated, Christ's words on the indissolubility of marriage are not in any way affected. They remain absolute, as is made clear by St Mark, St Luke and St Paul, and as is emphasised by the whole context of Christ's ruling on the matter. If the Church continues to denounce divorce and to declare that Christian marriage is of its nature unbreakable, it is not out of a puritanical severity or a lack of sympathy with the difficulties of married life. It is out of sheer loyalty to the teaching of her founder, Jesus Christ.[1]

---

[1] This is not to say that a number of the Fathers, both Latin and Greek, were not able to interpret the phrase as offering a real exception to the indissolubility of Christian marriage. The Greek Church and the Churches of the Protestant Reform, basing themselves on that interpretation, continue to allow divorce and remarriage in cases of adultery, and regard the high moral standard demanded by Christ as an ideal rather than as an absolute law—an ideal which it is recognised not everyone can live up to.

General Index

A

Abraham, God's convenant with, 19

Achab, King, 156-7

Adam: victory of sin through, 147

Agabus, 40

Agrupneo, meaning of, 201

Ananias: baptism of Paul, 58

Anazopurein, meaning of, 202

Animals, sacrificial, 26

Annas, visit to, 100

Anointing with oil, 26, 28-9; the sick, 180 and n.; as described by St James, 181

Antioch, church at, 177

Antioch in Pisidia, church at, 178

Antiochus Epiphanes, 140

Aphesis, use of word, 141 n.

Apostles: suffering and persecution of, 43; mandate of the risen Christ to, 54; at Pentecost, 55; authority to teach what was forbidden or allowed by God, 166-7; authority to decide on doctrine and moral conduct, 167-8; as denoting priesthood, 187-8; as God's plenipotentiaries, 188

Arabia, nomadic tribes in, 18

Aramaic, as spoken language of Palestine, 232

Asam, use of word, 106 n.

Asthenes, meaning of, 176

Audet, Jean-Paul, 210

Augustine, St, 54; on remission of sins, 154; on sinners and heretics, 166 n.

Azymes, feast of, 96

B

Balaam, 34

Baptism: relation to Christ's death, 49-50; theology of in St John's Gospel, 52-4; as an illumination, 52; conception of by primitive community, 55-7; 'in the name of Jesus', 57-9; 'with the Spirit and fire', 60; uniting the Christian with Christ's death and resurrection, 62; forgiveness of sins committed after, 136-7, 139; remission of sins through, 137-8, 147-8; relation to sacrament of Penance, 139; effect on the flesh and the spirit, 151; uniting Christ with individual soul, 245

Baptism, Johannine, 46-7

Barnabas, selected by Holy Spirit, 40

Barrett, C. K., 73 and n., 83-4

Benoit, P., 117, 240 n.

Bernard, J. H., 80

Bethany, the anointing at, 97, 98, 100

Bethzatha, cure at, 74

Betrothal: unique force of, in Jewish antiquity, 231 ff.

Bible, the: as source-book for the ministry, 207–8

'Bind and Loose', interpretation of, 166–7

Blindness, man's, meaning of, 108–9

Boismard, M.-E., 87 n.

Bonsirven, J., 140 n.

Borgen, P., 65

Börnkamm, 178 n.

Bread, as an image, 79–80

Buchsel, 167 and n.

Bultmann, R., 65

C

Cain: his banishment, 107

Cajetan, 78

Calvin, John, 78; on Johannine baptism, 45

Canticle of Canticles, 212, 231–8; original use as song, 232; allegory of love between Yahweh and Israel, 233–4; title, 234–6

Catholic Truth Society, 247 n.

Cazelles, H., 22 n.

Celibacy, 206; St Paul on, 248

Charity: as priestly virtue, 192–6, 204; nature of, in priests, 193; humility as part of, 194–5

Christian life, the, 131

Christianity: element of drama in, 160; as sect of Judaism, 177 n.

Chrysostom, St John, 54, 203

Church, the: as continuation of Christ, 43; building up of by Christian sacraments, 60; as the Body of Christ, 151–2; task of, to impart and increase the life of Christ, 164

Circumcision, 19–20 and n.

Clement of Alexandria, St, 78

Communion, the sacrifice of, 22–3, 26

Community, good of, Paul's concern for, 151, 153; Israel's sense of responsibility for, 157–8

Compassion: as priestly virtue, 196–200; of our Lord, 200

Condon, Kevin, 172

Confession, 132–3; as most onerous part of Penance, 135; to God, 165; as penitential practice demanded by the Church, 170; public, 184–5

Corinth, church at, 40; ask St Paul's advice on marriage, 248–9; their soulless asceticism, 250

Cornelius, 56

Courage, in the priest, 203

Covenant, the, 17; meaning of to ancient Israelites, 17–18, 124; relationship between God and man, 19 ff., 125

Creation, God's covenant with, 19; two accounts of, in Genesis, 220–7

Creed, the, earliest forms of, 138

Cullman, Oscar, 52 n.

Cyprian, St, 137–8

Cyril of Alexandria, St, 54, 138

D

Daniel, 240; penitential practices of, 158–9; prayer to God, 163

Daube, D., 64 n., 67–8

David: anointed with oil by Samuel, 29

Davis, Charles, 184 n.

Dead Sea Scrolls, 94 ff.

Death: as consequence of sin, 108, 141–4; spiritual death, 144–5; wide meaning of, 145–6; as understood by the Jew, 145 n.;

Death—*Cont.*
intimate relation with sin, 146; idea of preparation for, 184
Derbe, church at, 178
Deutero-Isaiah, 125 n., 133, 229
Deuteronomy, Code of, 256
Didache, the, 53, 185
Didascalia Apostolorum, 101
Disciples: given power over evil, 112
Divorce: Christ's words on, 247–8, 254–5; 'except it be for fornication', 252–64
Dodd, C. H., 63 n., 73 n.
Dubarle, A.-M., 145 n.
Dufour, X.-L., 65

E

Easton, B. S., 174 n.
Egeirein, use of words, 182
Elders, in the early Church, 177–8
Elephantine: marriage contracts of, 229 n.
Elias: commanded to anoint Eliseus, 29; tradition of return of, 46
Eliseus, anointed by Elias, 29
Energy, in the priest, 203
Ephesus: the elders of, 40; public confession at, 184
Epiphanius, 101, 102
Eucharist, Holy: and the second coming, 48; in I Corinthians, 69; as remembrance of Christ by Christian community, 69–70; intrusion of personal interests into, 70–1; St John's treatment of, 71–7; its significance for each individual, 72, 76–7; supernatural character of bread in, 75; eternal life through, 76
Eusebius of Caesarea, 78

Evangelists, the: their theological purpose, 98–9
Excommunication, Paul's teaching on, 150
Exomologesis, use of term, 165
Expulsion, of sinners, from the Church, 168–9
Ezechiel, 37, 229; individualism of, 116

F

Faith: as gift of God, 75; and works, St James on, 173, 174; essential part of healing, 180; as priestly virtue, 189–90
Faithfulness, as priestly virtue, 196, 200 ff.
Family: and the individual, 217–18; in Jewish antiquity, integrated with the people, 219; relationships, St Paul on, 239
Fathers of the early Church: and juridical power of forgiving sins, 135 ff.
Feuillet, M., 233 n.
Fidelity. *See* Faithfulness
Fire, as metaphor for action of Holy Ghost, 203
Firmilian, Bishop of Caesarea, 138 n.
First fruits, the giving of, 25
Five thousand, feeding of, 63, 73, 74–5, 82, 91
Forgiveness: achieved by sacrifice and suffering, 133; on sins, after Baptism, 136–7
'Fornication' meaning of, 259–64
Four thousand, feeding of, 91
Fraine, J. de, 116
Fruitfulness, blessing of in Old Testament, 214; in Genesis account of creation, 222–3

G

Gärtner, Bertil, 63 n., 66 n., 68 n., 92 n.

Gedeon, 34

Genesis: on the creation of man and woman, 212; importance of genealogy of tenth chapter, 213–14

Gerson-Kiwi, E., 235 n.

Gnosticism, 251

Gnostics: baptism of oil among, 180 n.

God: his convenants with men, 19 ff.; union of with man, 31; spirit of, 31 ff.; becomes man, 38; primitive man's conception of, 119–20; as he appeared to Israel, 124; his love and mercy, 124–5; his compassionate forgiveness of sinners, 153–4; reconciliation with, through penitential practices, 155; use of his name in prayer, 175; his plan for mankind in genealogical framework, 214–17

Gomer, wife of Osee, 230, 231

Gordis, R., 235 n.

Grace, of the priesthood, 202–4

Greek intellectualism: threat to early Christianity, 250

Guilt: as consequence of sin, 106–7; revealed through sufferings, 107; close connection with bodily sickness, 107–8

H

Haggadah, 66–7 and n.

Hamartia, aspects of meaning of, 105 and n.

Hata, use and meaning of, 121, 129–30

Healing: the sacrament of, 172 ff.; power of, among the presbyters, 179–80; spiritual and bodily, 185

Herod Agrippa, 174 n.

Hillel, 256, 257

Hippolytus, 138

Holiness, 27, 42

Holocaust, the, in sacrifice, 22–3, 24–5, 26

Holy Ghost, or Spirit, 39–44; dwelling in the Christian, 152–3

Hope, as priestly virtue, 190–2

Humility, demanded of the disciples, 194–5

I

Idumean dynasty, the, 140

Incarnation, the, 39

Individual, the, development of, 218

Irenaeus, 53

Isaac, blessing of Jacob, 16

Isaiah: warning against Egypt, 33

Israel: pre-biblical conventions incorporated into way of life, 123; dedication to God, 126; and law of the Sabbath, 128; belief in sin as ultimate cause of all suffering, 161; requests to God to manifest himself to the world, 162–3; conception of love, 226; love relationship with Yahweh, 227 ff.; Canticle considered as allegory of, 233–4

J

Jacob: Isaac's blessing of, 16

James, St (son of Alphaeus), 174 n.

James, St (son of Zebedee), 174 n.

James St ('the Lord's brother'):

James—*Cont.*
on anointing of the sick, 172, 175, 181–2; and their salvation, 182–4; on way of life pleasing to God, 173; enigma of, 174;
Jaubert, A., 94–5 n.
Jephte, 34
Jeremiah, 136, 229
Jeremias, J., 63 n., 139 n., 168 n.
Jerusalem, Council of, 259, 261
Jerusalem Church, baptismal teaching of, 59
Jesus Christ: on the Spirit, 38–9; revelation of God to the world, 43; his anointing by John the Baptist, 48–9; his baptismal teaching, 50, 53; significance of piercing of his side, 54; as bread of life, 66–7; as source of eternal life, 73–4, 75; historical settings of his teaching, 91–3; his criterion of morality, 130; as conqueror of sin, 140–1; as living proof that God had freed men from evil, 146–7; as apostle and high priest of God, 188; complete identification with human beings, 197; his answers to 'trick' questions, 255
Jews: humiliations and sufferings in period preceding Christ, 139–40; marriage outside their own race, 158; their legalism, as threat to early Christianity, 250
Job, 33
John, St: interpretation of meaning of creation, 44; and the spirit of the Last Supper, 64; and the significance of Jesus, 72, 73; and the meaning of the bread and wine, 72–3; his treatment of miracles, 73; on faith, 75; on salvation, 75; arguments against

his referring to the Eucharist in Chapter 6, 78 ff.; on baptism, 82; his historical reliability, 82–4; his interpretation of events, 84; adaptation of Christ's words, 91–2
John the Baptist, St: conception of in first three Gospels, 45; as prophet of Christian baptism, 47; his messianic anointing of Jesus, 48–9; conception of in fourth Gospel, 49–50; invites baptism for remission of sins, 141
Johnston, L., 94, 119, 239
Jouon, P., 236 n.
Joy, received from Holy Spirit, 42–4
Jubilees, Book of: as basis of Qumran calendar, 95
Judas, 98
Judgment, 41–2
Judith: penitential practices of, 158–9; prayer to God, 162–3
Justice: Christ's new principle of, 41
Justin, St, 53

K

Kelly, J. N. D., 138 n.
Kilmartin, E. S., 63 n., 68 n.
Kingdom of God: the Christian's membership of, affected by sin, 168
Koehler, L., 107 n.
Kramer, S. N., 226 n.
Kutsch, E., 28 n.

L

Lagrange, M.-J., 52 n.
Last Supper, the, 64; difficulty of

Last Supper—*Cont.*
    dating, 94 ff.; suggested new in-
    terpretation of Gospel account
    of our Lord's last day on earth,
    97 ff.; new chronology of, 100–3
Law, the, 22; as expression of will
    of God, 23; violations of, 24;
    teaching on cleanness, 27–8; as
    the expression of God's will,
    124; fulfilled by Christ, 130; St
    Paul's comments on, 142–4
Lazarus: purpose of his sickness, 109
Leeming, Bernard, 139 n., 166 n.,
    184 n.
Leviticus, Book of, 127
Loaves, miracles of, 63, 73, 74–5,
    82, 91–2
Locusts, plague of, 157–8, 163
Love: the life of, 39–40; of God
    and neighbour, 131; God as,
    131; as presented in the Bible,
    211–12; ascribed to God, by
    Israel, 226
Luke, St, on 'finger of God', 37
Luther, Martin, 45, 78
Lyonnet, S., 142 n., 169 n.
Lystra, church at, 178

M

Man and woman, first, blessing of,
    222–4
Mandeans, the, 181 n.
Manna, considered as type of the
    Eucharist, 63, 64
Maritain, J., 16 n.
Mark, St, on John the Baptist's
    work, 45
Markosites, the, 181 n.
Marriage: ancient Jewish concep-
    tion of, 215–20; as seen by Osee,
    229 ff.; as Old Testament sym-
    bol of relationship between God

and his people, 239; applied by
    St Paul as symbol of Christ and
    the Church, 239, 244, 251–3;
    as reproducing the Church in
    microcosm, 245; part played by
    in mystery of salvation, 246;
    St Paul's observations on,
    248–54; advice to the Corin-
    thians, 248–50; sacramental
    nature of, 253–4; Christ on,
    356–7
Matrimony. *See* Marriage
Matthew, St: on 'spirit of God', 37;
    description of Christ's mission
    of the twelve, 51; his explana-
    tions of words of Christ, 261–2
Meal offering, in sacrifice, 22, 25
Meer, P. van der, 214
Messiah, the: and the spirit of God,
    36; his conquest of sin and evil,
    112, 114, 240; the Jews' longing
    for, 140
Meyer, A., 174 n.
Michl, J., 181 n.
Miracles, the: conception of in the
    synoptic Gospels, 50–1; develop-
    ment into theology of Christian
    sacraments in St John's Gospel,
    51–2, 73; to shew power over
    sin, 111–13; of healing, 141
Mishna, the, 97, 101
Moses, 34; God's covenant with, 21
Mystery, the Christian: varying
    meanings of, 240; as set forth by
    St Paul, 240, 251; Christ as
    centre of, 241
Mythology, as expression of man's
    confusion, 120

N

Nabal, use of word, 130
Naboth, murder of, 156–7

New Testament accounts of anointing with oil, 180–1

Nicodemus: Jesus's conversation with, 53

Noah: sacrifice offered to God by, 24; genealogy of his sons, 213, 214

O

Oil, anointing with, 26, 28–9

Old Testament: part played in development of Christian theology, 154 n.; teaching on penitential practices, 155 ff.; attitude to love and marriage, 210–11

Olethros, meaning of word, 150

Origen, 78, 136 n.; on public confession, 165–6

Osee, 227; on love relationship between Yahweh and Israel, 229 ff.

Othoniel, 34

Oza, 121

P

Palmer, Paul F., 172 n., 184 n.

Pasch, the, and the Last Supper, 94, 96

Pascho, meaning of word, 198

Passion, the: varying accounts of, 98–100; chronology of, 100–3

Passover, the: Christ's teaching at time of, 92–3

Paul, St: on the power of the Holy Spirit, 39–40; on the Eucharist, 48; account of his own Baptism, 58; on the nature of Baptism, 59; his baptismal theology, 61; on bodily weaknesses resulting from sin, 110; 'sufferings of sin',

113; on the remission of sins, 141–7, 148 ff.; on the law, 142–4; his teaching on the incestuous man, 149–51; teaching on the priestly virtues, 196 ff.; on marriage, 239, 244, 248–54

Peace, received from Holy Spirit, 42–4

Penance, sacrament of: following repentance, 133; relation with Baptism, 139; remission of sins through, 164–71. *See also* Confession

Penitence: Old Testament teaching on penitential practices, 155 ff.; as outward manifestation of results of sin, 161; to underline God's power and love, 161–2; as means to an end, 163; the penitent, in the early Church, 166; public, 169. *See also* Repentance

Pentecost: experience of the apostles at, 55–6

'People', meaning of word, 217 n.

Pesha, meaning of, 123

Peter, St: on prophecy of Joel, 37; exhortation to Baptism, 39; inspired by Holy Spirit, 42; his denial, 100; on repentance and Baptism, 147; warning against the devil, 148; upholding faith of priests, 190; on marriage, 253

Pharisees, conflicts with, 99

Philip, St: directed by Holy Spirit, 40

Philo, 197

Pilate, Pontius, 101

Ploeg, J. van der, 24, 118 n.

Pontificale Romanum, 169

Porneia, meaning of, 259–60

Porschmann, B., 136 n.

Prayer: effect of, in a 'just man', 185; as essential to priests' work, 191–2

Preaching: and priestly virtues, 206–9; as explanation of Scripture, 207

Presbyters: modern meaning of, 176–7; their power of healing, 179–80

Priest, the: meaning of term, 188; need for faith, 189–90; hope, 190–2; charity, 192–6, 204; compassion, 196–7; faithfulness, 200–1; grace, 202–4; prudence, 204–5; purity, 205–6; preaching the word, 208–9

Prophecy, spirit of, 37; in New Testament, 40–2

Prophets, the: view of God, 124–5; view of sin as rebellion against God, 126–7; on devotion to God and his law, 128–9

Prudence: as priestly virtue, 204–5; St Paul's meaning of, 204–5

Purification, with water, 26

Purity, as priestly virtue, 205–6

Q

'Qoheleth', 32, 33

Qumran: the Covenanters of, 24 n.; Calendar, 95 ff.; and chronology of the Passion, 100–3; question of intercalated days in, 103; literature, 240

R

Redemption, doctrine of, 133–4

Religion: as union of God with man, 31; the practising of, 129

Repentance, 132–3; acceptance of suffering in, 133; penance, 133; Christian life as, 133–4

Resurrection, the, 44

'Rib'; conception of in ancient cultures, 225–6 n.

Richards, H. J., 247

Robinson, J. A. T., Bishop of Woolwich, 84 n.

Roman rule, over Jews, 140

Rougement, D. de, 212 n.

Rowley, H. H., 229 n.

Rûah, significance of Hebrew word, 31–3

S

Sabbath, law of, adopted by Israel, 128

Sacrifice: the nature of, 22 ff.; prophets' view of, 132; forgiveness through, 133

Sacrifices, as signs, 22 ff.

Salvation: St John's teaching on, 75–6

Samaria, Philip's evangelisation of, 57

Samaritan woman: Jesus's conversation with, 53

Samuel, 34; anoints David, 29; anoints Saul, 29

Saul, 34; the anointing of, 29

Scheil, V., 226 n.

Schmidt, W., 22 n.

Schmitz, O., 26 n.

Schurmann, H., 65 n.

Scribes and Pharisees: their authority to interpret the law, 168

Scripture, 31 n., 45 n., 63 n., 69 n., 94 n. 105 n., 119 n., 135 n., 172 n., 187 n., 210 n., 239 n., 247 n.

Service, dignity of, 195–6

Shammai, 256, 257, 258

Sick, the: to be saved from death and raised up to life through prayer, 181–2

Sickness: connection with sin, 107–8; as result of power of evil, 111; treatment of in ancient world, 176; prayer and, 179–80

Signs: nature of, 15 ff.; in St John's Gospel, 73

Siloé, cure of blind man at, 52

Simeon, 37

Simon Magus, rebuke to, 39

Sinai, covenant at, 124

Sin: offering, in sacrifice, 22, 23–4, 26; nature of, 41; word embracing many different aspects, 105–6; consequences of, 106; sickness as punishment for, 107–8; final purpose of, 108–9; use of word in New Testament, 110, 113; need to seek revelation of, 114–15; need to translate revealed teaching into other terms, 115–16; corporate punishment for, 116; 'original', 117, 130 n.; primitive man's conception of, 120–1; in the Old Testament, 122–3, 129, 131, 156; St Paul on, 143–4; intimate relation with death, 146

Sins, remission of, 135 ff.; through Baptism, 57, 137–8, 147–8; when committed after Baptism, 136–7, 148–54; through Christ, 139–47; through penitential practices, 154–64; through sacrament of penance, 164–7

Sirach, Jesus, 173

Smith, W. Robertson, 21 n.

Sozein, use of term, 181–2

Spicq, C., 145 n., 187

Spirit of God, 31 ff. See also Holy Ghost

Stanley, D. M., 99 n., 147 n.

Stendhal, K., 167

Stephen, St, inspired by Holy Spirit, 42

Stephen, St, Pope, 138 n.

Suffering: acceptance of, 133; as result of sin, 156

Sumpatheo, meaning of word, 199

T

Talmud, the, 188

Taylor, V., 98 n.

'Temptation', use of word, 199–201

Tertullian, 136 and n., 165; on chastity, 206

Theology Digest, 95 n.

Titus: instructions on presbyters and bishops, 178 n.

Tournay, R., 235 n.

Trent, Council of, 45, 135 n., 240

Trinidad, John T., 240 n.

Trinity, the, 240–1; revelation of, 37–8; belief of primitive Church in, 58–9

U

Uncleanness, ritual, 26–7

V

Victorinus of Pettau: De Fabrica Mundi, 102

Villien, P., 169 n., 171 n.

Vogt, E., 95 n.

W

Water: 'living', 53–4; immersion in, as symbolic reunion with God, 132

Wikenhauser, A., 78

Winter, Michael M., 169 n.

Wisdom, and the Spirit of God, 35

Word of God, 16; need for doctrinal instruction by priest, 206–7
Worden, T., 105, 135
Words: as signs, 15–16; of blessing
and cursing, 16–17
World, the: primitive man's conception of, 118, 119

Testament thinking, 47; meaning of, to Israel, 123–4; as one
all-powerful God, 156, 163; and
creation of man and woman,
224; love relationship with
Israel, 227 ff.
Yaron, R., 229 n., 232 n.

Y

Yahweh: as source of all holiness,
29; signs and symbols in religion of, 29–30; as spirit of
God, 33; judgment of in Old

Z

Zacchaeus, 140
Ziener, G., 68 n.
Zorell, 23 n.
Zwingli, on Johannine Baptism, 45

Index of Scripture References

(arranged alphabetically)

ACTS:

1: 5, *50*, *55*; 8, *206*
2: 2–4, *37*; 3, *203*; 3–4, *55*; 16–17, *48*; 38, *57*, *141*, *147*; 47, *56*, *60*
3: 19, 36, *141*
4: 27, *48*
5: 31, *141*
7: 60, *110 n.*
8: 5–17, *57*; 10, *58*
10: 30, *154 n.*; 38, *48*; 43, *141*; 44–6, 48, *56*
11: 15, *56*; 28, 40; 30, *177*
13: 38, *141*; 52, *43*
14: 23, *178*, *189*
15: 2, 4, 6, 22, *178*; 7–19, 20, *260*
16: 4, *178*
17: 30, *141*
19: 4, *47*; 4–6, *58*; 18, *185*
20: 17–38, *178 n.*; 18–35, *178*; 28, *189*
26: 20, *141*

AMOS:

7: 4, *47*

BERABOTH:

18, *145*

CANTICLES:

8: 7, *193*; 16–17, *233*; *passim, 252*

COLOSSIANS:

1: 14, *147*; 15, 18, *219*; 18, *146*

I CORINTHIANS:

1: 11, *26–8*, *70*; 12, 13–15, *59*
3: 16, *39*
4: 1, *189*; 2, *201*; 8 ff., *70*
5: 1 ff., *70*; 1–5, *149*
6: 1, 7–8, *70*; 19, *39*
7: 5, *154 n.*; 1–11, *249*; 25–35, *194*; 35, *205*
10: 1–2, *62*; 17, *70*, *151*
11: 23, *96*; 24, *188*; 26, *48*; 27–9, *71*; 30, *72*, *144*, *176*, *185*
12: 4 ff., *132*; 4, 6, 11, 28, *179*; 13, *61*, *152*; 28, *189*
15: 15, 29, 32, 35, 42–4, 52, *182*; 55, *146*

II CORINTHIANS:

1: 9, *182*
2: 5–11, *149*
4: 7, *191*; 14, *182*
5: 4, *204*; 5, *44*; 14, *193*; 18–20, *206*; 19, 20, *188*; 21, *110*
6: 6, *205*
7: 10, *145*
10: 3–5, *204*
11: 7, *110*; 28, *201*; 29, *200*
12: 9–10, *190*; 21, *149*
14: 13, *189*

DANIEL:

3: 28 ff., *133*
9: 3, *159*; *passim, 162*

275

DEUTERONOMY:
  4: 7, *31, 124*; 7–8, *36*; 24, *252*
  6: 4–5, *125*
  12: 23, *28*
  24: 1, *256*

EPHESIANS:
  1: 7, *147*; 3–14, *240*; 13, *44*
  2: 2, *110*
  3: 8, *189*
  4: 3, 40, *153*; 4, *152*; 11, *189*
  5: 3–5, *59*; 14, *52*; 22 ff., *239,
    252*; 22, 244 n.; 26–32, *241*

EXODUS:
  19: 5, *155*; 6, *177*
  24: 4, *21*; 5, *21*
  30: 22–5, *28*; 23, *28*; 26 ff., *28*

EZECHIEL:
  11: 24, *37*
  16, 228 n., *252*
  23, 228 n., *252*
  33: 11, *169*
  36: 23–8, *36*

GALATIANS:
  2, *174*; 2: 9, *174*
  3: 27, 61, *147*
  4: 6, *152*; 14, *188*

GENESIS:
  1–3 *passim, 213, 219*; 1–11
    passim, 214; 1: 1–2, 4, *43*;
    1–2, 4, 26–31, *220*; 27, *228*;
    27–8, *214*; 31, *227*
  2: 4–25, *220*; 23–4, *238*; 23, *242*
  3: 1–24, *220*
  4: 11–16, *213 n.*; 13, *107*
  9: 9–11, *19*
  11, *216*
  12, *216*
  15: 18, *19*
  17: 2, *19*; 10, *20*
  18: 12, *253*
  27: 27–9, 39–40, *213 n.*

28: 33, *16*
31: 47, *17*
45: 27, 202

HEBREWS:
  1: 9, *48*
  2: 4, *40*; 10–16, *196*; 15, *145*;
    17–18, *197*
  3: 1, *188*; 2, 5, *200*; 2–6, *201*
  4: 14–15: 10, *198*
  5: 7, *198*
  6: 4, *52*
  9: 14, *145*
  10: 32, *52*
  11: 1, *189*
  12: 1, *113*
  13: 1–12, *201*; 4, *253*

HENOCH:
  5: 8, *140*

ISAIAH:
  1: 2–3, *125*; 21–6, *252*
  4: 2–4, *36*
  6: 3, *125 n.*
  10: 16, *35*
  11: 2, *36*
  30: 27–30, *47*
  32: 15–18, *36*
  40: 3, *46*
  42: 1, 6, *36*
  50: 1, *252*
  53 *passim*, 26; 4, *76*; 12, *50*
  54: 1–10, 228 n.; 6–7, *252*
  58: 3–4, *160*
  61: 1, *29*; 1–2, *51*
  62: 1–12, 228 n.
  64: 2, *162*

JAMES:
  1: 1, *174*; 1–18, 19–29, *173*; 6,
    18, *183*; 5, *110 n, 113*

JAMES—*Cont.*

2: 1–13, 14–26, *173, 174 and n.*;
9, *110 n.*

4: 1–12, 13—15; 6, *173*; 17, *110 n.*

5: 7–20, *173*; 7, 16, *182–3*; 14,
175; 14, *201*; 15, *110 n.*; 16,
129 n.

JEREMIAH:

2: 1–4, *228 n.*; 2, *252*

3: 1–12, *252*

8: 4, *137*

30: 22, *229 n.*

31: 1–22, *228 n.*; 31, *127*; 33,
229 n.

JOEL:

1: 8—2: 13, *158*

2: 28, *37*; 19, *158*

3: 1 ff., *48*; 5 ff., *47*; 5, *58*

JOHN

1: 6–8, 15, *46*; 14, *73, 79*; 18,
189; 26–7, 31, 33, *49*; 29, *50*

2: 11, *73*

3: 5, 8, 13, *53*; 5, *57, 81*; 12, *74*;
13, *76*

4: 13–14, *53*; 14, *74*; 25, *206*

5: 20, *74*; 21, *75, 145*; 35, *203*

6: *passim*, 63 ff., *78–93*; 34, *73*;
37–40, *193*; 51, *75*; 54, *76*;
26–58, *86–90*

7: 38, *74*; 38–9, *54*

8: 14, *53*; 12, *51, 74, 79*; 21, 24,
110; 32, *204*

9: 1, 5, 7, *52*; 3, *108–9*; 39, 53,
109; 41, *110*

10: 7, 11, *79*; 10, 27–8, *74*; 38,
73

11: 4, *176*; 4, 39, *109*; 25, *79*;
25–6, *74*

12: 26, *195*

13: 1, 13–14, *195*; 17, *90*

14: 1, 12, 13–14, *191*; 1, 24, *90*;
6, *79*; 8–10, 91–2, *188*; 11, *73*;
16, *41*; 17, 25–6, *190*; 21,
193

15: 1, *79*; 4–7, *91*; 5, 18–25, *190*;
7, 16, *192*; 9, 12, *193*; 15,
189; 16, *193*; 27, *189*

16: 7–15, *190*; 23–4, 26–7, *192*;
27, *193*; 31, 32, *190*; 33, *191*

17: 2–3, *91*; 6–8, *190*; 16–19,
193; 17–19, *188*; 18–19, *209*

19: 35, *54*

20: 21, *188*; 23, *135, 136 n., 137*

21: 15–17, *193*

I JOHN:

1: 9, *185*

2: 1, *41*

3: 3–9, *110 n.*; 16, *194*

4: 11–14, *39*; 13, *39*; 9–10, *188*

5: 2–3, *193*; 4–5, *191*; 6–8, *54*;
14, *183*; 16, *110 n., 176*

JOSHUA:

22: 10, *21*

JUDE:

1, *174*

JUDITH:

9: *passim, 162*; 1, *158*; 14, *163*

I KINGS:

19: 16, *29*

21: 27, 29, *157*

II KINGS:

1: 8, *46*

8: 1–5, *202*

9: 3, *29*

19: 7, *34*

LEVITICUS:

1 *passim, 24*; 1; 9, *22 n.*

5: 1–7, *22, 23, 24, 25*; 4 ff.,
121; 17, *24*

13: 45, *107*; 13–14, *107*

14: 19, *107*; 49–53, *122*

17: 8–18: 26, *260*

18: 8, *149*

26: 12, *229 n.*

LUKE:

3: 22, *49*; 23–38, *215*

4: 18, *48*; 18–19, *141*; 40, *111*

5: 15, *176*; 17–26, *184*

6: 20, *261*

7: 38, 46, *180* n.; 21 ff., *111*; 22, *141*; 36–50, *98*; 37 ff., *140*

8: 2, *111*, *176*; 48, *180*

9: 51—19: 27, *254*

10: 34, *180* n.; 49, 51–3, *50*

11: 14–23, *99*

12: 29–31, *85*; 48, *202*; 49, *193*; 50, *50*

13: 11, *176*

14: 42, *201*

15: 7, *160*; 7, 10, *137*

16: 10, *201*

22: 1–3, *98*; 19–80; 24–7, *194*; 28, *199*; 31–2, *190*; 61, *100*

24: 47, *139* n.; 49, *55*

I MACCABEES:

13: 7, *202*

MALACHI:

3: 1–5, 22–3, *46*; 3 passim, *247*

MARK:

1: 1, *45*; 4, 46, *141*; 5, 47, *185*; 17, *192*; 31, *182*; 34, *111*; 35, *246*

2: 1–12, *184*; 5, *176*; 5, 11, *182*; 19, *239*

3: 10, *111*; 14, *192*

4: 11, *109*

5: 28, 34, *182*; 41, *182*

6: 5, *112*; 13, *180* and n., *181*; 52, *92*; 56, *182*

8: 11, *91*; 13–16, *92*

9: 23, *180*; 27, *182*; 29, *154* n.; 37, *188*; 38, *181*

10: 1–12, *254*; 38, 45, *50*; 52, *182*

11: 22–4, *180*

12: 13–37, *67*; 34, *67*

14: 3, *180* n.; 16, *198*; 24, *80*; passim, *97*, *98*

15: 25, *96*–7 n.

16: 16, *139* n., *180*; 18, *179*

18: 18, *183*

MATTHEW:

3: 6, 47, *185*; 11, *46*, *47*

4: 23, *111*; 14 ff., *51*

5: 3, *261*; 6, *262*; 7, *197*; 14, *189*; 32, 247 n., *254*, *259*

6: 17, *180* n.

8: 17, *176*; 22, *145*; 29, *51*

9: 1–9, *184*; 2 ff., *141*; 5–7, 21, 25, *182*; 13, *139*; 22, *180*; 35, *111*

10: 1, *51*; 1, 8, *112*; 40, *188*

11: 5, *145*; 14, *262*; 19, *139*; 29–30, *195*

12: 1–30, *99*; 7, 40, *262*; 22, *111*; 32, *110* n.

13: 11, *189*, 240 n.; 14, *262*

16: 12, *92*; 16, *137* n., *262*; 18, *135*; 19, *166*, *167*

17: 11, *46*; 16, 18, *112*; 18, *176*; 21, *154* n.

18: 18, *135*, *166*, *167*

19: 3–9, *255*; 9, 247 n., *260*; 10, *258*

21: 2, *262*; 21, *180*

22: 1–14, *252*; 15–45, *256*; 30, *248*

23: 8, *167*; 13, *168*

24: 30, *262*

26: 1–13, *252*; 7, *180* n.; 20, *188*

28: 16–20, *189*; 16 ff., *139* n.; 18–19, *54*

NEHEMIAH:

9: passim: *162*; 2, *185*; 8, *200*

13: 13, *200*

NUMBERS:

19, *28*

OSEE:

  1: 3–9, *230*

  1–2, *252*

  2: 4, 25, 228 n.; 16–22, *231*; 18,
     228; 21, 229 n.

  6: 6, *137*

  11: 1–9, 228 n.

I PETER:

  1: 12, *206*

  2: 5–9, *177* n.; 22, *110* n.; 24, *110*

  3: 1–7, *253*

  4: 14, *43*

  5: 8, *117*, *148*

II PETER:

  2: 14, *110*

PHILIPPIANS:

  2: 3, *196*; 9, *58*; 17, *206*

  4: 14, *190*; 18, *206*

PROVERBS :

  9: 5, *79*

PSALMS:

  8: 6, 221 n.

  13: 1, *129*

  18: 16, 32 n.

  22: 23–7, *26*

  32: 3–5, *106*

  38: 5, *107*

  41: 10, 25

  44, *252*

  48: 8, *32*

  50: 13, 22

  51, *35*; 7, *145*

  78: 24, *65*, *66*, *67*, *68*

  104: 30, 33

  135: 17, *32*

  143: 10, *35*

PSALMS OF SOLOMON:

  17: 41, *140*

ROMANS:

  3: 9, *113*

  4: 13, *142*; 19, *145*; 25, *62*

  5: 12, *113*, *141*; 13, 14, *143*; 20,
     142; 21, *113*

  6: 2, *117*, *145*; 3–5, *62*; 12, 14,
     23, *113*; 8–11, *134*; 16, *144*

  7: 5, 17, *113*; 5–6, *152*; 7, 16–17,
     24, *144*; 8, *143*

  8: 4, 8, 10, 26, *152*; 3, *110*; 5, 8,
     113; 14, *40*; 15, *145*; 19 ff.,
     117; 23, *44*; 27, *41*; 28–30,
     219

  10: 9, 13, *58*; 14–17, *206*

  11: 32, *113*

  12: 1, *206*; 8, *189*

  15: 15–16, *188*, *206*; 30, *40*

I SAMUEL:

  2: 25, *136* n., 35, *201*

  10: 6, *29*

  16: 13, *29*

SIRACH:

  24: 21, *79*

  25: 24, *108*

  39: 21, *109*

  48: 1–11, *46*

I THESSALONIANS:

  1: 5, *203*

  4: 4–8, *283*; 8, *42*

  5: 12, *189*; 12–22, *153*; 19, *203*

II THESSALONIANS:

  3: 14, *149*

I TIMOTHY:

  1: 5, 7, *204*, *208*; 8, *203*; 12, *201*;
     19, *209*

  2: 4, *207*; 7, *208*; 15, *253*

  3: 2, *205*, *207*; 5, *178* n.; 15, *208*;
     16, *206*

  4: 1–11, *253*; 6, *207*; 6–15, *208*;
     12, *204*, *205*; 13, *206*; 14, *178*,
     179 n., *202*

  5: 1–3, 22, *205*; 17, *178* n.; 22,
     206

  6: 3, *207*; 11, *204*; 20, *208*

II TIMOTHY:

   1: 6, 202; 10, 13, 207

   2: 1, 203; 2, 206; 9, 14, 24, 207; 15, 208; 22, 204

   3: 14–17, 207

   4: 2, 206; 6, 207

TITUS:

   1: 1, 9, 207; 3, 206; 5, 208; 5–9, 178 n.; 13, 208; 14, 208

   2: 1–10, 15, 205; 5, 207; 15, 206

   3. 6, 203; 8, 207; 14, 208

   4: 3–4, 209

WISDOM:

   2: 24, 108

   4: 16, 176 n.

   9: 10, 11, 17, 35

   10: 14–16, 17

   15: 9, 176 n.

   16: 6, 53

ZACHARIAH:

   7: 9–10, 160